While the world waited for Hitler's dowr   ght
the six battles of the Courland Pocket in ꞁ

Blood in the Forest builds a vivid picture of a savage episode at the end of the Second World War through eyewitness accounts and stories told here for the first time.

In October 1944 Nazi forces pushed back from the Eastern Front were cut off and trapped with their backs to the Baltic. The only way out was by sea: their only chance of survival to hold back the Red Army.

Latvians fought on both sides – some against a second Soviet occupation, some against the Nazis. Many had no choice, forced into battle against their fellow countryman – sometimes brother against brother. Hundreds of thousands of men of all nations died in unimaginable slaughter. When the Germans capitulated, a partisan war against Soviet rule continued from the forests for years afterwards.

An award-winning documentary journalist, the author travels through Courland meeting veterans, survivors of the Holocaust, former partisans and a refugee who later became President. He also discovers the true story of Crocodile Dundee, a soldier who survived this hell.

This is the tough, uncomfortable story of the place where the final surrender of the Second World War was signed, and of a nation both consumed by war and at war with itself.

Vincent Hunt is a writer and award-winning BBC documentary maker who gathers his material face-to-face in his search to get to the heart of a story.

He has crossed America, Europe and Africa making documentaries about key moments in world history, including post-colonialism in Africa, the US civil rights movement, and the Troubles in Northern Ireland.

In *Blood in the Forest* he travels through western Latvia meeting eyewitnesses to the overlooked chapter of the Second World War known as the Courland Pocket. He goes deep into the forests to hear graphic accounts of long-forgotten battles and terrible atrocities and meets 'Diggers' still recovering the fallen from their battlefield graves.

This is Hunt's second book about the end of the Second World War. His first, *Fire and Ice* (The History Press, 2014) was praised for its meticulous research (*History of War* magazine) gathering stories of the Nazi scorched earth retreat through northern Norway in 1944.

BLOOD IN THE FOREST

The Shores of Kurland (Kurzemes krasts)

By Veronika Strēlerte

Dimly and vaguely there came into vision
Blurred ship masts, phantom-like frames,
Twilight unbroken stretched endless and vast;
Suddenly sorrow they broke overcast:
Kurzeme, distant, appeared amidst flames.

There it remained, land of hopes, of our freedom,
Of glory and creed a shattered shrine.
Thou that in exile risest and sleepest
Carry, when foreign darkness is deepest,
Firmly engraved this fiery sign.

Ringing of bells has brought peace to nations.
Is there a bell that for us proclaims?
On all the crossroads and fateful turnings
We feel in thirst and smoke-choked yearnings;
Kurzeme beckons to us through flames.

This book is dedicated to Jānis Kamerads of Jaunpiebalga.

BLOOD IN THE FOREST

The End of the Second World War in the
Courland Pocket

Vincent Hunt

Helion & Company

Helion & Company Limited
Unit 8 Amherst Business Centre
Budbrooke Road
Warwick
CV34 5WE
England
Tel. 01926 499 619
Email: info@helion.co.uk
Website: www.helion.co.uk
Twitter: @helionbooks

Published by Helion & Company 2017. This revised edition published in paperback by
Helion & Company 2020
Designed and typeset by Mach 3 Solutions Ltd (www.mach3solutions.co.uk)
Cover designed by Paul Hewitt, Battlefield Design (www.battlefield-design.co.uk)

ISBN 978-1-913336-03-5

British Library Cataloguing-in-Publication Data.
A catalogue record for this book is available from the British Library.

For details of other military history titles published by Helion & Company Limited contact
the above address, or visit our website: http://www.helion.co.uk.

We always welcome receiving book proposals from prospective authors.

Contents

List of Plates

List of Maps

Preface

This is a book of social memory, an oral history of events that occurred during the final months of World War II in Latvia. It's set in the west of the country on the Baltic coast, where German and Latvian soldiers were cut off and contained in an episode of the Second World War known to historians as 'the Courland Pocket'.

Courland – Kurzeme to Latvians – was of little strategic importance by 1945 and so historians have understandably focused on the bigger stories: the fall of the Reich, the end of the Nazis, the discovery of the concentration camps. The Western Allies would not resist Stalin's ambitions in the Baltics and so Latvia was absorbed for a second time into the Soviet Union.

Enemies of Moscow and opponents of the Soviet system were filtered out and removed. Fifty years of occupation followed, but it is still possible to find Latvians who fought in the Courland Pocket. Their tales of combat, capitulation and post-war punishment are brutal, tough and often tragic, echoing time and again in the population as a whole. I am grateful to my contributors for telling them.

My journey through Courland unfolds in chronological battle order and is intended to make sense for a visitor wanting to see these places for themselves – a journey that yields great rewards. I was lucky enough to make several trips to Courland. It is a beautiful and charming place, though the scars of its turbulent history are still evident.

Much has changed in Latvia since 1944, including the geography. Agriculture was collectivised, huge numbers of people were deported and the land and living accommodation was re-organised and centralised – but still the stories survive, and that's my focus.

I was particularly interested in how veterans remember their fallen friends after such a long period under Soviet occupation of being unable to. The wartime experience was so profound and so deeply embedded in Latvian families that almost everyone I spoke to had a similar story. It's common to find families with relatives who served on opposing sides, making this war akin to a civil war.

My journey led me to the brave officers of the EOD bomb squad still clearing up the munitions from that war and to Klaus-Georg Schmidt, Michael Molter and the *Legenda* Diggers, who are working today to bring closure to the fallen of Courland and of course to their families.

I regret not meeting Red Army veterans, despite requests and appeals in newspapers. Time has swung against them, and they preferred not to be interviewed. So this is not a definitive history and it does not have a political purpose. It's a reconstruction through social memory of vivid and unforgettable images in a landscape that has in essence changed little, in a country that has changed enormously.

Latvia has survived the loss of a generation in the war, the extermination of its Jewish population, the deportation of opponents to Soviet rule, the fifty years of occupation that followed the war and then an exodus of the grandchildren of the war generation in the economic collapse of 2008. All these events, and many more, are part of this complex story.

After 25 years of independence – the longest in its history – Latvia is emerging from the shadow of a century of bloodshed and turmoil. In the 21st Century it is a happier place: a capital of European culture, with a growing collection of boutique hotels and upmarket restaurants in Old Town Riga. Perhaps this is a return to the style and elegance Latvians displayed in the 1910s and 1920s when the art nouveau city was known as 'the Paris of the East'.

The future looks bright for Latvia, with its multi-lingual new generation keen to absorb ideas from all corners of the world and with family connections everywhere due to their own particular diaspora – but this is a glimpse into their past. This is what happened, in the words of people who were there.

Vincent Hunt
Riga, January 2016

Acknowledgements

A great number of people helped me with the gathering and writing of this book, over several years. I am deeply grateful to all of them.

Tukums Museum director Agrita Ozola offered advice, translation and expertise and arranged interviews for me with key people. Emīls Braunbergs, Arnolds Šulcs, Karlis Vārna and Leonhards and Līvija Stanga were kind enough to share their stories with me thanks to her. She has made an enormous contribution.

Jelgava Museum Head of Collections Aldis Barševskis was unstinting in his generosity and enthusiasm and placed his museum's entire photographic archive at my disposal; Ilgvar Brucis showed me round his amazing collection of Courland Pocket military finds in Zante.

Artis Gustovskis applied his considerable energy to finding veterans in Kuldīga and Skrunda: my deep thanks go to Antons Leščanovs, Fricis Borisovs, Žanis Grīnbergs and Jānis Blums for their interviews and the Kuldīga branch of *Daugavas Vanagi* for their time and hospitality. Herberts Knēts in Kuldīga deserves a special mention because of his painstaking efforts to preserve this awful history.

In Priekule, Mārtiņš Cerins and Lidija Treide were invaluable in explaining why this small town was the scene of such loss of life. Talking to them would not have been possible without the efforts of Kristine Skrivere. Artūrs Tukišs and Kristina Graudina added greatly to my stories in Ventspils and introduced me to some valuable written sources, as did Toms Altbergs at the Railway Museum in Riga.

Roberts Sipenieks was kind enough to show me the secrets of the forests around Zvārde and to take me to the capitulation museum at Ezere, run by his grandmother Biruta Sipeniece. I am grateful to them, and to Legionnaire Roberts Miķelsons whom we interviewed that day.

In Saldus EOD bomb squad officers Oscars Lejnieks and Aigars Pūce took a break from their valuable work gathering leftover explosives from the war and the Diggers of *Legenda* – in Saldus Dmitrijs Mežeckis and in Riga Andris Lelis and Yngve 'Inka' Sjødin – described their efforts recovering the forgotten fallen of the Second World War. Klaus-Georg Schmidt and Michael Molter added important detail about their experience as relatives of German soldiers who fell in Courland. Michael's website www.kurland-kessel.de is a valuable resource for those searching for information about German units serving there.

In Liepāja I am grateful to Ilana Ivanova, Andžils Remess from the *Kurzeme Vards* newspaper and Rita Krūmiņa and Maija Meijere at the city's museum, which generously allowed me to reproduce pictures of the war-damaged city and also their historical postcards. At Karosta Prison Juris Raķis opened up especially to see me. Several people, including Latvia's President, told of the terrible bombing raid on Liepāja on 9th October 1944. I am extremely grateful to the publisher Verlag Slezak of Vienna for allowing me to reproduce a photograph taken the following day by German Army photographer K. Wenzelburger.

In Dundaga I am grateful to Aina Pūliņa and her daughter Ālanda as well as Jautrite Freimane. They gave me a guided tour of the village and brought much of its wartime history to life. My visit to the Popervāle area gave me an insight into the experiences of Dr Margers Vestermanis, Holocaust survivor, partisan and founder of the Riga Jewish Museum, who gave an astonishing and priceless four-hour interview.

Another notable interview is that of Vaira Vīķe-Freiberga, twice President of Latvia, who fled the country during this Courland Pocket period. She was generous enough to revisit these memories.

I would like to record my thanks to the University Press of Kansas for permission to use extracts from *In Deadly Combat: A German soldiers' memoir of the Eastern Front* by Gottlob Herbert Bidermann, translated and edited by Derek S. Zumbro, and to Pen and Sword for allowing use of extracts from *Stormtrooper on the Eastern Front* by Mintauts Blosfelds, edited by Lisa Blosfelds.

Roger Bender Publishing kindly gave approval for extracts from *Latvian Legion* by Artūrs Silgailis and John Federowicz of JJ Federowicz Publishing generously allowed me to use excerpts from Franz Kurowski's *Bridghead Kurland*. I would like to thank Jānis Elksnis for permission to use translated extracts from *Kareivja gaitas Latviesu legiona* by Andris Gribuska, published by The Publishing House of Latgalian Culture Centre.

For their time, expertise and advice I am grateful to many staff at museums across Latvia. Māra Zirnīte at the National Oral History Archive at the University of Latvia in Riga directed me to vivid eye-witness accounts from Courland; Evita Rukke at the Occupation Museum in Riga assembled a collection of images perfectly illustrating life and death in combat in Courland, and special thanks go to Māris Locs and Edvīns Brūvelis for allowing me to use images from their personal archive. Valdis Kuzmins at the Riga War Museum gave me good advice at the beginning of my journey.

Daina Pormale, director of the Lūcija Garūta Foundation, authors Zigmārs Turčinskis and Sanita Reinsone, historian Karlis Dambitis, Ilya Lensky at the Jewish Museum, Margriet Lestraden, Dr Jānis Kalnačs and Joachim Bonitz were also valuable sources of information and advice. In Jelgava Astrid Zandersons translated accounts of the battles there specially for me: Aija Alba gave me a personal tour of the Stūra Māja KGB building in Riga, which was chilling.

Many thanks go to Kristine Zuntnere and Viktors Sopirins at the Latvian Football Federation and Ronald Gelbard at SC Hakoah, Vienna for their help with my research on football coach Otto Fischer, as well as to Ilana Ivanova for the photographs and anecdotes. I am also grateful to Andrew Reeds for help correctly identifying weapons, medals and unit badges in some photographs and to Sasha Skvortsov for translating the Heroes headstones of the Soviet fallen.

A special mention must go to Uģis Sarja who generously gave his time and expertise drawing the six maps illustrating this collection of stories. He did this because he believes these stories should be told. Copious thanks go to Dace Bērziņa for her wisdom, help, guidance and on occasion, lifts. I thank my sister-in-law Kristīne Kamerāde for keeping me sane and taking me out in Riga, and I'm grateful to Ralfs Jekabsons for his translation work and to my son Mārtiņš Vītoliņš for keeping me grounded. I am especially grateful to Duncan Rogers and his team at Helion for their efforts and expertise in bringing this book to publication.

However, the person who deserves my deepest thanks and who offered unstinting support, advice, companionship and translation services at all times day and night and even made phone calls on my behalf is my wife, Dr Daiga Kamerāde-Hanta. She was there for me in the dark times and helped make sense of the contradictions of Latvia's tortuous history.

My grateful thanks to all.

Vincent Hunt
Riga, January 2016

Notes on Language

The Latvian language has some rules that are quite different to English, so here is a brief guide to the correct pronunciation of some of the places in the book and the names of the people telling their stories.

Ā: a stripe over the a, as in Liepāja, makes it long, so pronunciation is 'Leea-paaya'.
    In Jānis: aah, but the J is pronounced Y ... so 'Yaanis'. Popervāle: Popervaaleh.
Ī: an ī as in Kuldīga is 'ee', so pronunciation is Kul-dee-ga. Riga is the same.
Dž as in Džūkste is pronounced like the j in jungle, so 'Jook-ster'
Š as in Arnolds Šulcs, Aldis Barševskis for example: <u>sh</u>
Ž as in Žanis: a soft 'j' so 'Janniss' ... Dmitrijs Mežeckis is Meh-jetskis
Č as in Turčinskis: a 'ch' sound so 'Tur-chin-skis'
Ē: a stripe over the e makes it long, so Herberts Knēts is pronounced 'Ker-nairts'.
A ķ means a 'chir' sound, so in Juris Raķis, the surname is pronounced 'Rah-chirss'
A stripe over the ū as in Brūvelis equals 'oo' so 'Broo-velis'. Stūra Māja: 'Stoora Maa-ya'
A normal u is short, like in 'put'
Ai is pronounced as in 'fine'. Au is pronounced like 'loud' as in Jaunpils: 'Yown-pils'
Ei is pronounced like 'play'.

Source: English-Latvian Phrase Book by Gunta Strauhmane, Zigrīda Vinčela, published by Zvaigzne ABC

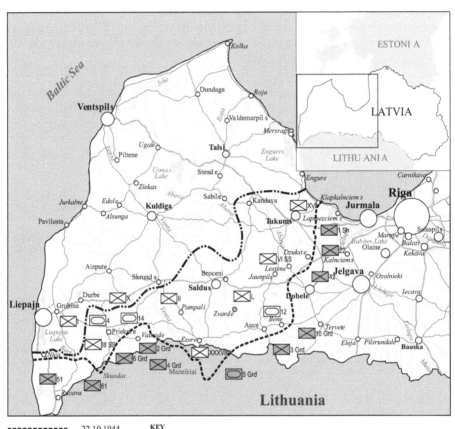

Map 1 Western Latvia and the Courland Pocket, October 1944 to May 1945.
The area between the lines is the extent of the Soviet advance following the six battles from
October 1944 to May 1945.

1

Maybe it's Easier to Forget

Seventeen floors above street level, the view from the roof of Riga's Academy of Sciences is spectacular. It's possibly the best in town.

Like a 1950s nicotine-stained version of the Empire State Building with cousins in Moscow and Warsaw, the Academy is a symbol of fifty years of Soviet power; a period of alien occupation, repression and suppression which ended only in 1991 with the restoration of Latvian independence.

Few tourists come here, but many should. There's a bird's eye view to the east over the Daugava, the wide and rolling river that flows through Riga to the Baltic. A tall red TV tower rises from an island in the middle of that blue ribbon which divides Latvia as it flows from Russia and Belarus into the Gulf of Riga.

To the west is the five-arched railway bridge into the city, an icon in metal which brought to Riga industry, machinery, trade, wealth and, perhaps most significantly, people. Further to the west are the symbols of the new Riga: an enormous glass and steel national library, the 27-storey smooth glass cylinder Swedbank building known as The Sun Stone, and a little further to the right the beautifully-weighted Valdemara Street suspension bridge across the river.

The Academy of Sciences stands alone on the Old Town side of the Daugava as a magnificent monstrosity: a classic Soviet-era monolithic skyscraper gifted to the city by the Kremlin, its tower narrowing in stages as it rises into the sky.

From the viewing platform there is a glorious panorama through the centuries of Riga's existence. The tall spire of St Peter's Church and the Riga Dome are landmarks on the cobbled streets of an Old Town dating back to the 13th century. By day they buzz with the conversations of tourists in bars and restaurants in the picturesque squares. By night they echo to the drunken shouts of stag parties and the thumping beats of basement nightclubs.

When the visibility is good – like today – it's possible to see Riga unfolding for several miles in each direction before the forests begin. They are dark, dense fringes of pine trees skirting the suburbs, marking the boundaries of urban habitation.

People say there are two Latvias: Riga, and everywhere else. But there's also the Latvia of the towns and the land of the forests. Both are utterly different.

The forests are a world of silence, stillness and secrets. In the cities material things move on – the cars, the clothes, the phones – but in the forests time has stood still.

There are far fewer tourists at the top of the Academy today than are leaning out from the viewing deck of St Peter's, one of the plum platforms for casual city visitors. The Academy tower lies outside the safety of the Old Town in a poor, rundown area called the Moscow suburb. There's a feeling of dodginess in the streets around here that would be enough to put off those who prefer sightseeing in absolute safety. Independent travellers say a market round the corner from here is the first place that stolen mobile phones re-appear. It's one of the most desperate markets I've ever seen. Part-worn bicycle tyres, junk furniture, second-hand clothes, car parts: on my first visit I couldn't quite believe the stuff displayed in the canvas-covered stalls actually had a price.

The Moscow suburb is, like Latvia itself, a crossroads of history. The junction of Gogola Street* close to the market is a classic example. The imminent arrival in Riga – then part of the Russian Empire – of Napoleon's forces on their way to Moscow triggered such a crisis that the houses to one side were cleared to allow a greater field of fire to stop them. In the end, Napoleon never arrived.

On one corner of that junction a savage episode in Latvia's more recent history was played out when Nazi troops torched the Great Choral Synagogue as one of the first acts of the Holocaust. Having forced the Red Army out of Riga, the Nazis began the systematic genocide of European Jews with Riga the epicentre of the killing machine.

Within days of the German occupation in late June 1941 anti-Jewish pogroms in Riga started. Fascist Latvian thugs encouraged by their new Nazi masters roamed at will, beating up Jewish women, children and old men, raping and humiliating them. Then the killing started.

Historians disagree on the exact number of dead but just 200 metres from where I am this synagogue was set ablaze on the evening of 4 July 1941. The event was filmed for use in Nazi propaganda newsreels. The story goes that as many as 300 Lithuanian Jews, mostly women and children, were locked in the basement by a squad of pro-Nazi Latvian auxiliaries known as the *Arājs Kommando*. Led by former policeman Viktors Arājs the 200-300 volunteers in the *Arājs Kommando* shared anti-Soviet, anti-Semitic political leanings and from the earliest days of German rule embarked on a vicious and drunken rampage of hatred and death.[1]

The synagogue fire was just the start. Before long their missions of murder spread out across the Latvian countryside. They drove from town to town in blue transit buses, rounding up Jews and forcing them to dig their own graves before shooting them, aided and guided by the notorious Nazi *Einsatzkommando* mobile killing units.[2]

Some historians estimate the *Arājs Kommando* volunteers were responsible for the deaths of 26,000 people, mostly Jews.[3]

By the end of February 1942 the SS reported 65,000 Latvian Jews executed, most by *Einsatzgruppe A* and their Latvian auxiliaries. Altogether only 1,000 Latvian Jews survived the war out of a pre-war population of 70,000; only 100 were left alive in Riga.[4]

In the years 1941 to 1944 the streets of this district were designated as the Riga Ghetto, where the city's Jews were gathered. From here men, women and children alike were marched off to the forests at Rumbula in November and December 1941 for one of the most appalling chapters of mass murder in World War II. Here

*   Named after the Russian writer Gogol, in Latvian *Gogoļa iela*.

25,000 Jews were killed in two massacres by soldiers from the personal staff of SS *Obergruppenführer* Friedrich Jeckeln. He had organised the mass killings of Kiev's Jews at Babi Yar a few months earlier. They were helped by 1,500 Latvian accomplices, including 800 Riga police, who cleared the ghetto, marched the Jews to the forest and sealed off any escape routes.[5]

The descriptions of what happened in the forest are unspeakable, like a glimpse of hell. Men, women and children were forced to undress and lie in a pit before being shot. The next victims were ordered to lie on top of them then they too were shot, with an officer administering a *coup de grace* to anyone not killed outright. This method was known as 'sardine packing'. The process was repeated endlessly, with soil thrown over each layer of victims until everyone was dead. As the murderers marched away the mass grave twitched and groaned for a while, then fell silent. Amazingly two or three women survived by pretending to be dead, and crept out of the pile of corpses when night fell. Only one survived the war, Frida Michelson, whose account is harrowing.[6]

Ruthless and brutal, Jeckeln was decorated for his work in the forest. I will hear accounts of many more murders ordered by him before my journey through the Latvian battlefields is complete.

I am travelling west from Riga along the front line of the final frontier of World War II, across a region called Courland. The Germans called it Kurland, the Latvians know it as Kurzeme. It's a land of dense forests, of lakes and rivers and sandy, unspoilt beaches – it's a lovely place to have a holiday. But seven decades ago this land was the last battlefield in a cataclysmic fight to the death between two massively armoured ideologies, pressing anyone within reach into serving their cause.

The once-triumphant Nazi armies were pushed back by their Soviet enemy to a corner of the Baltics where, with their backs to the sea, they resisted six unimaginable onslaughts from land and air aimed at dislodging their grip on the final two ports that offered a way out. Alongside the Germans were a generation of Latvian men, many no more than schoolboys, fighting in Nazi uniforms as *Waffen-SS* and known as 'the Latvian Legion'. Once the Nazis started taking heavy casualties in the East, men of fighting age in the lands they had captured were seen as ready replacements. For many Latvians the choice they were given was simple: a combat unit, a labour battalion or a concentration camp. Formed in early 1943, the Legion consisted of two divisions of *Waffen-SS*, the 15th Grenadiers and the 19th. The 19th ended up trapped in Courland and was forced to capitulate: the 15th was shipped west to help defend Germany. Despite the 15th taking huge casualties, many men managed to surrender to the Allies and thus survive both the war and the post-war reckoning.

The Legion remains controversial to this day as its ranks included *Arājs Kommando* men responsible for the murder of tens of thousands of Jews in the Holocaust in Latvia. One of its founding fathers was Lieutenant Colonel Voldemārs Veiss, who, along with Arājs, energetically murdered Communists, Jews and political enemies in 'cleansing' operations in Riga.

Army officer Artūrs Silgailis fled to Germany in 1941 after being removed as unreliable by the Soviets and was groomed by the *Abwehr*, German military intelligence.

He returned with the Nazi invasion and helped set up the Legion, eventually becoming chief of staff to Inspector General Rūdolfs Bangerskis, nominally the highest-ranking Latvian officer but still under German command.[7]

As well as being an eye-witness Silgailis was a key player in the conflict in Courland. His memories are quoted throughout this book.

There were many Latvians in the Red Army too. Some were volunteers, some were Jews who went east to escape the Nazi invasion in 1941. Many were men press-ganged into a Red Army uniform as areas of Eastern Latvia were freed from Nazi control after 1944. The casualty lists in Courland record many Latvian Jews dying in Red Army service fighting the Nazis.[8]

My journey will take me across a land stained with wartime tragedy, revealing a nation still traumatised by its recent and not-so-recent experience. Even now Latvia is mourning its war dead … but grieving for so much loss in so many ways in such a short space of time that it is scarcely believable.

This is the story of a world at war in a small, forgotten part of a land at the cross-roads of history. There are Russians and Germans, but there are Latvians too, and Spaniards, Swedes, Kazakhs, Norwegians, Ukranians, Dutch, Lithuanians … a united nations of men fighting for fascism and Adolf Hitler pitted against a united nations of men fighting for Joseph Stalin – whether they wanted to or not.

Sometimes brothers of different ages found themselves on opposing sides, facing each other across the battlefield. Civilians were grabbed from the street and sent to Germany to build defences. Boys were taken from the classroom, pressed into uniform and sent to the front line: they were often dead within days. The future President of Latvia escaped in a truck laden with refugees, dodging a hail of bullets from Soviet planes strafing the road to the coast.

The forests became places of refuge, escape and resistance as well as of ambush. Several times entire Soviet units were caught in the woods and wiped out. In the deep forests, casualties of the war have been found unburied even recently, resting for one final time against a tree. Now, just bones remain.

The forests were dangerous places, concealing deserters, partisans and armed and desperate men of all allegiances. They shared the sanctuary of the trees with refugees and people with nowhere else to go. Awful, unspeakable things were done to defence-less and vulnerable people.

Infants and their young mothers, grandmothers and grandfathers were murdered, mutilated and raped by Nazi and Red Army soldiers alike in a frenzy of bloodlust. Pro-Soviet partisans took revenge on local fathers for the bravery of their sons in a Nazi uniform. When a group of nationalist partisans, the Rubenis Battalion, killed 300 Nazi troops in a running battle through the forests and were fed and watered by people living in that area, German revenge squads slaughtered them all. The name of Zlēkas should rank alongside the worst brutalities of the Nazis. It's sick-ening: babies, teenagers, the elderly – 160 civilians murdered. And there's hardly a word about it.

These brutal episodes are a glimpse of the bloodlust, murder and crazed killing that visited this small region of western Latvia. They do not feature heavily in official histories but are remembered in great detail by the locals, recorded for this book.

'I hope you have a strong stomach,' the ageing history teacher said, clutching bulging folders of records painstakingly copied by hand from Soviet-era archives – and then kept away from the prying noses of academics.

Before I started my journey I asked one friend why there weren't more memorials to the terrible things that happened in Latvia during the war. 'Maybe it's easier to forget,' she said. 'The country would be littered with memorials. There wouldn't be time to get on with things that need doing today'.

Latvian history has been twisted by victory and ideology. Archives which survived the bombs and flames of war were shipped out of the country. The men who fought on the losing side were sent off to Siberian mines for decades. Many never returned. Latvia was rebuilt by prisoners of war to Soviet plans and standards. The memorials today in the graveyards of Latvia to Soviet 'heroes' who fell in the fight against fascism are sometimes to men who actually drank themselves to death. The countryside is littered with decaying collective farms built in the middle of nowhere, with blocks of appallingly constructed brick-built flats slowly collapsing nearby.

Those who survived had an alien peace imposed upon them. They weren't free to grieve: enormous statues to their liberators were erected in public places; sometimes, as in Dobele, built over monuments to their own dead. Even today elderly men are abused as they remember friends who fell. But though they pulled the triggers of Nazi guns they are defiant to the end: 'We were fighting for Latvia', they say.

Having travelled around Courland, met people who were there in the war and heard these stories, I now see what my friend means. For a long time it wasn't easy to understand.

Six apocalyptic battles from October 1944 to May 1945 make up the period known variously as 'the Courland Pocket' or 'Kurzeme Katls' (Kurland Kettle) or even 'Kurland Cietoksnis' (Courland Fortress or Stronghold). Each variation has the core idea of an army being trapped or contained – apart from the only term Hitler allowed, that of the less negative 'Kurland Bridgehead'.[9]

Those six battles centred on Soviet attempts to break through German lines and capture the crucial western port of Liepāja on Latvia's Baltic coast, which could be supplied directly from Germany and German-occupied Poland. Had that happened in October 1944 the scale of the military defeat would have surpassed even Stalingrad. The dogged resistance of the German and Latvian forces against overwhelming Soviet superiority kept open not only Liepāja but also Ventspils further north. Those ports offered an escape route for soldiers desperately needed to shore up the Reich's eastern approaches, as well as getting the wounded home and shipping out forced labourers and prisoners to build defences.

For the Germans it was a defensive war to buy time to get as many of their men back home as possible before the inevitable defeat. From that perspective the Courland Pocket was an important operation, even though the sacrifice of 200,000 men as prisoners was a high price.

Holding Courland was also strategically important for the Nazis to build a new generation of 'super U-boats' operating out of Baltic ports. These boats were faster, more advanced and better protected than their predecessors, which had performed so well at first in the Atlantic. Hitler's naval chief Dönitz hoped they would tip the balance of the war back in Germany's favour. Ultimately this was thwarted by the disruption to production caused by Allied bombing of German submarine assembly works and ports.[10]

In the few Latvian newspapers that survive from this time there are stirring calls to arms from German commanders for the Latvians to fight, accompanied by promises that the Germans will stand with them 'to the end'. By the end almost the entire country had been mobilised on the German side. The fighting strength of both German and Soviet armies in Courland was roughly a quarter of a million men each, including the vast numbers of Latvians pressed into service on either side. The fields, swamps and forests of Courland would become graveyards for many.

There were artillery barrages of unimaginable, unending ferocity; mass tank assaults, salvo after salvo of rockets that sucked the air from mens' lungs and crushed their skulls in their trenches. There were suicidal charges towards German machine gun positions that left piles of dead Soviet soldiers lying in front of them. The waves of attackers were forced forward by NKVD [KGB] agents brandishing pistols and threatening instant death to those who refused to obey. Either way they ended up dead. In Moscow's Museum of the Great Patriotic War the Courland battles barely get a mention.[11]

Ripped apart in combat, the Latvian 15th Division was pulled back to Germany to help defend Berlin against the unstoppable Soviet offensive. Up to half their number perished in the onslaught – but the men who survived this far were about to see a glimmer of hope. As Nazi defeat became inevitable, some commanders refused to accept German orders any longer and headed for the American and British lines to surrender. Thousands managed to reach safety this way.[12]

After years in Displaced Persons' camps alongside civilians who also escaped, they were offered fresh starts in America, Australia, Germany, Canada or Britain. Some Latvian populations in these areas are directly descended from these men.

Another exodus from Courland, this time in fishing boats, took refugees and members of the Latvian Central Council – in effect, a gathering of anti-Soviet nationalist politicians and intellectuals who knew victory for Moscow spelled the end for them – into exile in Sweden via the island of Gotland, 140 kms off Latvia's Baltic coast. These boats ran a gauntlet of fire from both sides, with many casualties.[13]

The German and Latvian soldiers who survived the carnage but couldn't get away faced a choice – to go into captivity and hope they survived years of forced labour in Siberia, which a significant number didn't, or to take to the woods and fight on, which a significant number did.

As many as 12,000 men took up arms against Soviet rule as partisans, operating from bases and bunkers in the forests, calling themselves 'Forest Brothers' or *Meža Brāļi*.[14] They were systematically hunted down by vast numbers of NKVD secret police who snuffed out any remaining pockets of resistance. Once eliminated, the bodies of the partisans – men and women alike – were dumped in the market squares of towns across Courland as a warning to others. In 1949 a mass deportation of partisans, nationalists and those resisting the collectivisation of Latvian agriculture in accordance with Soviet principles was designed to break support for the partisans. Some partisan groups, hopeful of Allied support, fought on until 1953.[15]

I make my way down from the Academy's tower and walk towards the Old Town. To my right as I cross the road in front of the main entrance is a billboard showing images celebrating 25 years since the 'Awakening'; the resistance to Soviet rule which led eventually to the second period of independence.

The protests that began in Latvia in 1989 were characterised by human chains across the country. People linked hands from one city to the next, along the main roads and into the countryside, my future wife among them, making a personal statement of a wish for freedom and for change. This human chain stretched across the Baltics, marking the fiftieth anniversary of the secret deal between Nazi Germany and Soviet Russia that condemned their parents and grandparents to decades of surveillance, poverty and oppression.

One picture of these human chains shows a girl at the end of a long line of people – several hundred, possibly – linking hands along a road leading out of a small village. The girl is holding a sign which shows the hammer and sickle emblem of the Soviet Union alongside the swastika of Nazi Germany. The implicit message is that both these ideologies were equally evil in their enslavement of Latvians from 1939 – a period of captivity from which the country was trying to free itself. That picture was a quarter of a century ago. The girl, if she'd had children, would probably be in her late thirties or early forties now. Her children will have grown up free, but what do they know of their country's history?

Almost every Latvian family has a story from the Courland Pocket time. There were Latvians serving in the front line in the Legion and as auxiliaries known as *Hiwis* (*Hilfswillige*) – labourers, drivers and men in construction battalions who serviced military units, constructed airfields and dug fortifications. There was a 1,200-strong Latvian Air Legion formed of two squadrons of bombers and one of fighters, which was used in the summer of 1944 in operations against the Red Army in Jelgava, a city south of Riga. Latvian personnel made up ground crews manning anti-aircraft flak batteries. As many as 146,610 Latvians served the Germans in various capacities: the strength of the Legion at July 1944 was 31,446. Ethnic Russians under German rule – 7,700 men – were mobilised into the Vlasov Army, commanded by the former Russian general and prisoner of war Andrei Vlasov.[16]

I know now, from speaking to men who were there, that the six battles of the Courland Pocket were hell on earth, whichever side you were on. It was a time of savagery, incomprehensible slaughter and suffering. It is a complicated, cruel and painful story stained with the blood of hundreds of thousands of Russian, German and Latvian soldiers, and countless Latvian women and children. It's a war that didn't end in freedom for anyone.

Much of what happened goes to the absolute core of the Latvian nation but the true horror has not crossed into the English language. In many ways, remembering all this is the painful route. Maybe it's easier to forget.

What follows will give you nightmares.

Notes

1   V. Lumans, *Latvia in the World War II*, p.237.
2   Lumans, p.204.
3   Lumans, p.241, quoting Ezergailis 'The Holocaust in Latvia'.
4   M. Paldiel, *The Path of the Righteous: Gentile Rescuers of Jews During the Holocaust*, p.260.
5   B. Press, *The Murder of the Jews in Latvia: 1941-1945*, pp.105-107, quoting 'I Survived Rumbula' by Frida Michelson.
6   Ibid.
7   Lumans, pp.287-289.
8   The Museum of the Jewish Soldier in the Second World War: Latvian Jews at the Fronts of Struggle against Nazism at www.jwmww2.org.
9   Buttar, *Between Giants: The Battle for the Baltics in World War II*, p.280.
10 Grier, *Hitler, Dönitz, and the Baltic Sea: The Third Reich's Last Hope, 1944-1945*, (chapter 9).
11 Author's visit, March 2015.
12 Lumans, p.370.
13 Buttar, p.325.
14 Plakans, A. *The Latvians: A Short History*, p155.
15 Zigmārs Turčinskis, *The Unknown War*.
16 Lumans, pp.292-5.

2

Leaving Riga

From the Academy of Sciences I walk through the market at the back of the train station, past stalls selling cheap clothing from all corners of Eastern Europe and China. There are tables laden with enormous watermelons, plastic tubs filled with honey, glass jars full of blueberries and boxes of garlic, dill, forest mushrooms and vegetables fresh out of the ground, brought into the capital in vans from all corners of the country. The food is fresh, good and cheap: Latvians live very close to the land still. The buzz of the food trade is particularly keen in the former Zeppelin hangars which house Riga's Central Market. Transplanted here from a First World War Zeppelin airbase at Vaiņode in Courland they have become a focal point for the city through thick and thin, a symbol of Riga and, along with the Old Town, a UNESCO World Heritage site.[1]

I am heading for another symbol of Riga, the Freedom Monument on the edge of the Old Town. It's a tall column topped with a female figure of liberty, holding three stars above her head representing the regions of Vidzeme, Latgale and Kurzeme which came together to form Latvia at the end of the War of Independence with Bolshevik Russia between 1918 and 1920. The monument is a memorial to those who died fighting for Latvian freedom during that war. The granite memorial was unveiled in 1935: five years later that freedom had gone.

I am meeting one of Latvia's most famous sculptors, Arta Dumpe. She built her reputation during Soviet times but since the return of independence in 1991 has used her artistic talents to commemorate the intense grief experienced by Latvian families and by the nation as a whole during the war. Among her many pieces on that theme is an immense piece of granite carved into an angular statue of Mother Latvia grieving for her child lost to the war, the focal point of the Legionnaires' cemetery – *brāļu kapi*, or brothers' cemetery in Latvian – in Lestene, Courland.

The fields around Lestene and the battered, patched-up church alongside the cemetery are where some of the most bitter fighting of the Courland Pocket period took place, including the Christmas Battles which pitted Latvians fighting for the Red Army against Latvian Legionnaires fighting alongside the Germans. It was slaughter here: massed tank attacks, artillery bombardments, hand-to-hand fighting, defensive lines stretched to breaking point. The damage to the church alone tells how fierce the onslaught was. Since the cemetery's consecration in 2003 Lestene has been the national focus of remembrance for the Legionnaires who died fighting for Latvia – albeit having sworn allegiance to Hitler, wearing German uniform and ending up on the losing side.

We sit in a café near the Freedom Monument as Arta tells me her story. She was born in 1933 in Talsi, a town close to Lestene. Her father was mobilised into the Legion and sent to fight at the front near Leningrad, leaving her mother and the family living in Pilsblīdene, between Jaunpils and Saldus. In 1945 that area became a no-man's land between the opposing front lines, Soviet and German.

> The monument in Lestene is a thank you to the Legionnaires who in spring 1945 saved me and my family. My father was in the Legion and fought at Volkhova and was wounded there – we didn't know where he was. We lived in Remte parish near Pilsblīdene and we ended up between the two front lines. One morning in March my mother went to the stable where the cattle were kept while my sister and I were having breakfast. Around 11am a battle started. We heard machine guns and artillery shells being fired so we got under the table with our dog. There was a crash and the window shattered and a powerful draught came in: we didn't know what had happened to our mother.
>
> But she came back from the stable and found us under the table, crying. The eight houses around us are all on fire. Grandma is so scared she starts singing hymns – 'God is our fortress'. Mum packs some bags with flour and smoked meat and we hide in the loft area above the fire. Around 11pm shells are still flying overhead when we hear someone saying in Latvian: 'Are there still civilians here?' Around 20 Latvian Legionnaires came into the house and found us. They started making jokes and washed themselves and drank some milk. They told us to grab some things and be ready to go with them.
>
> These guys who could die at any moment appeared calm, carefree, nonchalant – but they saved us, taking us away from the front line through the forest. I was 12. I took a little doll I had carved out of wood with a knife. I remember that the sun was rising when we got to Remte and then suddenly there was a plane overhead. We all threw ourselves into a ditch next to the trunk of a horse chestnut tree.
>
> It was spring. At night the roads froze and by day they melted. This spring they were melted so much I'd never seen mud like it – liquid, like porridge. Heavy Belgian horses were stuck in mud up to their bellies. They couldn't move and so the wagons they were pulling with field kitchens and wounded got stuck as well. We saw things like this every day.

We order more coffee and Arta moves on to talk about the end of the war and the capitulation of German and Latvian forces.

> One day in May I heard my godfather August shouting 'The Russians are coming!' Grandma locked the girls into a pantry so the soldiers wouldn't find them. We were scared to death. A soldier came into the house and started to speak in very good Latvian, so we calmed down a little. He gave us orders: 'Boil potatoes! Bake bread!' We were cooking and baking so much because there were lots of mouths to feed. Then a second wave came. They did not ask any more but took anything they saw. They broke the fence, broke the gate, drove into the

flowerbeds, took the cover off the well and … took August the godfather and our horse. I don't remember how long he was away, but he came back.

We stayed with our aunts and waited to see what will happen. On the night of 8th May we were woken up by loud noise. Rockets were being fired into the sky and there was lots of cheering: 'The war is over! Berlin has capitulated!'

The morning of the 9th May was quiet and sunny. I ran to the stream to gather white flowers and mushrooms and nearly stepped on a mine! Across the fields I saw a column that looked like a very long snake. They were prisoners of war, holding white shirts as flags of surrender. Once proud and standing tall, the invaders had changed beyond recognition. When they came closer they whispered: '*Alles kaput* – everything is over'.

After the mines were removed from the fields and all the debris of war was cleared we could return to our house. There were bodies and bits of bodies to collect, burned-out tanks, skulls and ripped uniforms lying around in the fields for a long time. The storage space we'd hidden in was blown apart by a shell and the stable had no roof. One side of the house was still all right though, so we could live there.

The forest we were led through by the Legionnaires had been chopped to just two or three metres high by all the shells and bullets. All the fields had craters in them from the exploding shells. But there was something nice too. Between the damaged trees in the forest there were strawberries ripened like never before! I have never seen strawberries like that anywhere since.

I ask what gave her the idea for the statue of Mother Latvia at the Brothers' Cemetery. It exudes not only a mother's love for her child, but also a great sense of loss.

When a competition was announced for a statue at Lestene I thought it was my responsibility to enter. I can say that it is built for those who saved my life.[2]

The trauma of Latvia's experience from those times has taken its toll on the population. One family lived for 50 years after the war thinking their loved one had fought for the Germans, only to find out he'd been killed in action serving in the Red Army. Another woman told researchers at the War Museum in Riga she remembered her father saying goodbye to her as a four year-old and leaving to fight. He never returned. She spent the next six decades searching for him, hoping to find at least a grave, but she never did. Eventually, into her seventies, she walked into the War Museum and told her story, handed over his photograph and walked out. 'It's over,' she said. She has never been back.

I walk across Riga that evening musing on the stories I have heard so far. Courland is not far from here. I could be in Pilsblīdene in 40 minutes at this time of night. In less than three hours I could drive all the way across the front line to the Baltic coast.

Courland is a triangle, surrounded on three sides by water. The Baltic Sea lies to the west, the Gulf of Riga to the north and the river Daugava to the east. To the south lies Lithuania and the Eastern European mainland. Water, forest and flat land are the dominant features in the region.

Most of the significant towns run in an arc across the middle of the triangle from east to west – the district towns of Tukums, Saldus, Kuldīga and Aizpute – ending in the huge Baltic port of Liepāja. The second western port, Ventspils to the north, connects to another scattering of smaller-scale towns and villages in the heavily-forested area at the top of the triangle: Piltene, Pope, Ugāle, Dundaga, Talsi, Valdemārpils.

Though barely registering as a significant destination for visitors today, Ventspils during the Second World War was of huge strategic importance for Nazi Germany. It was one of the few supply lifelines from the Reich and also a place where boats out of the Courland nightmare could be boarded.

Along the coast to the north and west, at the top of the triangle between the Baltic Sea and the Gulf of Riga, are the fishing villages of Lielirbe, Mazirbe, Kolka and Melnsils, home until the Second World War to the Livs, indigenous inhabitants of northern Latvia and southwestern Estonia for more than 2,000 years, albeit in relatively small numbers. When Latvia was incorporated into the USSR in 1940 the Livonian coast was declared a closed military zone and the Liv people were driven from their homes. Stopped from fishing, many went to Sweden. The end of the war and the subsequent Soviet occupation led to deportations and the suppression of Liv culture, language and lifestyle.[3]

To the south of the band of significant towns linked by the ribbon of today's main road, the A9, are countless smaller towns like Priekule, Dobele, Skrunda, Lestene and Bunka which on the surface have little to attract modern visitors other than their country town simplicity and hospitality. That impression is deceptive. This is where war on an almighty scale arrived.

Here the roads are very straight across flat or gently undulating plains inter-rupted by stretches of dense pine, birch or spruce forests. Swamps and marshy regions are common: they were significant factors in slowing down the Red Army and forcing attacks into bottlenecks where defensive fire could be concentrated, like at Priekule.

As I look at my road map and delve deeper into the episode of violence and death that was unleashed here seven decades ago these names will crop up time and time again, growing to assume a strategic importance I had never imagined ... along with a capacity to absorb blood and devastation that I could barely believe.

I have walked back across Riga's Old Town almost to the Daugava. I turn into an old street close to St Peter's Church and then down some stairs into a popular cellar bar called the Folk Club Ala. I'm having a drink here with a man with a very distinctive perspective on the war in Courland.

Andris Lelis is a slim, carefully-mannered man in his twenties. He's a military collector and dealer fascinated by the equipment used by those soldiers but he has a deeper connection still: he's a long-standing member of a group of enthusiasts called *Legenda* who search for soldiers still missing in the fields and forests. They're known as 'Diggers'. We sit in the vaulted cellar sipping glasses of honey beer and nibbling pickled savouries as he tells stories of recovering the fallen.

It can be compared to the Western Front. The fighting was incredibly intense. You see it from the amount of splinters and mortar fins. When you go with a metal detector in the forest you hear a low sound from the splinters. In the fields you hear this sound all the time. If you take a piece of earth from that field about a third of it will be splinters. There are more mortar splinters than stones. Mortars were exploding all the time.

We have a few helmets which were found lying on the battlefield. We don't understand how they are held together. They have more holes than iron in them.

There are about 20 active members in *Legenda*. It's a privately-funded group. The idea is that you follow the legend 'over there, by the tree'. You go to the countryside, find an old lady and talk to her and she says: 'My father buried some Germans here at the end of the war, by the apple tree. But I don't remember which one'. And there are twenty apple trees. But we will search for that soldier.

We don't call them 'Russians' or 'Germans', we call them soldiers from the Soviet side or soldiers from the German side, because we can't tell nationality. Soldiers from more or less the whole of Europe fought on the German side; from the whole of Eastern Europe on the Soviet side.

It's very difficult to identify Soviet soldiers if they don't have any medals. Often they don't have documents, unless you are lucky. Soviets were atheist, so no crosses. The Soviet dead were buried in mass graves, in a line. Germans were buried in individual graves. And the German paperwork is much better than Soviet paperwork.

In the best case it's only about ten per cent of Soviets who can be identified. The Germans are about 90 per cent. That's because of the dogtag, but in the last few years the zinc dogtags are starting to destroy themselves. The Latvian soil is so aggressive that it attacks the zinc and means it can't be read. We dig them out very fast because when air gets in the grave and reaches the dogtag it can be destroyed in minutes. It almost disintegrates in front of you. We scrape them to see the stamp but by the time you've read the tag it's almost dissolved, because the metal becomes as thin as foil and it's impossible to read.

We found two Soviet pilots from an Ilyushin attack plane, deep in a swamp. They still had their documents in their pockets, completely readable. They had money in their pockets – everything. In the swamp everything is preserved, as new. But working in the swamp is difficult. We have to pump out the water and the dirt and the swamp comes in the hole all the time. Working with bodies that still have flesh on them is not pleasant. It's dirty and stinky. It's much easier with skeletons. They are clean and easy to handle.

I drain my glass and we order another honey beer. The scale of the slaughter in Courland and the impenetrability of the terrain – swamps, dense forests, harsh winters with deep snow – means that Latvia has become attractive to bounty hunters seeking unsalvaged war relics and equipment. *Legenda* is one of the few groups licensed to dig and has strict codes about not taking anything from the soldiers they find. Remains, artefacts and dogtags are handed over to the authorities. Illegal diggers – known as 'black diggers' – are less scrupulous. Stories circulate about 'black diggers' stripping graves and leaving bodies which cannot then be identified. In at least one distressing instance 'black diggers' contacted the families of fallen soldiers they had located and demanded money in return for information about where the body was. The 'Black Diggers' are frowned upon by legal excavators like Andris.

> The number one rule in everything I do is: Do not take anything from the dead. If I know a digger is a grave robber then I won't buy anything from him. The unofficial diggers don't have papers and they rob graves. The Germans won't have anything to do with them. They refuse to deal with them. So they place the bones back in the forest and sell the dogtag.
>
> We have tried to educate the diggers about what to do when they find a soldier. We need bones and identification material. If you want the dogtag, keep it. But give us the number. If you want the medal, keep it – but give us the number. So in this way we get the soldier and we get his name. If we insist on the dogtag then we won't get anything.
>
> All the diggers in Latvia know that no-one earns money out of it. And if local diggers find a grave-robber in the forest, there's a good chance that he'll be beaten up. Grave-robbing here is not popular. There's a group in the northeast of Latvia that we can't do anything with, but there's not many soldiers there. In Kurland 99 per cent of soldiers found are given to the authorities.

With the arrival of another beer we move on to discuss examples of *Legenda* diggers finding fallen soldiers. One famous story among the diggers is that of 'Panfilov's Men', a Kazakh division honoured for bravery in the defence of Moscow in November 1941 whose commander, Ivan Vasilyevich Panfilov, was killed shortly after they'd beaten back the Germans. Andris tells me that in the later stages of the war this unit – the 8th Guards Rifle Division – were part of a Soviet offensive from the south into the forests of Pampāļi, where they were surrounded and systematically wiped out.

> We think between 3,000 and 5,000 men died in the Pampāļi forest. Only 300 escaped. The Germans knew they would attack there and so ambushed them. They encircled them and slaughtered them, bit by bit. They brought *nebelwerfer* rocket launchers in, big rockets, some with high explosives, some with something similar to napalm. And they just kept firing them. The *nebelwerfers* have such powerful explosives they suck all the air out. They are pressure rounds which collapse everything. It destroys lungs, skulls … everything. Our pictures from our first dig in the forest show helmets and skulls lying on the surface. We found a large number of bodies just lying on the ground. One of the guys saw something bright on the surface: it was a skull. Under the skull he found a helmet, and under that a greatcoat. When we dug out the site we found he was at the centre of a group of twenty other men, possibly who'd been wounded and who'd been left there to die because they were so badly injured. They were laid out calmly. They hadn't been killed in action. He was probably the first to be taken there, then another, then another.[4]

It's all rather sobering. This slaughter in a remote corner of the Baltics, way off the main highways of military or political importance, was just the final act in the settling of scores between Nazi and Soviet forces that characterised the fighting on the Eastern Front.

Less than twenty years after the Latvian War of Independence pushed first the Bolsheviks out of Riga and then the Baltic Germans out of Courland, ending 700 years of domination, the Molotov-von Ribbentrop non-aggression pact carved up the Baltics, secretly assigning Latvia to the Soviet sphere of influence. Hitler invaded Poland in September 1939 to claim the territory promised him in that deal. Moscow forced Latvian politicians to accept 30,000 Soviet troops being based in the country for the duration of the war. On 17 June 1940 the first Soviet troops occupied Latvia and took control. In July a pro-Soviet Parliament was elected which requested that Latvia be incorporated into the USSR. Moscow agreed.

A wave of political purges began, reminiscent of the bloody score-settling of the 1919 occupation of Riga by the Bolshevik forces of Pēteris Stučka. This time 34,250 Latvians would be killed or deported in a 12-month period known as 'The Year of Terror' [the *Baigais Gads*]. Among those who would be forced into wooden railway wagons to die in Soviet prisons was the President, Kārlis Ulmanis.[5]

Hitler's attack on the Soviet Union, *Operation Barbarossa*, was launched on 22 June 1941. The *blitzkrieg* ripped through unprepared Russian defences and by 1 July the Nazis controlled Riga. Coming less than two weeks after the mass deportation of 15,000 Latvians to Siberia by the Soviets on the night of 13-14 June 1941, Latvians celebrated the arrival of the Nazis as liberators. Liepāja, home of the Red Fleet in the Baltic, held out for a week before it fell. German advance forces moved on Daugavpils in the east, the gateway to Leningrad, taking it quickly. But joy at being freed from Soviet occupation soon disappeared as the Nazis pulled down the Latvian flags, outlawed the national anthem and began the eradication of the Jews. Another reign of terror was about to begin, against an ancient enemy Latvians had already hated for 700 years.[6]

The following morning I walk across the stone bridge over the Daugava to the Riga Railway Museum to talk about the strategic importance of the railway network in wartime Courland. Ahead of me in a vast space of swampy parkland rises a tall fluted column decorated with Soviet stars. Around the base figures of Soviet soldiers wave PPSh machine guns victoriously. This is the Monument to Soviet Victory in *Uzvaras Parks* [Victory Park], an area originally intended to mark the victories that led to Latvian independence but designated late into Soviet times as the site for this now-controversial memorial, built in 1985. Even the process of remembrance is a cause for an argument in this land.

I turn into the museum to meet Toms Altbergs, an expert on Latvia's railways. He tells me the rail network in Courland was a major factor in the way events unfolded during the war.

The people who had most to fear from the Soviet occupation [of 1940-41] were the stationmasters. In the independence time of the 1920s and 1930s the stationmaster was responsible for order around the station and more or less all of them were *Aizsargi*.[*] So many of them escaped. But train drivers were just normal. Some evacuated the Soviet military personnel and equipment [in 1941] and didn't come back from Russia. Some came back in 1944 and 1945, even bringing the locomotives back. Not all came back though – some disappeared without trace. Maybe killed? Nobody knows.

In Liepāja one locomotive driver worked first in the Latvian independent times, then during the Russian occupation in 1940-41 and then throughout the Second World War as a driver for the Germans. The system kept going according to German civil rules. Later in 1944 he was in Liepāja and drove the train to Saldus. There'd be a driver, an assistant driver and a German guard. He'd keep an eye on how they were working. The train drivers drove the trains, and there were no problems, nothing to fear. They just drove trains. German train, Russian train… who cares?

German engineers built a narrow gauge railway in northern Courland during the First World War. Now their sons found themselves running it, carrying out phenomenal feats of engineering to keep the German transport and supply routes functioning as the Soviet stranglehold on Courland tightened.

When the Russian Army moved into Courland in 1944, they cut the rail links between Riga and [the port of] Ventspils. The Germans added a loop to link the line with the Riga to Liepāja track and managed to evacuate 20 or 30 locomotives before the Russians closed this gap. Then, in just three months, the Germans laid 110 kms of track between Ventspils and Liepāja.

Because of the rudimentary engineering, the locomotives couldn't operate at high speed but chugged along at 10-15 kms an hour. It was important that locomotives could get to Liepāja for repairs. In Liepāja there were railway workshops, locomotive fabrication shops and mechanics – in Ventspils there was just a loco shed.

Toms goes to his office and collects an armful of books, which he lays out on a table.

The railway from Liepāja to Belarus and Ukraine is a very old line, dating back to 1870 and the Tsarist time. The Russians rebuilt sections of the line to run 180mm railway guns up and down to shell Liepāja. From September 1944 when the front line became intense, the Germans literally laid railway lines on the ground to get troops out of areas that were too hot to hold. Sleepers were laid on a bed of sand and then tracks clamped into place by Wehrmacht engineers helped by prisoners.

They literally laid lines on any level ground they could find. Prisoners of war built the track and camouflaged the line with Christmas trees. The rails weren't

[*]   Home Guard, so considered authority figures, and often executed by the Soviets.

even fixed properly to the sleepers sometimes so there were derailments. There was a derailment on the line from Džūkste to Berzupe on 16.9.44 – it had only opened the day before. But they evacuated 30 locomotives that way.

Post-war records show big differences between the number of locomotives operating during the Courland Pocket period and those tallied by the Soviets at the capitulation, Toms says.

It's thought there were approximately 1,000 locomotives during the Courland Pocket but according to official Soviet archives in Minsk and Moscow, they only recovered 250 locomotives. One opinion is that the Germans evacuated many locomotives by sea. Every locomotive has a value – they needed to get them on the boats out. But I have never found a person yet who has confirmed 100% that the Nazis took all those Latvian locomotives back to Germany with them.[7]

Before I leave Riga for Courland I watch a film about the Latvian Legion sent to me by a Latvian friend. It's been funded by The Soros Fund and scripted by the respected Latvian historian Uldis Neiburgs, in whose footsteps I will follow on occasions during my journey. It's a chilling introduction to some of the themes I am about to become familiar with.

One man who volunteered to fight the Soviets, Valters Skuja, describes his experiences during the 1940 *Baigais Gads* repressions.

Our neighbours were arrested, murdered and after that their bodies were found in the Central Prison. The same happened to my father's relatives ... they were sent to Siberia. Also a family near Jugla Lake. They had hung out a Latvian flag when the Germans were coming in. The Russians, who were retreating, took them and shot them all, down to the last family member. Even little children – just their little legs sticking out of the ground.

That disturbed us so much that my father said: 'Let's go, brother. Let's go, son. Let's fight the Russians and make sure they don't come back, for otherwise it will mean death for all of us'.[8]

Another volunteer speaks, Arvīds Nusbergs:

We hoped that the Allies would understand that Latvia cannot be occupied a second time by the Red Army and then we, by holding Liepāja and Ventspils, would be preserving an independent Latvia.[9]

And then Tālivaldis Grinsbergs, who was a conscript.

If the Allies had come here we would all have gone over to the Allied side. If they had made but one landing, say at Liepāja, then the Latvians would have instantly turned their rifles on the Germans.[10]

Janis Niedritis was a Latvian conscripted into the Red Army with a brother fighting for the Germans.

> It happened that my brother was called into the German Army because he was older and I was younger. So I got into the Russian Army. How can someone feel about this? To know that your brother is on the other side? I didn't feel good about it, but it was a chance for an 18 year-old boy to stay alive.
>
> On 23 December 1944 the [Christmas] battle began and on that fateful day my brother fell. I remember my brother on February 18. That is his birthday.

When interviewed about this fifty-five years later he is still so emotional that he chokes up.

> During the fifty years [since then] the Legionnaires were no better than war criminals and they even went to Siberia and everything, and now they are Legionnaires. And now those who fought in the Soviet Army – they are also supposedly worthless. As if they could have refused. No. We couldn't. We had to go.[11]

His sister Zenta Niedrite explains the torment of having brothers fighting on either side.

> Our family was heavily affected by the war. My older brother was in the Legion and fought in Kurzeme [Courland] and my younger brother was called into the Russian Army. And he also fought. It turned out that in many families brother fought against brother. The last news we received was that he was in the 19th Division, that he was in Kurzeme – and then the letters stopped. When we heard from his comrades that he had fallen we didn't celebrate Christmas for a long time after that. It made us too sad.[12]

As I sit watching the film, the torment these people have been through shows in their eyes. Many are close to tears. Statistics roll, revealing the scale of suffering.

- Latvia lost one third of its population in the Second World War.
- 30,000 were arrested or deported in the first Soviet occupation.
- 80,000 were killed in the German occupation.
- 80,000 were casualties in the German and Russian armies.
- 130,000 fled to the West.
- 150,000 were repressed during the Soviet second occupation.[13]

A former Resistance man, Ansis Ēlerts, offers his thoughts.

> If today we look at and talk about those Legionnaires and also those who served in the Red Army, my thinking is that we had no heroes. We were all victims. The Legionnaire was a victim because he fought in the interests of others, a

foreign country's interests. And he who was called into the Red Army fought for foreign ideas and in the interests of another country. We were all victims.[14]

But it's the final words of Valters Skuja that shocked me then, and they still shock me now. He was taken prisoner by the Soviets at the end of the war along with his wife and son. What happened next is barely imaginable.

I was taken to a filtration camp and brought to a house. They had black uniforms – I don't know who they were, but they were Russians. They started to speak in Russian and I understood nothing that they asked me.

They called for an interpreter and in the end when I gave them my proper name that told them I was Latvian, they grabbed my wife from the other room with our infant in her arms and took them away.

They stabbed my wife with a bayonet and then killed our little boy. Slammed his head against the door: grabbed him by the legs and slammed his head. It was crushed. They held me, tied up, and then brought me back to the barracks. I no longer cared after that.[15]

Notes

1   UNESCO World Heritage list at http://whc.unesco.org/en/list/852.
2   Arta Dumpe, interview with author, Riga, January 2015.
3   Liv Cultural Centre website at http://www.livones.net.
4   Andris Lelis, interview with author, Riga, January 2015.
5   G.J. Neimanis, *The Collapse of the Soviet Empire: A View from Riga.*
6   J.P. Himka and J.B. Michlic, *Bringing the Dark Past to Light: The Reception of the Holocaust in Post-Communist Europe.*
7   Toms Altbergs, interview with author, Riga, January 2015.
8   from *Latvian Legion* film.
9   Ibid.
10 Ibid.
11 Ibid.
12 Ibid.
13 Ibid.
14 Ibid.
15 Ibid.

3

God, Thy Earth is Aflame

The Soviet offensive in 1944 that pushed the Nazis back west from the USSR through eastern Latvia and into the Courland Pocket was codenamed *Operation Bagration*. It inflicted one of the worst defeats of the war on their enemy. By the end of it the five huge offensive fronts of Red Army soldiers had cleared Nazi forces from most of the western USSR and stood on the edges of Poland and Romania ready for a final thrust towards Berlin.

More than 1.25 million Soviet troops fought in *Bagration*, supported by 24,000 artillery guns, 4,000 tanks and 6,300 aircraft. Facing them were 800,000 Germans, 9,500 artillery pieces, 553 tanks and 839 aircraft. To the south, with the target of Lublin, Brest and Warsaw, were another 416,000 men of the Red Army equipped with 1,748 tanks, 8,335 guns and mortars and 1,500 aircraft.

The offensive began on 22 June 1944, three years to the day since the Nazi invasion of the USSR. It was an irresistible force as it swept west. The Germans suffered catastrophic, astronomical losses. German casualties in the fall of Minsk alone were close to 100,000 and an entire corps of 30,000 men was destroyed in the encirclement of Vitebsk.

More than 300,000 men were lost in two weeks of fighting between 22 June and 4 July. Another 100,000 casualties followed in the subsequent weeks, bringing German losses to a quarter of its Eastern Front manpower.[1]

The 57,000 Wehrmacht survivors taken prisoner were paraded through the streets of Moscow later that month in front of crowds to show the world the scale of the defeat inflicted.[2]

In July 1944 Red Army advance units gathered in Lithuania ahead of their next assault. This time their objective was the Latvian city of Jelgava, a key prize in the drive north to the capital Riga and west to the Baltic coast.

Jelgava was an important railway hub for routes across Eastern Europe and into Russia. Pushing the Nazis out of the city they called Mitau would disrupt their control of supply lines across Courland and leave the Red Army within striking distance of the important port of Liepāja. More importantly, if the land corridor from western Latvia along the Lithuanian coast could be closed, the 200,000 German troops in Courland would be cut off, inflicting another morale-sapping and strength-weakening military defeat.

The battle for Jelgava began in July. The German and Latvian units defending the city put up stiff resistance. Huge artillery bombardments, heavy bombing and street-to-street fighting cleared the defenders by early August but left Jelgava like a Latvian Stalingrad – a city in ruins.

Soviet tanks pressed north to reach the Gulf of Riga and briefly cut the roads west out of the capital. German counter-attacks broke the encirclement and cleared a way out. For some, it would be a lifeline and an escape route to the Baltic coast. For others, it was a journey to their grave.

I should be on the way to Jelgava now, but I have become fascinated by a period about five months before this, in March 1944, where, in the area of Riga around Gertrudes iela, a short walk north east of the Old Town, an extraordinary piece of music was premiered.

It's called *God, Thy Earth is Aflame** – a cantata, composed by pianist Lūcija Garūta who'd been a teenager during the turmoil of Riga in the power struggles of World War One. Her family stayed in the city as control switched from nationalist to Bolshevik and back, and in 1919 she went to study music at the Riga Conservatory. She drew inspiration from the renaissance of cultural expression in the newly-independent Latvia, but also mourned the descent into chaos and suffering the second war brought. Despite illness she drove herself to compose and perform in public and was acclaimed as one of the best pianists in the country.

In the spring of 1943, a competition was held for a cantata to be written to express the religious experiences and emotions of the Latvian people in the harsh wartime conditions. Among those entering lyrics was Andrejs Eglītis, a poet before the war who'd become a war correspondent and had worked with Garūta previously. In June 1943, the jury awarded first place to *God, Thy Earth is Aflame* and another piece by Eglītis in which the poet's words were interspersed between lines of the Lord's Prayer.

The winning cantata was due to be announced in May 1944 but with the front approaching Garūta couldn't wait and started work. The premiere was set for 15 March 1944 in St Gertrude's Church in Riga, with Alfrēds Kalniņš – a famous composer who wrote the Latvian nation's first opera – playing what was then the finest organ in the country.

But Kalniņš fell ill so Garūta, a fine pianist but no organist, had to sit down at the organ and rehearse the piece for the premiere later that day. The performance was broadcast live on radio across the country with a cast list of the top singers and musicians in Latvia, including Mariss Vētra (1901-1964) singing tenor, Ādolfs Kaktiņš (1885-1965) singing baritone and Teodors Reiters (1884-1956) conducting the huge massed choir he'd developed since the 1920s.

The church was packed for the performance. Mariss Vētra wrote later that it was almost as if listeners were gripped by a mass psychosis. The same church was filled to capacity for a further four performances through March and April, and the cantata was toured through Courland: in Kuldīga and Liepāja; in Ventspils at Easter, in Ārlava, Stende and three times in Talsi. On May 6, 1945, two days before the war ended, the cantata was performed in Stende at 11am and in Talsi at 5pm.

---

*   In Latvian: *Dievs, Tava zeme deg!*

Many of those involved subsequently fled to Sweden to escape Soviet victory. Eglītis retreated to Liepāja with the 19th Division, escaped by boat and founded the Latvian National Foundation in Stockholm with other exiled writers and political figures. Mariss Vētra – real name Moritz Blumberg, who as a teenager fought in the War of Independence – went first to Sweden then to Canada, where he formed the Latvian National Foundation there.

A hugely powerful and emotional experience, the cantata was banned by the Soviets but found new symbolism in the period of the Third Awakening of the late 1980s when it came to represent the longing of Latvians for freedom and an end to their exile. It was revived for the 1990 Latvian Song Festival when it was performed by more than ten thousand singers and is now used to commemorate the thousands deported by the Soviets.[3]

I find a critique of the work by the director of the Lūcija Garūta Foundation, Daina Pormale.

> In his candid and piercing poem Andrejs Eglītis reveals the tragic fate of a nation on the brink of non-existence, when emotions oscillate wildly between hope and despair. The composer Lūcija Garūta expresses all this in music that is deeply Latvian at heart, in combination with the enlightened power of intense spiritual experience, which gives hope and faith. The authors of the cantata express the heartbreaking situation existing in their homeland and give it the dimensions of a universal tragedy of mankind. Music and poetry have become inseparably entwined. Seeking refuge, a nation joins in prayer.[4]

A recording of the premiere performance remains, released on vinyl in 1982 in Stockholm by one of Garūta's students, the composer and musicologist Longīns Apkalns. There is a recording of the performance on You Tube, in which the sounds of battle can be heard in the background.[5]

Too absorbed in the intense emotions of a Latvia sliding helplessly towards oblivion, imagining the crowds emerging from St Gertrude's drained and uncertain of what will happen next, I realise I have lost track of time. I'm supposed to be in Jelgava tonight, and the train I meant to catch leaves in twenty minutes.

I run through the Old Town, along the subway to the Central Station, up through the station concourse and onto the platform. There's a minute before my train departs. I jump onto the metal stairs of the passenger carriage and climb inside. As I sit down the carriage door slides back behind me. The train slips gently out of the station and takes me away from Riga.

An hour later, drowsy from my exertions, I arrive in Jelgava. It's November 11th, Lāčplēsis Day, the day of remembrance of the liberators of the country. On that day in 1919 the newly-formed Latvian Army, supported by Estonian armoured trains and the British Navy, defeated the forces of the Baltic German nobility, the Bermontians, which had helped eject a Russian Bolshevik invasion post-First World War but then seized power. The Battle of Riga (3-11 November 1919) finally ended the War of Independence, led to the signing of a peace agreement with the Soviet Union the following year, and established Latvia as an independent parliamentary republic.[6]

Everyone on the train is wearing the red-white-red ribbon of Latvian remembrance. Latvians wear the ribbon with the bow downwards and the two ends upwards, like a flower or the branches of a tree, representing the one nation all the fallen came from.

Opposite Jelgava station is a monument to the liberators of Jelgava. It's a statue of a man with head bowed, leaning on a sword. The base of the statue is covered with flowers and candles in glass dishes, decorated with these red-white-red ribbons. The paths through Grēbnera Park leading up to and away from the statue are lined with candles too. It's 7pm, and families with their children have come out to look at the scenes. Many people who were on the train with me have produced candles which they are lighting.

I watch for a while then turn and walk to my apartment up Zemgales Prospekts, once a grand avenue for Tsar Alexander. I shut the double doors on the outside world after another day of intense history and prepare for the next.

The ancient city of Jelgava splits roughly east and west on either side of the river Lielupe. The main tourist attraction, Jelgava Palace (or *pils*), is built on an island in the centre of the river. From the 14th century until 1737 the Livonian Knights had a castle here, until it was blown up to make way for this sumptuous palace residence, designed for the Duke of Courland by the Russian court architect Rastrelli.

When the Tsar took control of Jelgava in 1795 the Palace became the governor's residence until it was burnt down in 1919 by the Baltic German Bermontian forces retreating from defeat in Riga, torching houses and killing civilians in their path. Restored, badly damaged in the Second World War and restored again, this time as a home for Latvia's Agricultural University, it is one of the most outstanding palaces in Latvia, ranking alongside the Baroque Rundāle Palace near Bauska, the summer palace of the Dukes of Courland, also designed by Rastrelli.[7]

Little now survives of the old city on the west bank, rebuilt in grim Soviet style, but gradually the gems of Jelgava are being returned to their pre-war glory. The stunning white tower of the city's oldest church, the Holy Trinity Lutheran Church on Academijas Street is a recent addition to the highlights, restored in 2010. St Anna's Lutheran Cathedral on Liela Street is the oldest building left in the city, dating back to 1573. The Russian Orthodox Cathedral at Raina Street with its perfect onion domes is a beautiful sight, especially by night, and has been fully restored after extensive war damage. What's left of the original Old Town wooden housing district built between the 18th and 19th century at the junction of Dobeles Street and Vecpilsētas Street is now a national town planning monument.[8]

The history of the city is intertwined with that of its Jewish population, which had flourished since the days of the Duchy of Courland in the late 18th century. Then, one in five of Jelgava's population was Jewish and 70% of all Courland's Jews lived there.

In the late 19th Century industrial expansion and the development of Riga and Liepāja as rivals led to a steady decline in the numbers and wealth of Jelgava's Jews, coupled with a grain crisis and cholera epidemic. In 1915 the Jewish population of Courland was exiled to Russia and those who returned after the First World War were the targets of pogroms by local Germans. By 1935 just 2,000 Jews lived in Jelgava.[9]

When the Soviets arrived in The Year of Terror of 1940-41, the economy was nationalised and Jewish institutions and political parties were shut down, but it was the Nazis who would pose a much greater threat to Jewish survival. Recognizing this, many Jews fled with the retreating Red Army when the Nazis entered Latvia in June 1941.

The killing of Jews began almost immediately the Nazis reached Jelgava on Sunday 29 June. The Synagogue was set on fire and Jews separated from the rest of the town. In early July around 2,000 Jews were marched to a former Latvian Army base outside the city, forced to dig their own graves and then executed in groups, a method used by *Einsatzkommando 2* in other mass killings.[10]

Afterwards, signs were erected at the entrance to the town stating 'Jelgava [*Mitau*] is cleansed of Jews'.* According to one account, a county commissioner later reported that he'd been brought in to restore discipline among local policemen who had 'lost all moral restraints' as a result of their involvement in the execution of the Jews. He arranged for the transfer out of Jelgava of the 21 Jews who survived, he said.[11]

In 1970, 25 years after the war's end, Jelgava's Jewish population remained at that same level.[12]

Jews were not the only target of massacres though. In early September 1941 Nazi troops visited Jelgava's hospital for mentally handicapped people, drove about 240 patients into nearby woods and shot them all.

The liberation of Jelgava in July 1944 would be a fight to the death in baking summer heat between the Red Army and its Nazi and Latvian defenders. Jelgava station was the focal point of intense bombing by the Soviets. Here the Western gauge railway network met the wider Russian gauge rails. The city was an important staging post, supply depot and training base for the Germans, heading both to and from the Eastern Front.

Waves of Soviet Ilyushin IL-2 ground attack planes appeared in the skies, bombing, machine-gunning and rocketing tanks and vehicles, infantry positions, bridges and buildings, softening the defences up before vicious hand-to-hand fighting in the subsequent assault.

A train carrying 430 refugees from Vidzeme and Latgale in the east was caught in a bombing raid alongside a military train carrying fuel and munitions. The ammunition train exploded, causing a massive fireball which engulfed the refugees, killing them all. Even today no-one is entirely sure who was on that train. The victims are buried in cemeteries around Jelgava, the unfortunate and unknown victims of war.[13]

Men of all nationalities fought for the Nazi cause in Jelgava and across Courland. Alongside Latvians there were Italians, Flemish, Dutch, Swedish and a Spanish 'Blue Brigade'. Local people remember Italian fighter pilots being stationed at the airfield, but not engaging in dogfights with the Soviet planes. Instead the resistance came from Latvian night bombers – German Arado biplanes based mostly in Tukums – which supported the infantry by targeting Red Army tanks and supply vehicles and taking reconnaissance photos of Soviet movements.

*   *Judenrein*: free of Jews.

As many as 45,000 volunteers from Franco's Spain served on the Eastern Front from 1941 onwards. There was an artillery regiment and even an air squadron that shot down 156 Soviet aircraft. Estimates are that 4,500 Spaniards died in Courland. Allied pressure on Franco led to the recall of the force in 1943, but the 'Blue Brigade' of volunteers stayed, many fighting to the bitter end in defence of Berlin.[14]

Jānis Blīvis was a student living in Jelgava in the summer of 1944. His father was deported in the first Soviet occupation of 1940-41. After the war he interviewed many eye-witnesses to the battle for Jelgava.

Soviet air raids [on July 28] continued, aimed at Jelgava's airfield. It was an unequal struggle between a single anti-aircraft gun at the airfield and 62 Soviet bombers backed up by 56 fighters. Even so, the lone gun crew downed one bomber and two fighters.

Red Army tanks were ordered to advance on Jelgava and though their advance was stopped briefly by a German armoured train, by 5.30pm they were rolling into the southern outskirts of the city. Two crossed the Gaisa bridge but turned back when they realised they had no support. Fierce resistance greeted tanks which reached Grēbnera Park close to the ruins of the railway station.

Katyusha rockets rained down on Jelgava, stoking the fires still burning from the raids of the day before, but the Germans were recovering from their surprise at the intensity of the Soviet offensive.

An experienced military commander, *General* Kurt Pflugbeil, was sent to Jelgava to organise a defence. For the first time 18 German attack planes bombed Soviet forces on the outskirts. A joint meeting of Germans and Legionnaires ended with the declaration of Jelgava as a city fortress, to be defended at all costs.

In the early hours of 30 July another attempt was made to take Jelgava with a fierce attack aimed at the railway station from the southeast. Two Soviet divisions threw themselves against a small group of the city's defenders spread along a front 1km long. Through the day, 35 Latvian aircraft* made 300 sorties against Soviet positions, dropping more than 50 tons of bombs.

By the evening the railway bridge had been captured undamaged but the station remained in the hands of the defenders. Soviet attacks from three sides – the southeast, south and southwest – were suspended.

The storming of Jelgava was a failure – they could not take the railway station, nor get to the city centre.[15]

I sit in my apartment reading this account of the fighting, realising that I had walked home last night through the area where the battle raged most intensely. I have a file of pictures of the wartime damage in Jelgava from the city museum's Head of Collections Aldis Barševskis, who has promised me a tour. Tanks and dead soldiers lay scattered in the rubble of the city's streets. Entire buildings were demolished. I guess this is why it was known as the Latvian Stalingrad.

---

* Night Close Air Support Group 12 – *Nachtschlachtgruppe 12*.

Following the failure of the assault the commander of the First Baltic Front, Ivan Khristoforovich Bagramyan, a Soviet-Armenian veteran of Kursk and Vitebsk, ordered his men to take the city at all costs.

Fresh Soviet attacks began on 31 July, signalled by intense missile and mortar salvos. At the same time Bagramyan's advance units bypassed Jelgava and moved on Tukums, where his tanks made a beeline for the sea at Klapkalnciems on the Gulf of Riga, cutting the road from Riga west to Courland and leaving 38 German infantry and armoured divisions stranded.[16]

On Stalin's insistence, bottles of sea water were sent back as proof the tanks had reached the coast.

Mr Blīvis's account of the battle resumes as fighting continues for control of the Driksa bridge across the river by the Palace, amid reports on Soviet radio that Jelgava had been taken.

> On the night of August 1, German artillery cannon retreated to the Lielupe's right bank via the Driksa and Lielupe bridges and blew up both bridges behind them. A few dozen soldiers remained behind the city walls and continued to defend the city.
>
> A well-known story is told about the four Latvian men who stayed in their stronghold in St Anna's church tower, where they continued to fire at the invaders to the last bullet.
>
> The fighting continued on the Lielupe's right bank. On the night of 1 August Soviet forces used the remaining undamaged Lielupe bridge, came over to the river's right bank, took the sugar factory, Pastu Island and Jelgava Palace but encountered fierce resistance and were forced to retreat back to the left bank.
>
> The next night, the Soviets repeated the operation upriver using rafts, but were forced back. However Jelgava Palace finally fell into Soviet hands. Eye-witnesses say Red Army soldiers dragged artillery guns into the Castle, firing them through the windows at German and Latvian positions on the Kalnciema Road [across the river]. In turn, the German heavy artillery turned their barrels on the Palace, reducing it to rubble.
>
> At this point Soviet troops dug in to defend their gains along the left bank of the river while other units moved on to keep the offensive moving.
>
> Several days later, on August 3 and 4, the defenders of Jelgava were strengthened by reinforcements from Riga. After heavy artillery fire the following nights – August 4 and 5 – they secured bridgeheads over both the Lielupe and Driksa rivers, threw a pontoon bridge over the water and sent troops in to re-take the city centre.
>
> Outraged, Bagramyan ordered that the city was to be re-taken and resistance crushed absolutely. For the next two days an onslaught of aerial bombing and artillery and mortar bombardment battered Jelgava before Soviet troops and tanks swept back into the city and this time snuffed out opposition entirely.
>
> By August 7, what was left of Jelgava – which wasn't much – was under Soviet control.[17]

At 9am the following morning I am waiting outside the museum in my rental car. Mr Barševskis gets in.

'Morning Mr Hunt,' he says. 'Did you get a chance to look at the pictures of the fighting in the streets?'

I nod, and put the car into first gear.

'Yes, I did. Incredible. Those pictures are really dramatic'.

'Indeed incredible,' he says. 'We'll go to that spot first. Turn left here'.

Over the next two hours Aldis shows me where the battle for Jelgava was fought. The onslaught came first from the air and artillery in the woods to the southwest of the city, then Red Army infantry took on the defenders in their prepared positions, with a huge cost in lives.

From the outskirts of the city around Dambja Street and the Ģintermuiža district, advance Soviet troops closed in on the station, first sending tanks to crush resistance in Grēbnera Park. But the defenders inflicted a heavy toll on the Soviet armour and repulsed the infantry time and again, often in bitter and bloody hand-to-hand combat.

One small triangle of the southern city at the corner of Kļavu and Smilšu Street changed hands six times in a day, as local people fled or sought shelter in basements. At each location Mr Barševskis describes in detail what happened.

> Jelgava is not a large city, but it's complicated for street fighting. It's surrounded with parks and woods, so it was easy to hide artillery and re-group forces, but then difficult to attack dug-in positions in the city. Stalin's tactics were to outnumber and overwhelm the Germans, sometime three to one, five to one, seven to one – but the tactics weren't designed to preserve life. Some of the Soviet soldiers had fought their way to Jelgava from the counter-attack at Stalingrad. They were very tough, and hardened in battle.
>
> In Grēbnera Park Latvian Legionnaires stopped Soviet tanks and soldiers crossing the railway line and taking the railway station. There was heavy hand-to-hand fighting and people killed with bayonets close by here at the viaduct. Recent excavations have found evidence of how intense the fighting was, from injuries to the skeletons. The Legionnaires fought very hard to defend the station, and re-took it a number of times after being beaten back.

We stop at the old hospital, where Mr Barševskis tells one of the legends of the battle for Jelgava.

> The chief of this hospital was Ringolds Čakste, the son of the first President of Latvia, Jānis Čakste [who served from 1922 – 1927]. In the war this was the only place where a water tap was working. During *Operation Bagration* in July and August it was very hot in Latvia. Very large forces of Russians and Germans clashed here, and of course there were many buildings on fire and lots of flames. At this point it was like the jungle. One soldier, a German maybe, would run

up and drink and no-one would fire. Then his enemy, a Russian, would run to drink. And no-one would shoot, as there was nowhere else to get water.

We move on, pausing briefly at the railway station and then at St Anna's church, where the four Legionnaires fought to their death in its tower. We drive on to the Palace and walk through the courtyard of this magnificent 670-window red and white building, buzzing with the comings and goings of student life. Seventy years ago every one of those windows was shattered as the fighting raged across the river. Mr Barševskis has sent me pictures of the ruined Palace with gaping shell holes in the walls.

> The city fell to the Soviets on August 6th and Jelgava was only re-opened to civilians on the 28th October 1944 when the front line stabilised. Between August and October we have no record of what happened here. The Soviets used trophy-searching brigades, searching everywhere, maybe looting. People ran away leaving everything. Family albums were destroyed, lots of homes were burned. We just don't know what happened.
>
> People who lived in Jelgava as children after the war remember the rats, a lot of rats – because there were bodies in basements and corpses that hadn't been found and they were food for the rats … and some of these rats were huge. One man remembers walking down a street with his friend and seeing a big column of rats crossing the street, going from one house to another. You understand why? It was a war city, and people had died and not been found, and food was left out. And they had to take action against the rats, to poison them.

In Aldis' office later that afternoon we look at maps and pictures of the damaged city to get a sense of the human scale of the battle. Pictures of the wartime damage show church towers and factories without roofs or windows, sometimes without four walls. The Police headquarters in the Market Square was almost entirely destroyed. There are prisoners sifting rubble and loading it onto big Soviet lorries to be carried away. Working alongside them are crews of civilians, some women. Russian soldiers with machine guns watch them working. The gangs clearing the rubble are still there in photographs dated 1948.

I need to think about moving on. We walk slowly down the stairs to the street talking about Jelgava's wartime past. The loss of control over the teaching of their history has caused problems for the post-war Latvian nation, Aldis says.

> As boys we were all fascinated with the war. What had it been like to be a Legionnaire? There was no official information available and the books by Latvians abroad in New York, Melbourne and Stockholm were illegal. We all pretended to be Legionnaires fighting the Russians and we were all heroes.
>
> 'Crocodile Dundee' is a Latvian who fought in the war and escaped to Australia, where he bought some opal mines. His real name was Arvīds Blūmentāls and he was from Dundaga, a country boy working in the woods. He was a good strong boy who fought at the front line with the 15th Division in Germany which surrendered to the Allies.

Some men became guards at the Nuremberg trial. They were good soldiers. That was one of the arguments against Latvian Legionnaires being Nazis. They were just soldiers, and most of them were forcibly included in the Legion or the Red Army, under pressure to join up – repressions against their family were threatened and so on.

We didn't know much about our war history for many years after independence. People didn't really start to feel safe until Latvia joined NATO in March 2004. Many were scared that the Russians would come back, so they didn't talk in public.

Only in the late 1990s did these stories start coming out, when the situation stabilised. Then some old people gave me photos and material and told stories, and a year or two later they died, but it was documented. Very many people were repressed, and they were suspicious and scared that they were in danger. They suffered, and they don't want to speak and perhaps put their families at risk.

Maybe now in this 21st century it's time to re-write our history. Our military history, the history of Jelgava, our national history. I search the internet for what happened in Jelgava but it's still not enough. Maybe one day.[18]

It's time for me to go. I thank Aldis for his time, get in my car and steer out into the street.

Notes

1   D. Glantz & J. House, *When Titans Clashed: How the Red Army Stopped Hitler*, p.201.
2   G. Roberts, *Stalin's Wars: From World War to Cold War, 1939-1953*, ch. 7.
3   D. Pormale, *Lūcija Garūta. Andrejs Eglītis. Dievs, Tava zeme deg!* [God, Thy Earth is Aflame!]. Foreword.
4   D. Pormale, 'God Thy Earth is Aflame'.
5   'God Thy Earth is Aflame' on You Tube: https://www.youtube.com/watch?v=rttecfu1NBQ.
6   J.D. Smele, *Historical Dictionary of the Russian Civil Wars 1916–1926*.
7   Latvia University of Agriculture website: http://eng.llu.lv/?mi=579.
8   Jelgava City tourism website at http://www.jelgava.lv/for-visitors/sightseeing/historical-sites/.
9   M. Meler, *Jewish Latvia, Sites to Remember*, p.142.
10 Ibid, pp.143-145.
11 C.R. Browning, *The Origins of the Final Solution: The Evolution of Nazi Jewish Policy, September 1939-March 1942*, p.274.
12 Jewish Virtual Library online at http://www.jewishvirtuallibrary.org/jsource/judaica/ejud_0002_0011_0_10064.html.
13 Aldis Barševskis, interview with author.
14 S. Payne, *A History of Fascism*, p.434.
15 Jānis Blīvis, *Memoirs* translated for this book.
16 Buttar, p.196.
17 Jānis Blīvis, *Memoirs*.
18 Aldis Barševskis, interview with author

4

A Taste of What's to Come

When Soviet tanks reached the Gulf of Riga and cut the roads west out of the capital, the war entered its final chapter. Defeat was inevitable: the only question now was when it would come. German counter-attacks broke the encirclement and cleared a way from Riga to Courland but everyone knew the Russians were now on the doorstep.

The return of the Soviets was something many Latvians were determined to resist. For centuries Latvia had been dominated by either Germany to the west or Russia to the east. The Second World War merely intensified this. Latvia repeatedly proclaimed its neutrality while both Germany and the Soviet Union prepared for what was to come. After Hitler re-occupied the Rhineland in 1936, the Baltic states became even more important to the Soviets as a buffer against German expansion. When in 1938 the Nazis annexed Austria and then demanded the Sudetenland, Stalin saw Latvian neutrality first as pro-German and then as no defence against a German strike against the Soviet Union. The pressure on Latvia from Moscow led first to a Treaty of Mutual Assistance, then an occupation, and then the 'Year of Terror'. The nightmare had arrived.[1]

When the Red Army occupied the country in June 1940 the Latvian Army was absorbed into it. The officers were arrested by the NKVD [KGB] and eliminated the following June. More than 500 were deported to a slave labour camp at Norilsk deep into Arctic Siberia, where most died; 80 were shot in Riga and, on 14 June 1941, 200 were executed at an Army base in the forests at Litene having been sent there on the pretext of a training exercise. According to some accounts more than 4,500 Latvian Army officers, NCOs and enlisted men were arrested, deported or murdered in the Year of Terror.[2]

Civilians branded 'bourgeois nationalists' or opposed to the Soviet takeover were deported to the USSR, with 15,000 people sent to Siberia on the night of 13-14 June 1941 in wooden cattle wagons. The majority would not return. Latvia's Ministry of Foreign Affairs includes an account of this night on its website:

> People to be deported were awakened in the night and given less than one hour to prepare for the journey. They were allowed to take with them only what they could carry, and everything left behind was confiscated by the state. The unfortunate were herded into already prepared cattle or freight railroad cars, in which they spent weeks and months. Many died on the way, especially infants, the sick and the elderly. Men, totalling some 8,250, were separated from their families, arrested, and sent to GULAG hard labour camps. Women and children were

taken to so-called 'administrative settlements' as family members of 'enemies of the people'.[3]

The only news families had of what happened to their loved ones came from the notes scribbled on pieces of paper and dropped out of the railway wagons. The newspapers, now controlled by Soviet censors, didn't even mention the deportations.

> Conditions in the hard labour camps were inhumane. Food rations were meagre and did not replace the calories expended through work. People grew weak and were crippled by diarrhoea, scurvy and other illnesses. Winters were marked by unbearable cold. Many did not survive the first one. Only a few of those deported in 1941 later returned to Latvia. The families had to fend for themselves in harsh conditions; the death rate among the very young and the elderly was likewise high.[4]

Hitler's strike against the Soviet Union was seen by some as an opportunity for Latvians to get revenge for the repression and deportations of the Year of Terror, and to re-establish an independent state. The infantry leader and later chief of staff of the Latvian Legion Artūrs Silgailis had been removed from his officer rank by the Soviets, who viewed him as unreliable. He fled to Germany in January 1941 where he was groomed for a position in the Latvian Self-Administration of the Nazi occupation and was a key figure in creating and organising the Legion.[5]

Silgailis survived the war and published a history of the unit, explaining why Latvians chose to fight alongside the Nazis.

> They didn't like the Germans after 700 years of German domination: forcible annexation of Austria, Czechoslovakia and Klaipėda did not enhance Latvian-German relations. Relations were so strained that no cultivated propaganda nor other means could have changed the Latvian sentiments. However, only one year of Soviet occupation of Latvia was sufficient to drastically change them. At the outbreak of war between Germany and the USSR, when the first German Army units crossed the Latvian border, the Germans were greeted wholeheartedly as liberators from the communistic reign of terror.[6]

When the huge numbers of casualties on the Eastern Front began to drain resources from Germany, men of fighting age from the occupied nations were pressed into service. The Latvian Legion – part of the *Waffen-SS* – was operational by March 1, 1943. Men mobilised into the force were obliged to swear an oath of loyalty.

> I swear by God this holy oath that in the struggle against Bolshevism I will give the Commander-in-Chief of the German Armed Forces, Adolf Hitler, absolute obedience and as a brave soldier I will always be ready to lay down my life for this oath.[7]

Legionnaires were sent immediately to the Leningrad Front where two Latvian divisions fought together on 16 March 1944, the date celebrated as 'Legionnaires' Day'. They were pushed back by the Soviet offensive in summer 1944 to Riga and by autumn to Courland.

During the German Occupation, the country was run by the collaborationist Latvian Self-Administration government, headed by General Oskars Dankers.

Decorated in the War of Independence, he'd fled to Germany when the Soviets occupied Latvia in 1940 and was groomed by the Nazis as another 'yes man' for when they invaded.[8]

Dankers agreed repeatedly to provide more and more Latvian manpower and resources for the German war effort. With the arrival of the Red Army on Latvian soil once more, the involvement of civilians in this struggle for survival was ratcheted up another notch.

On 17 August 1944 Dankers issued orders for all men under 60 and all women under 55 to report for work on fortifications 'for a few weeks'. They should bring bedding and food for two days as well as shovels, axes and saws. Those who didn't comply faced hanging as saboteurs. As many as 15,900 Latvians were sent to Germany as forced labourers during the occupation. In the month before the Nazis withdrew from Riga 6,000 civilians were seized in the city.[9]

By September 1944 the Germans began pulling out of Riga for defensive positions in Courland. A coastal corridor south through Klaipėda in Lithuania was still open, a precious land route back to the Reich. On 24 September Red Army commander Bagramyan received new orders to close the escape route and cut off the Germans. He was given six days to prepare for the attack and eleven to finish the operation, which involved moving half a million men, a thousand tanks, 10,000 guns and mortars and all their associated supplies 120 miles across roads already heavily degraded by the fighting of August and September.[10]

Vast amounts of men and munitions were moved into position by night. Recruits conscripted from newly-liberated areas under Soviet control such as eastern Latvia were quickly trained and pressed into the front lines to replace the heavy losses of the summer. The Soviet forces launched against the German defences in the fog on the morning of October 5th included a substantial Latvian contingent.[11]

The German defenders resisted: civilians fled. Some escaped, others were overrun by Soviet soldiers. Survivors who fled the village of Priekule told terrifying tales of rape and murder.[12]

When Soviet forces reached the Baltic coast at Palanga five days later, the German 16th and 18th armies were cut off. Again, bottles of sea water were sent back to superior officers.

The German and Latvian Legion forces east of Riga had been fighting a losing battle for several weeks holding back the Red Army advance. To release enough forces for a breakout from Courland, the German Army commander Ferdinand Schörner persuaded Hitler to allow the evacuation of Riga, now within range of Soviet artillery.

Operation Thunder involved a withdrawal through the city and over the bridges across the Daugava west towards Courland while a rearguard held off advance Soviet troops. When the last soldiers were over them, the bridges would be blown.[13]

Mintauts Blosfelds was a 20-year old legionnaire from Jelgava who had been wounded as the Russians pushed into Latvia. When his casualty station near Cēsis was evacuated, he was sent back to Riga.

> Walking wounded had to walk along the highway towards Riga. When I left the hospital the enemy were quite near the town and I could hear the sounds of battle quite clearly. Some soldiers were looting a shop and handing out bottles of drink, tinned food and biscuits through a broken window. German sappers were busy blowing up the larger buildings and mining the streets.
>
> The road to Riga was packed with troops, transport vehicles and wagons and civilian refugees. It was actually quicker to walk through the fields off the road. Now and then Russian aircraft flew low along the road shooting up and bombing the traffic.[14]

When Blosfelds got to Riga he found a former textile mill in the district of Jugla converted into a makeshift hospital, with beds laid out dormitory style. The wounded were sorted. Some were given travel passes to Germany to convalesce: others were ordered to report to local hospitals where the chances of being killed or captured would be much higher. Blosfelds got a pass to Germany – and was delighted.

> I did not want to stay in Latvia any longer. It was obvious to me by now that the Germans were unable to stop the Russian advance and I had no wish to be killed or taken prisoner by the enemy. I had also passed the heroic stage which would have urged me to remain out of patriotism and sense of duty to fight to the end. All I wanted was to preserve my life and get away from the constant threat of capture by the Russians. When I was handed my travel warrant I was glad to have it and realised that my future depended on that one piece of paper.[15]

The next morning Blosfelds was taken by bus to the harbour in Riga, ordered to dump his weapons and board a large ship sailing to Danzig.*

> The stream of soldiers boarding the ship seemed endless. The Germans were glad to leave Latvia and return to their 'Fatherland'. Whereas they laughed and joked, passed around bottles of drink and were merry, the Latvians on board were more restrained and serious. They all realised they were leaving their country, if not forever, then certainly for a considerable time to come… It was Monday 25 September 1944 and I was leaving Riga and Latvia, a Latvia which had failed to keep out the Russian reign of terror already engulfing half the land, and which would soon have complete control of the entire country and its people.[16]

---

*   Now Gdansk.

Among the German soldiers retreating was Gottlob Herbert Bidermann, a gun captain who had fought his way across Russia and back.

> We were provided the dubious distinction of observing the once-beautiful city at our backs experiencing its death throes. The primitive roads were choked with the dusty columns of trucks and tanks. Lines of refugees with wagons and handcarts piled high with belongings filed through the Latvian capital day and night. The bellowing of confused and weary herds of cattle filled the air as they were driven westwards over the brick-paved streets.
>
> The foreboding sight of Russian fighter-bombers became a constant reminder of our dire situation as they screamed over the tiled rooftops, the five-pointed red star clearly visible on the shining silver fuselages.[17]

The German withdrawal from Riga began on 6th October, with an entire army heading west along the only way out, a corridor 45 kms long and 6 kms wide between Riga and Sloka.

> Any abandoned equipment was destroyed. Pony carts piled high with wounded, intermingled with civilian refugees – the flotsam of war – creaked slowly toward the sea in a vain effort to escape the Red Army. The flames rising in the heart of the city from the Opera House danced against a black sky, casting ghostly shadows on the grey columns treading over the ancient bridge as a once-conquering army withdrew in tatters.[18]

The withdrawal from the East became a scorched earth retreat as the Germans destroyed everything of strategic value that might be of use to the pursuing Red Army and took anything they could haul away. Grain fields ready to harvest were burned as were forests full of valuable trees. Livestock that couldn't be taken along were killed. Railway stations, telegraph and telephone stations, buildings of no military value – even churches – were demolished. The country was plundered, pillaged and destroyed by the very people who had vowed to protect Latvia from the return of Soviet terror.

The Latvian commander Rūdolfs Bangerskis complained to Schörner, who ordered the looting to stop. But the destruction of strategic facilities continued, including an attempt to blow the Kegums hydroelectric dam on the Daugava river east of Riga, the pride and joy of Latvian pre-war economic development.

SS police chief Jeckeln told Bangerskis the Germans wouldn't leave anyone in Riga who could help the enemy. Prisoners of war, soldiers and civilians alike were rounded up and taken to Courland to dig trenches and prepare defences.

The evacuation from Riga took place mostly at night, sailing from Daugavgrīva in ships escorted by German naval boats. The Russians often bombed the refugee ships with incendiaries, and several were sunk. The rural population either walked to Courland or went by horse and cart. Riga fell to the Russians on 13 October 1944. Gottlob Bidermann was among the last to leave the city.

At 0500 the dawn brought a wet and cold day. As the sun attempted to penetrate the thick grey horizon, an officer from a pioneer unit pushed the charging handle of an electric blast machine wired to the demolitions placed within the Duna Bridge.*

> A gigantic ball of flame shot into the air over the river and the atmosphere was rent by an enormous explosion as the bridge finally collapsed into the Duna, severing us once again from the Soviet Army. Some 100 metres distant a ferry carrying the last remnants of the rear guard was completing its crossing of the river. As the bridge sank into the swiftly moving current with a roar, large pieces of stone rained down onto the vessel, striking and severely injuring some of the withdrawing soldiers. Thus *Operation Thunder* had reached its ominous end.[19]

At this same moment a six year-old girl, Vaira Vīķe – who six decades later would become President of this country – was among the refugees on the trucks heading for Courland. Her stepfather had been wounded at the front and returned to Riga just as the fall of the city to the Soviets became inevitable. On October 10th he packed his family onto an open truck packed with refugees heading for Liepāja.

> By sheer accident Dad had found out that at the end of the street where we lived a small convoy was being formed and that one truck would take civilians, along with one of the last columns of the retreating German Army. The Germans were leaving Latvians at the front and retreating first. The truck was loaded full and there were nasty quarrels about who could get in. One man wanted to take his bicycle. He said it was his most precious possession and it was new, but the people already in the truck said they would take a family, not luggage, so they threw the bicycle out.
>
> There was me, my step-father and my mother with a baby in her arms; my sister Marite. I was six. I turned seven in Liepāja. Marite was born in May, so she was just six months old. By January she was dead, only ten months old. From pneumonia. And, I think, to some extent, starvation.
>
> I was right on top of a piled-up pyramid of suitcases and parcels and was worried about falling off. It was scary. Planes attacked us several times on the road, machine-gunning the convoy. We would jump off the truck – I was lifted off – and lie in a ditch or try and find some trees or some cover and hope that we wouldn't be killed. We had three or four attacks on the first day before we stopped at a farm and slept in a barn full of hay. It was cold too – it was October.
>
> We arrived in Liepāja on the night of the biggest bombing raid on that city, when two or three munitions trains were hit and blown up, with loud explosions going on constantly. We all took shelter in the cellar of a brewery. My dad ran out to get diapers from our suitcase for the baby and shrapnel started flying about so much that he couldn't get back into the cellar. He hid in a huge empty

---

*   Duna is the German name for the Daugava.

beer vat in the inner courtyard. He went as deep as he could in the vat and there was shrapnel hitting the oak walls but not penetrating them.

Bombs were raining down. First one train blew up, then the next. The noise was absolutely deafening. When it was finally over and the All Clear was sounded, he came down into the cellar all pale and shaken up. It took several days to get his hearing back. At first he thought he'd lost it forever.[20]

Less than twenty minutes drive from Jelgava and I cross into Courland, the wind-screen wipers flicking away big fat drops of country rain. The roads are mostly straight two-lane highways with a centre line, unlit outside the towns, with drivers dodging and weaving to get past slow, heavy lorries. Road accidents are regular and often fatal.

I'm not in a hurry. One of the things I love about Latvia is the geography: dead straight roads shouldered by forests, flat fields edged by forests, sand roads through forests. The forests go right up to the beach and are a different, magical world.

It's one road all the way to Blīdene. This road I'm on – the A9 – cuts across the country from east to west, more or less exactly where the front line was. To my left and right the fields have been ploughed and the soil is heavy, full of clay. Tight rolls of hay lie scattered across the fields, and here and there small copses of trees gather by the roadside. It reminds me of the landscape of the Western Front in France and Belgium.

This peaceful country scene seems a world away from the horrors and hardships of the Courland Pocket. Gottlob Bidermann and his battle-hardened comrades some-times covered 20kms a day on their march west, passing columns of refugees, strafed by Soviet ground attack planes and existing on meagre rations sometimes supple-mented by horsemeat from badly wounded equine casualties of the Soviet harassing fire – baked with onions, as goulash, or smoked.[21]

Riga was evacuated in ten days from October 5th to the 15th, when the Germans finally abandoned their defensive line in the southwest suburbs. Along a single road and railway line west from Riga, and to the north of the forests between here and the border with Lithuania, passed 35 Army divisions, thousands of refugees, 80,000 motor vehicles, countless more horses and carts and 100,000 tons of supplies.[22]

The towns and villages on either side of this road would become landmarks in six furious battles in as many months: Džūkste, Lestene, Tukums, Dobele, Jaunpils, Saldus, Skrunda, Vaiņode, Priekule, Bunka, Ezere. Very little territory would change hands, but a great deal of blood would be spilled, especially in the belt of green lying east to west across Latvia just north of the border with Lithuania and below the A9; the three forests of Pampāļi, Kursīši and Zvārde.

Here the land is flat and swampy, punctuated by lakes and edged with deep forest. There are few roads, even today. When temperatures drop in winter the ground freezes as hard as rock.

The commander-in-chief of German forces in Courland, Army Group North, was *Generaloberst* Ferdinand Schörner, based a short distance north of here in Pelči Castle near Kuldīga. Decorated for his service in the First World War, he was a veteran of the Munich beer hall *putsch* and one of the men who turned the *Waffen-SS* into a serious fighting force. He was known by his own men as 'Bloody Ferdinand' for his willingness to hang anyone shirking frontline combat.[23]

The Nazi leadership didn't permit use of the term 'Courland Pocket' as it implied that the Germans were trapped there. That led quickly to comparisons with Stalingrad with consequent negative effects on morale.

The approved term was 'Courland bridgehead', as this suggested that Courland would be a springboard for a new offensive driving east again once the present difficulties had been overcome.

As mid-October approached, Schörner was certain that a Soviet attack was imminent. Tank divisions were positioned at Priekule and Grobiņa to defend the vital port of Liepāja, defensive lines 40kms and 20kms from the city. One division was held in reserve further inland at Aizpute, ready to respond if the Soviets threatened to break through in either place.

The first battles of the Courland Pocket began on 15th October. There was a powerful Red Army attack southeast of Liepāja and a fierce drive towards Džūkste at Dobele, south of Blīdene. In fighting near Putnakrogs, the Soviets lost 26 tanks in one small sector alone.

Making little headway, with both sides suffering heavy casualties, the Soviets switched the offensive slightly east. Battles raged for control of a small hill, identified as Hill 65.3, which changed hands several times. Tanks broke through the trench defences but the defenders mowed down the oncoming infantry. The tanks became isolated and were either destroyed or had to fight their way out. Few gains were made for vast loss of life. Latvian Legion commander Artūrs Silgailis wrote:

> During those eight days of fierce fighting the Russians had gained only a 2km deep and about 10km wide strip of terrain for which they suffered complete carnage of four infantry divisions and two armoured brigades.[24]

After the battle Schörner, a tough disciplinarian, sent military police units and a judge to the area to question soldiers who had fallen back without orders. Hanging stragglers on the spot and enforcing absolute unquestioning obedience was a measure designed to stiffen backbone, harden resolve and prevent panic. One regimental account paints a vivid picture of what life was like for the soldiers in late October 1944.

> The night sky was constantly aglow with the discharges of Stalin organs (truck-mounted *Katyusha* rocket launchers) and the muzzle flashes of enemy batteries. Artillery rumbled on a broad front from Dobele to Saldus.
>
> In cold soaking rain and on muddy roads the companies marched around Lake Lielauce to their new employment [relieving a badly battered unit unable to hold its position].
>
> The exhausted soldiers could only sleep for brief periods of a few hours in overcrowded farmhouses along the route. During the night one squad ... occupied a farmstead. The soldiers had hardly got themselves organised when a

Russian T-34 moved up out of the night and into the farmyard. The Germans ducked into cover around the corner of the house and cautiously kept an eye on the monster. Suddenly the Russian crew dismounted, hauled a cow from a stall, tied her to the back of their tank with a rope and drove off at walking speed back to the Russian lines.[25]

As November began the 19th Latvian SS were ordered to launch a pre-emptive attack on a Soviet mechanised corps but two soldiers from a penal battalion building defences deserted to the Red Army. A spoiling attack began the next day to break up Latvian preparations but Red Army commander Bagramyan called off the offensive shortly afterwards. In three days his troops penetrated only six kilometres into enemy defences, facing bitter fights for every piece of high ground and every farm.[26]

Combat like this would take a heavy toll over the next six months, with little or nothing to show for it. The fighting was remarkable for its intensity and the dogged determination of the Soviet generals to keep on attacking, despite an incredible price in lives.

Pēteris Stabulnieks was a soldier in the Latvian Legion who fought against the Red Army at Pilsblīdene. He survived the war and was sentenced to years in a Siberian gulag as punishment. On his return he wrote a vivid account of his combat memories in which he described joining up for the Legion imagining war to be 'a playground, in which you do as you please and have a good time. I was very happy. I was just waiting for enlistment day. I had no hate or anger towards the Russians'. He was soon to get a taste of what was to come.

I steer my car along the roads that Stabulnieks marched along to his positions. Pilsblīdene nowadays is no more than a railway station,* a few houses and a small civilian cemetery. In 1944 it was right in the middle of a war – as was Stabulnieks.

After four days we had to swap with the Germans at Pilsblīdene. We sent quartermasters but the Germans refused to come out of their positions because they were set up very carefully and it was quiet around this area. In the evening everyone gathered in Pilsblīdene to watch a film but as soon as it started all the Latvians were instructed to go outside where we were greeted by trucks. We knew when we were being transported by trucks it wasn't to a nice place. What a surprise. The Russians had broken through the defences near Blīdene and we were being sent there to stop them.[27]

There were, however, moments when stomachs ruled amid the fighting.

Not too far from here we found abandoned homes whose owners had escaped, leaving all their belongings inside. Even the goat was still there. We did think of taking it. In the cupboard we found flour, a bottle of milk and we already had

*   Blīdene.

butter and fat: we decided to make pancakes. It was dangerous but the temptation was unbearable and it was very rare to stumble on these kind of things, so we lit the fire and started to cook.

The Russians saw the smoke and started to fire their artillery at us. As we had managed to cook a few pancakes the shells started falling in the yard. Despite the explosions we continued to cook. However, a shell landed right inside the house. Vevers was wounded and screamed: the room was full of smoke and it was impossible to see or hear a thing.[28]

Stabulnieks grumbles about fighting alongside the Germans, beginning with complaints about the Germans getting better food, but before long he notices that 'wherever the fire was the hottest, they [the Germans] pushed the Latvians'.[29]

Shells are falling to the right, to the left, in front and behind. Everything is covered in smoke: bits of dirt and stones are flying through the air.

I wait for a bullet or a piece of shrapnel to hit my body. A good number of our men already lie dead or are heavily wounded. My only thought is that if I'm hit, it's in a way that will kill me.

After more than 100 metres the tank ditch hits a large turn and it seems like no tank can catch us now, not even the one right by the ditch. We jump into water deeper than our knees. Now we are much safer, but it's hard to move quickly. We pause at some houses halfway back to the regiment headquarters. Our commander had been wounded at the start of the battle and we found him here. I stayed to help him because the hospital attendant and the paramedic who came with us were wounded.

Having taken care of our wounds we headed back. The commander couldn't run. A soldier ahead of us was caught in the back by an anti-tank shell and blown into the air. When we got to headquarters … orders were given … that the Russians could not be allowed so close to the regiment headquarters, as with another push they will be here. But dinner had just been delivered and we were allowed to have a bite. For some this dinner was their last. As soon as they shared out the soup the Russians started to shell the forest we were in.

One shell exploded right near us and containers went flying everywhere. A second shell landed next to that one, badly wounding three men and killing the soldier who'd brought the food. As soon as we'd eaten we went back to the battle.[30]

Seventy years later I'm driving along the same dirt tracks. These were the roads behind the German and Latvian front lines. Across the railway line the roads lead to Remte, Irlava, Džūkste, Lestene – places that in 1944 were no more than small villages and gatherings of farms, but whose soil is rich with the blood of men, mown down or blown to pieces here. What happened in these villages would alter the course of a country's history and generations of its people.

Notes

1   Lumans, pp.55-57.
2   Ibid, pp.132-133.
3   V. Nollendorfs, U.Neiburgs et al: *The Three Occupations of Latvia 1940–199: Soviet and Nazi Takeovers and their Consequences*, p.23.
4   Ibid.
5   Lumans, p.288.
6   A. Silgailis, *Latvian Legion*, p.4.
7   Ibid, p.25.
8   Lumans, p.181.
9   A. Plakans, *Experiencing Totalitarianism: The Invasion and Occupation of Latvia by the USSR and Nazi Germany 1939–1991*, p.150.
10 P. Buttar, p.255.
11 Ibid, p.261.
12 Ibid, p.268.
13 Bidermann, *In Deadly Combat: A German Soldier's Memoir of the Eastern Front*, p.243.
14 M.Blosfelds, *Stormtrooper on the Eastern Front*, pp.135-136.
15 Ibid, p.136.
16 Ibid, pp.137-138.
17 Bidermann pp.244-245.
18 Ibid, p.245.
19 Ibid, p.248.
20 Vaira Vīķe-Freiberga, interview with author.
21 Bidermann, p.253.
22 Kurowski, *Bridgehead Kurland: The Six Epic Battles of Heeresgruppe Kurland*, p.72.
23 K. von Lingen, p.45, Soldiers into Citizens.
24 Silgailis, pp.126-128.
25 Kurowski, p.88.
26 Buttar, p.287.
27 A. Gribuska *Ways of the Soldier in the Latvian Legions*, p.59.
28 Ibid, p.60.
29 Ibid, p.59.
30 Ibid, pp.50-51.

5

One Man's War Museum

I pull up in front of what looks like a brick-built school dating from the 1960s, two storeys high with glass and wooden panels. I have arrived in a small village in central Courland called Zante, home to an astonishing private war museum run by a former Territorial Army soldier, Ilgvars Brucis.

He is a tall, substantial man with a military demeanour and physique and a ready laugh. He is delighted to show me around the museum and tell a few stories. More or less everything on display here he has dug up from the surrounding fields.

This museum is his life's work: an obsession, a driven piece of collecting. Ilgvars has spent years tramping these fields collecting the detritus of war. He gathers it in glass cabinets here, washed and preserved. It is a mindblowing array of weapons and military hardware from all across Europe, spread across two floors – and an indication of how intense this conflict was.

There are heavy machine guns, light machine guns, rifles and pistols from Poland, Italy, Belgium, Czechoslovakia. There are German MP40 'Schmeisser' machine pistols, MG42 'bonesaw' machine guns, Russian PPSh submachine guns with their drum magazines, Luger pistols known to users here as Parabellums. This is top grade hardware that is much prized by collectors.

There are shells of all calibres and sizes, enough to blow this place to kingdom come. There are binoculars, pipes, slide rules, corkscrews, water bottles, dinner services – everything a soldier and his superiors needed to make the best of their life and death existence in these fields, through rain, snow and shells.

Perhaps the most teeth-jarring item on display is upstairs: a portable operating table from a field hospital. It's made of sheet metal in sections so it can be folded up and carried and it's drilled with holes to allow blood to drain off. It's adjustable at either end to allow a variety of positions for whoever is unfortunate enough to be lying on it. I shudder at the thought of doctors sawing off legs without anaesthetic and critically injured men moaning and bleeding as surgeons hastily prioritise which of them is most likely to survive.

With my teeth still on edge I walk back downstairs with Ilgvars and he begins to tell his story.

> The Second World War was a tragedy for Latvia. In 1940 when the Soviet Union occupied the Baltics the Red Army absorbed the Latvian Army, and its officers were killed in a massacre in Litene forest. The soldiers were absorbed into the Red Army, into regional corps. Even Latvians living in Russia since the First World War joined the Red Army.

When the Germans ran short of manpower in 1943 they set up the Latvian Legion, and when the Red Army broke German resistance in the east and moved through Latvia towards Courland, any men of fighting age were pressed into Soviet military units and often forced into leading assaults against German positions ... which were defended by Latvians.

From October 1944 this was the last front line in the Second World War. The Germans held the Russian Army back for six months in six big battles.

The Russians lost 800 planes and 1,200 tanks in six months to achieve virtually nothing in military terms. Roughly half a million soldiers were casualties in this little bit of Latvia. Sometimes the Russians attacked with ten times the number of soldiers defending. The Germans shot the first wave down but they just kept coming and coming.

The Latvians who were trapped in Courland were the 19th Division. The Latvian 15th Division was taken out in October 1944 to Pomerania. One of our neighbours who was in the 15th Division ended up surrendering to the Allies and was in a Displaced Persons' camp. Then he went to Britain, and worked in Corby at the steel works.

He points to a photograph of the man in a glass cabinet. Next to it is displayed the application to live in Britain he filled in while being screened in the camp.

One question asks: 'Desire to return to previous residence?' His answer reads: 'No, to an independent democratic Latvia'.

Mr Brucis laughs.

If you came back in Soviet times and you'd fought for the Germans you would have gone straight to Siberia. Sometimes one brother would be in the German Army, another in the Red Army. They ended up fighting each other at Džūkste, in the Christmas Battles. Latvians on one side knew their countrymen were fighting against them. Soldiers from both armies switched sides, there were deserters – they even sent letters to each other.

Some of these letters are on display in cabinets in the museum. There are call-up notices from the newspapers. In one cabinet there's a life-size model of a German soldier on guard duty holding a rifle wearing an enormous pair of felt boots. These were winter boots for guard duty which fitted over normal boots. When the time came for an attack, those boots were taken off.

There are whistles, belts, a box of matches, some German 'front money', cigarettes, cutlery, stretchers, first aid boxes, special paper to wrap bodies in.

But it's the stuff that doesn't kill that offers an idea of what life was like for those who made it out alive. There's an officers' kitchen and a kitchen for other ranks. The officers' kitchen has bottles of all types of alcoholic liquor, crockery and even a gravy boat.

There are cameras and film, lighters, corkscrews, a pipe in a blue glass ashtray, a signed copy of *Mein Kampf*, a pack of playing cards, a mouth organ; a packet of Bulgarian cigarettes with the brand name 'The Soldier's Friend'. There's a cut-throat razor, some hair clippers, a comb with some broken teeth, a pair of spectacles and a pocket watch, stopped at 1030.

There's a wardrobe full of uniforms and boots and a big heavy piano accordion lying on a table next to it. All of this was found in the fields around here, Mr Brucis says.

> I was born in Zante and since I was a child I've been going through the forests looking for military things. I've been fascinated with it all my life. All my life I have collected things, since I was a pupil at school. On one hand it's a shame I was born so late because the war had ended, but on the other hand, at least I survived. I was part of the Territorial Army, working in mine clearance, a sort of Home Guard.

In the corridor downstairs we pass a four-barrelled German anti-aircraft gun and a variety of air-cooled machine guns, some with belts of bullets fed through them. There's a German helmet with SS insignia on the side and another with Belgian markings – black, yellow and red badges. There were of course Flemish, Swedish and Dutch SS divisions here ... it was like a multi-national force of Fascists.

Here are signal pistols, rifle-fired mortars, a sniper's rifle with telescopic sight. Moving along; some stick grenades, round hand grenades, wire cutters and then – very rare – some anti-tank turf mines and anti-personnel glass mines. These had no metal parts so they were difficult if not impossible to detect with metal detectors. When a tank rolled over the turf mine, the pressure forced two chemical agents together, detonating the mine. Ilgvars found seven of them, but only one survived being dug out of the field.

Outside are artillery guns, most of a Junkers JU-52, the remains of an Ilyushin fighter-bomber he and a friend dug out of a field over three days – and most of a T-34 tank he managed to acquire as the Russians pulled out in the 1990s. In a barn there are Jeeps, old motorcycles and trucks. Beyond the barn are trenches and bunkers that were intact which he has restored and lined with wooden planking. Intrepid visitors can sleep in them overnight by prior arrangement for an authentic experience of front line Courland.

It's the most complete collection of military equipment I've ever seen, I think. I'm astonished that Ilgvars has gathered it all from this corner of the Courland battle-fields. His whole family is from Zante, dating back on his father's side to the 19th century and on his mother's side even longer. Like his father and his grandfather before him he grew up in this town. Like many Latvian families they have have been separated and traumatised by the war. His grandfather died of scurvy on the streets of Vladivostok after being banished there for serving as a Legionnaire. It's clear this is still a painful memory, never far from his thoughts.

We walk outside the museum and over to a statue Mr Brucis made as his personal tribute to the men who died in the war. Every Latvian I will meet on this journey knows of his museum, but few 'foreigners' do. They should. Mr Brucis taps the statue.

The war came to Zante only on 8 May. The Latvian Legion was in Gaiķi, on a crossroads near Remte behind the front line. Latvian Red Army soldiers came here.

The Russians accepted a capitulation bit by bit along the front line. In Ezere the main generals signed and then were taken to Kuldīga. There was a manor house 3kms from Zante called Plāņi and the 24th Division of Germans signed the capitulation there. There's nothing left of the house now.

When the Germans capitulated many men from the 19th Division took their weapons and went into the forest. Some fought for eight years against the Russians, from 1945 to 1953. They were in forests all across Latvia. The hope was the British had promised to free Latvia, so they stayed in the forest.

All the bodies that could be found were collected. The Russians came in and buried all their dead. The only military cemeteries [allowed] were Red Army cemeteries. The Latvian and German graveyards were flattened, sometimes with tanks. The crosses were broken. There was no sign of any other military cemetery.

There was a school in Zante built in 1925 which was used as a military hospital. There's a mobile phone tower in Zante now, and in that area dead German and Latvian soldiers were buried. But in Soviet times they built a pig farm over the graveyard. In 1998 [after independence] the pig farm was removed. Germans came here and found the remains of 229 soldiers and re-buried them. They were expecting to find 36 Latvians because one Latvian boy had written down all the names of the soldiers who died there, but they only found a few Latvian soldiers. The Germans couldn't identify many of the bodies.

Mr Brucis looks at his watch. His daughter was married at the weekend and he is expecting his new son-in-law any moment, but he has more to say.

At the end of the war the Germans didn't keep documentation – March, April, May 1945 – and not everyone kept their identity tags. The military hospital used to keep information in bottles about the injuries soldiers had, and who died.

If someone deserted from the Legion they swapped their identity tags with someone who had died. That way the family didn't get bothered by the security police because relatives of Legionnaires were deported too.

As soon as the Russians came in they started deporting people. The Home Guard, landowners. If someone had run away and they couldn't find them they took someone else. My own grandfather was deported. He was in the Legion, deserted and was hiding at his grandmother's [house] but they found him. He was sent to Vladivostok and he died there.

Every spring and autumn when people are working on their land, it's not only explosives coming up but also bones and bodies. There were lots of bodies that were never collected, on both sides. When the war ended people just buried the dead in shellholes and got on with their lives.[1]

As if on cue, Mr Brucis' new son-in-law arrives and I sense it's time to move on. We shake hands and I get back behind the steering wheel.*

Note

1   Ilgvars Brucis interview with author, August 2014.

---

* Mr Brucis' many years of hard work to create the collection at Zante were recognised by a Certificate of Gratitude from Kandava Regional District Council in November 2016.

6

Now it's Total War

The layers of the past seem to gather in the centre of Tukums, a market town 30kms northeast of Zante. It's an ancient place. The roads in and out are more or less unchanged since medieval times, apart from their modern surfacing. A castle stood here then, surrounded by craftsmens' workshops and shops run by German traders.

The town's life still revolves around the marketplace, a pleasant spot with a fountain and nice carved benches. Local traders, fishermen and farmers have brought their produce here to sell for seven centuries. The main road in Tukums – *Liela iela* [Main Street] – dates back to the 14th century, straightened in the 16th century to point towards Prussia, the direction of trade.

Streetlights lit up the road into Tukums from 1875 and the arrival of the railway from Riga two years later boosted growth enormously. By 1897 there were tanneries, wood carding mills, a glue plant, food production factories and a pottery business, as well as two windmills. With industry came bosses, workers and families. New housing districts were built – the rich to the east, the workers to the west. German, Jewish and Latvian investment underpinned much of the town's everyday life.

World War I brought revolution and a reckoning to the town. The modern police station in the Market Square has a chequered history which runs more or less in tandem with the ebb and flow of events – and blood – in Latvia.

In those days, it was a courthouse. Part of it was used as a jail. In 1919, when the Bolsheviks seized Tukums after the Armistice, they imprisoned 11 local German land-owning 'barons' in the jail before killing them, along with another seven from across Courland. A plaque to the barons stands on Cemetery Hill (*Kapu Kalns*).[1]

Stability came with the establishment of Latvia as a republic and the peace agreement with Russia in 1920. Tukums grew and developed over the next decade. By the 1930s the population hit 8,000 with more than 70 companies based here, two-thirds connected to food and food processing. There were eight textile companies, five timber firms, two ceramic companies, a stone processing firm, a chemical manufacturer, a printers and also gas, electricity and water companies. Then everything went wrong. The period leading up to the war and the war itself would transform this town forever.

The Nazi-Soviet Non-Aggression Pact of 1939 had a profound effect on the town. Hitler offered Stalin Finland, Estonia, eastern Poland and the northeastern part of Romania known as Bessarabia, while keeping Poland and Lithuania. He suggested splitting Latvia along the Daugava but Stalin wanted the ice-free Baltic ports of Liepāja and Ventspils. A secret clause split Eastern Europe from the Baltic to the Black Sea into German and Soviet spheres of interest, with a stipulation that neither party would raise objections to what the other did in their respective areas. The treaty was signed on the night of 23 August 1939: the Soviet Union denied the existence of the secret clause until 1989.[2]

Part of the deal involved re-settling 20,000 Baltic Germans from Estonia and 60,000 from Latvia to areas of Eastern Poland occupied by Nazi Germany in autumn 1939, allowing Stalin a free hand in Latvia.

Many ethnic Latvians realised that when the Baltic Germans left, the Russians would come in. When the ships arrived to evacuate them in late 1939 there was panic-selling of currency and a run on the banks. The export of luxury goods such as furs, jewellery and artwork had to be banned, and a rumour that there was a soap shortage in Germany led to panic-buying in Latvian stores.[3]

In October Latvia bowed to Soviet demands to sign a Treaty of Mutual Assistance offering protection from German expansion. This involved the clearance of a coastal strip 50kms deep as a Soviet military zone, the handing over of naval bases at Liepāja and Ventspils and the stationing of 30,000 Soviet troops throughout Latvia. On 23 October the cruiser *Kirov* and several other navy ships sailed into Liepāja. Six days later the first of the Red Army units crossed into Latvia at the Zilupe railway border.[4]

By 15 December 1939, the deadline for completing the re-settlement, 50,000 Baltic Germans had left for the Reich. The 13,000 who stayed did so on the understanding that they renounced their German nationality and became Latvian – with all that entailed.

The war took a tremendous toll on Tukums. Between 1939 and 1945 the population fell by 30 per cent. The town lost the majority of its German population, 400 of whom were re-settled to the Reich. Virtually every single Jew disappeared, fleeing to Russia before the Nazis came or falling victim to their death squads.

Jews had only been allowed to live in Tukums after 1795, when Courland became part of the Russian Empire. They quickly settled and by 1850 there were 2,887 Jews in Tukums and its suburbs, just under half the population. More Jews arrived from Lithuania in the late 19th century. The bloodshed and deportations of the First World War and the War of Independence led to an exodus and by 1935 the Jewish population of Tukums had fallen to under 1,000.[5]

When the Soviets annexed Latvia and marched into Tukums in June 1940 the doors of the jail in the market square were thrown open to welcome their opponents or those arrested after being denounced. During the first Soviet occupation, 103 'bourgeois nationalists' were deported, including 47 wealthy Jews.[6]

The fate of three of those deportees – two brothers running an acclaimed horticultural business and a millionairess socialite publisher – gives an insight into what constituted a crime worthy of deportation in Soviet eyes. What happened to them echoes the tens of thousands of personal tragedies in Latvian society during the first Soviet occupation, which some might characterise as a 'class war'.

One of the big firms in Tukums in the 1930s was the specialist plant nursery run by the Krauze brothers, Mārtiņš and Andrejs Juris. Both brothers had nurseries in glasshouses covering 1,300 square metres. Andrejs Juris dealt in roses, dahlias, chrysanthemums and *lefkojas** as well as bouquets and funeral wreaths. Mārtiņš Krauze was best known for his orchids. These were highly prized throughout Eastern Europe, acclaimed as the largest orchid collection in the East. Mārtiņš was a regular traveller and his orchids were collected in many countries, especially in South America.[7]

Demand rocketed when Latvia's most famous woman, the publisher and million-aire socialite Emilija Benjamin was pictured wearing an orchid as a buttonhole.

Emilija got her start in newspapers working as a theatre critic and advertising agent for a German language paper in Riga at the turn of the century. Six years later she became involved with Antons Benjamin, one of the reporters. Although both were married to other people they took over the running of the paper – Antons as editor, Emilija as the business brains. In 1911, having persuaded all the Latvian-speaking journalists on the Russian and German papers in Riga to work for nothing, Emilija founded the country's first Latvian language newspaper *The Latest News*. This was a runaway success with a paid-for circulation of 200,000 – one in ten of the population of the time. Printing continued through the 1914-18 war until Riga was occupied by the Bolsheviks.

When peace came and independence with it, they launched an illustrated maga-zine called *Leisure* which became a window on the flourishing inter-war Latvian culture. They invested their vast profits in substantial real estate holdings in Riga, a factory in Ķekava and a beach house in the seaside resort of Jūrmala. But the Soviet occupation spelled the end for Emilija Benjamin and her family empire as well as for the Krauze brothers.

The Soviets nationalised all property and Emilija, the wealthiest, most famous woman in independent Latvia and one of the prime examples of the bourgeoisie, was removed from her luxury house by the sea in Jūrmala and sent to a Siberian labour camp in a cattle truck in June 1941. Her paper, which had backed parliamentary democracy, was closed down. Three months later, at the age of 60, she died of star-vation lying on a bed of bare boards, exactly as predicted by a Nostradamus-style fortune teller at a social party she had attended years before at the height of her glamour.[8]

The Krauze orchid firm was nationalised too and the brothers sent to Siberia.

Andrejs Juris died in 1941 aged 70. His son Ziedonis died in the same year. The younger Krauze brother, Mārtiņš, survived until 1944. The orchids were saved by the employees of the nursery.[9]

Today Emilija Benjamin's seaside house in *Juras iela* [Sea Road] in Jūrmala is consid-ered an architectural masterpiece. Built in 1938 at vast expense by the German archi-tect Lange, it was subsequently used by both Nazi and Soviet conquerors, including General Bagramyan, the commander of the Red Army in the Baltics. Another guest was Vilis Lācis, a former employee of Benjamin who became Interior Minister for the Latvian Soviet Socialist Republic in 1940. In a cruel twist of fate, he signed off the list of deportees – including her – that was sent to the NKVD. Deportees were

---

*   Stocks, or gillyflowers.

selected because of their social status and wealth and the NKVD decided whom to deport based on Lācis's list.

The house was declared a national monument by Kruschev in the 1950s and was used as a guesthouse for Soviet Presidents. It's significant in Latvian history as it was here that Boris Yeltsin recognised the independence of the Baltics, paving the way for Latvia to become an independent republic again in 1991.[10]

When the Red Army pulled out of Tukums on 27 June 1941 many left-wing Jews from the town went with them, no doubt anticipating what was to come next. There were 300 Jews left when the Nazis entered the town on 1 July. Streets were immediately re-named Adolf Hitler Street, Hermann Goering Street and so on. Once again the doors of the courthouse were thrown wide for an influx of new prisoners. Several well-known Jews, including a doctor, Louis Copenhagen, were accused of having Communist ties and organising deportations to Siberia and were murdered in woods at Vecmokas.[11]

The rest of the Jewish population were rounded up, stripped of their valuables and imprisoned in their own synagogue for a week before being taken to a forest near Valgums Lake and shot. Only one woman managed to escape the killings, which were carried out by the *Arājs Kommando*. The Tukums Self-Defence Squad was responsible for arresting and guarding those to be murdered. This was made up of members of the fascist *Pērkonkrusts* organisation, mostly men from the area aged between 30 and 40 wearing armbands in the national colours of red-white-red.[12]

The Roma too, traditionally based in the Tukums area, were butchered. The Nazis apparently quizzed them on how much travelling they did and how many lived in permanent accommodation – and then killed the travellers. Also murdered were 85 Soviet activists. Over the next three years, 1,543 people, considered opponents of the German regime, were locked up here.[13]

Harmonijas Street in Tukums is like stepping back in time. Low stone houses line a cobbled street in an area known as the 'Old Town' – in other words, it survived the war.

Most of the town centre is ground floor shops with flats above; drab, grey, flat-fronted, featureless buildings with a definite hint of post-war Soviet rebuild. But Harmonijas Street is different, probably because it's a throwback to what Tukums used to be like. If it wasn't for a modern car parked halfway down it, this could be a scene from the 1920s, even the 1820s.

I am here to meet two men who lived through the war in Courland, at the invitation of the museum director, Agrita Ozola, who knows both of them. She's kindly agreed to translate for me.

It's quite a welcome. There are pots of coffee and plates of biscuits laid out for us in her office so we arrange ourselves around a table and begin to talk. The younger of the two men, Arnolds Šulcs, was six in 1944 and lived nearby, in Irlava. To his right, Emīls Braunbergs was 13. His mother ran a successful grocery shop in the centre of town. In 1991 Emīls was an active participant in the Riga Barricades, the pro-independence protests of January 1991 that led to the eventual downfall of the Soviet regime and the second period of independence.

Sometimes they tell stories individually, at other times it's more like a conversation. There are moments when they are in complete agreement, such as when I ask if there were celebrations at the end of the war. Emīls looks at me sharply.

'We didn't consider the Germans as occupiers. They liberated us from Russian oppressors'.

Arnolds agrees.

'People joined the German Army to fight the Soviets'.

Accounts of the brief Soviet occupation of Tukums in 1944 read like a nightmare. They were a clear indication of what Soviet victory would mean.

> The Soviets unleashed a terror reminiscent of 1919. The Red Army rampaged, pillaged, shot civilians and raped women. All *suchmani,** *Aizsargi* [Home Guard], police, anyone collaborating with the Germans or even suspected of co-operating were executed without mercy. Latvians could clearly see what awaited them when the Soviets returned.[14]

Emīls grew up in Tukums but now lives on the coast at Jūrmala. After the war he became a surgeon and in later life, a painter. Arnolds works closely with the German authorities recovering fallen soldiers from the forests and ensuring that their families are notified. When they begin talking it's like the pages of history have been turned back. Emīls begins.

> There was an agreement between the Germans and Latvians in 1939 that the Baltic Germans would leave for Poznan [in Poland]. There were 500-600 Germans in Tukums and at least 450 left. Lots of elderly men were mobilised in Oct 1939 and simply disappeared.†
>
> In 1941 when the Germans came the division was based at the school in Tukums. They took all the furniture out of the school and stored it in the barn. They came into our house and asked for permission to wash themselves in the garden. Then they used our table to eat from, and afterwards washed all the dishes they'd used and put everything back.
>
> We didn't have much food but my mother put everything she had on the table, including the loaves of bread she had made in case we were sent to Siberia. I spoke good German: the soldiers were very surprised.
>
> Each soldier had a box of chocolates. Most gave them to children. The Russian soldiers didn't have anything like that.[15]

---

*   Nazi-controlled police and security, used to round up Bolsheviks and Jews.

†   When they were sent to the Eastern Front in 1941.

Arnolds is nodding. Although Emīls will dominate the conversation, Arnolds' contributions are worth interrupting him for.

> The food was strange. When the Germans came I had my first experience of instant coffee. I'd never seen cheese in a tube before. There was artificial honey, ersatz chocolate …[16]

He was six, and Emīls twice his age. Their memories reflect their age. Emīls continues.

> I could distinguish between the planes, artillery and tanks of either side. The Russian planes we called 'Ivans', the German planes 'Fritzes'. In summer 1944 Soviet tanks reached Jelgava.
>
> We saw that Jelgava was on fire and we were afraid. We lived on Raina Street in a two-storey house. We lived in the flat above Mother's shop so we had a good view. Beyond the forest we saw the sky lit up at night. We knew the Russians were coming.
>
> The Germans said to us: 'Don't stay here' so we went to Seme Lake about 10 kms to the west of Tukums where my mother knew some people, the Jursevics family, who had a farmstead there. We took sugar sacks and our personal belongings to Seme Lake and lived there for three weeks. The roads were full of German tanks and guns and trucks. We felt safe as we were out of town. The Russian Army took Tukums on July 30 and reached the sea at Klapkalnciems the next day, splitting Kurzeme from the rest of Latvia.
>
> I only saw two dead bodies during the war and it was then, in summer '44 at Seme Lake. A wounded soldier was brought into the house but he was too badly injured. In the morning he was dead. Two Germans brought him into the cellar on a stretcher but we couldn't do anything for him. I cried because I couldn't help. Maybe that was one of the reasons I became a doctor.

Arnolds nods.

> Everyone tried to pack up and run away. They killed their animals for food and left the rest behind. The Russians had them. Maybe it's a story but I heard the commander of the Russian Eighth Brigade [tanks] was ordered to send three bottles of seawater to the Kremlin to prove that the Russians had reached the coast.

Bypassing Jelgava in July 1944, Soviet T-34s carrying infantry and commanded by Colonel S.G. Kremer covered sixty miles in 48 hours, reaching the Gulf of Riga on the afternoon of July 30th, cutting the Germans links between Courland and Riga.[17]

Under the leadership of Stalingrad and Kursk veteran *Oberst* Hyazinth von Strachwitz, the German armoured *Gross Deutschland* division was sent to push them back. This was the northern tip of Operation *Doppelkopf,* an attempt from mid-August 1944 to re-open a corridor from Riga west to Tukums and Courland, relieve Jelgava and halt the Soviet advance through Lithuania. This tank force was bolstered by artillery cadets from the Latvian 15th Division and an SS panzer training unit.[18]

From close to the coast and guided by spotter planes the cruiser *Prinz Eugen* and four destroyers laid down a heavy bombardment on Soviet tanks in Tukums. The division re-captured Tukums and Džūkste and broke through to Army Group North, opening up a narrow corridor to Riga. Jelgava could not be reached.[19]

Emīls becomes animated.

> On 20th August shooting suddenly started in the west. The Germans pushed the Russians back helped by shelling from the *Prinz Eugen* [lying off the coast in Riga Bay]. The Russians were pushed back to Ķemeri.* After three days we went back to Tukums. It was tragic what we saw. All the doors of the flats were smashed open. The flats had been looted and the looters had even defecated on the tables and in the bath.
>
> We're not quite sure who did this but the Latvian tradition is to clean a house when leaving it. When the Russians left Latvia in 1991 exactly the same thing happened, so we think it must have been the Russians. Whatever: the toilets were demolished, everything was smashed up and there were human faeces in the bath. Our shop had been stripped bare. It was so bad that there and then my mother vowed that she wouldn't start again.

In September the Russians began bombing Tukums to destroy the strategic railway interchange. One line led to the port of Ventspils on the northwest Baltic coast while another two connected Tukums to Riga and Jelgava. These lines offered supply routes in and escape routes out. Again Emīls and his family were on the move.

> Our house was so badly damaged we couldn't carry on living there, so we packed everything onto a wagon and left Tukums again. This time we couldn't stay in Seme and it was too cold to stay in haybarns, so we moved 25kms to Dzirciems and the *Dreimani* farmstead. This was the farm of General Adam Kreicbergs, who had been deported to Siberia in 1941. During this time a relative of the Kreicbergs ran the farm. She was a good friend of my mother's so we stayed there all winter and through the spring until 9 May [when the war ended].
>
> Three or four days before the end of the war the house was full of German soldiers. Thirty to forty Germans, maybe more. I'm not exactly sure how many. They were sad because they knew about [the fall of] Berlin. They knew the war was over and now Russian rule would start.
>
> All round *Dreimani* there were German soldiers living in tents in the garden. The officers were in the house. There was a piano in the house too. One of the German officers was a music teacher. He asked if he could play the piano and when he did, he cried. He used to say: 'If I could go home I would waltz home'. Of course, he was from Vienna.

There was a fire going and soldiers were burning their old uniforms, their photos and their letters and personal effects – getting rid of everything: violins, accordions, cameras…they gave the instruments to me. There were no celebrations when the war finished.

After maybe three days after the capitulation some Russians arrived in American Jeeps and ordered the Germans to form a line. Then they marched them to Tukums.

We came back to Tukums in July 1945 to find our house repaired and full of Russian officers and their families. They'd thrown everything of ours out of the windows into the garden. We looked around and we found the documents proving our ownership of the house. We didn't say anything at the time but those documents would be very valuable when the Soviet Union collapsed fifty years later and we could prove the house was ours and get it back.

Arnolds has been smiling while Emīls told his stories, his face lit up as though remembering happy times.

Everyone had a harmonica. I did good business selling harmonicas after the war. Our family knew the deputy chief of Tukums District, a man called Uijerts. Just before the capitulation Uijerts escaped to Gotland in a rowboat. Three Latvian Legionnaires and three German officers rowed from Pāvilosta to Gotland on the 9th of May to get away from the Russians. Many people did. And the German officers just sat there and ordered the Latvians to do the rowing!

When the capitulation happened, in Grenči near Irlava, suddenly Russian soldiers started shooting in the air and shouting 'Urrah, Urrah!' After the shooting they spread out their loot – mostly watches – and they drank and ate, sitting around and chatting and telling each other how many watches they had.

They called them 'stones' because the number of diamonds a watch had in its mechanism affected its value. The more stones, the more it was worth. There's one story about a woman being stopped on Kuldīga Street by three Russian soldiers who saw her gold teeth and there and then they pulled them out.

[Near Irlava] there were two German officers who'd been killed near a farmhouse and their bodies were naked apart from their underwear. There were some Russians sitting near the house smoking. My dad asked them why the Germans were naked and the Russians said they wanted the uniforms so they could send the material back home to make working clothes for after the war. My dad and I carried the bodies to a bomb crater and buried them.

Before soldiers arrived in a village all the girls and the women started smearing themselves with mud, rubbing mud into their hair and making themselves look dirty. On some occasions they even rubbed horse poo into themselves. They literally stank. I thought it was odd at the time that they should do that but I understand why now.

Once one of the Russian soldiers started groping my mother so I began crying out. My father heard and rushed back in and the Russian soldier jumped clean through the window and ran off.

After the capitulation the road was full of Germans. It took all day for the soldiers to be marched to the prison camp at Tukums. The Latvians went into the forest. Some tried to go home; some became partisans.

The Russians organised their soldiers into chains and combed the town, the forests, the surrounding area. The whole of Tukums was combed through in May 1945 and the people they found were sent to filtration camps in each village.

If you had served in the German forces you were sent to Tukums, then Jelgava, then onto Russia. After that the prisoners were moved onto construction projects building either the Belomor Canal or the Baikal railway.

The politically repressed prisoners built the Baikal railway and the Pechora railway further south. The Soviets had a very good system of prison camps.

After we have finished talking Agrita arranges lifts home for the two men and asks if I would like to see anything else. I'm curious as to what newspaper archives have survived, so she leads me to a slim file containing a handful of wartime editions. These convey the sense of rising panic in the country at the time.

The front page of the *Tukums Ziņas* [Tukums News] from Saturday 20 July 1944 carried news of the total mobilisation of the country against the Soviet offensive under the headline 'All of Latvia to become a nation united in war'.

Underneath was a message to the population from the German SS commander and police chief in eastern and northern Russia, *General* Friedrich Jeckeln.

> Latvia is in danger. The aim of the Bolsheviks is to use their masses of people and material power to cut off all the Baltics. Then they intend to attack Latvia from all sides and crush it.
>
> The Red enemy is already celebrating, believing that within another 'Cruel Year'* they will be able to murder Latvian youth, burn beautiful towns, destroy well-tended fields and murder women and children … and if there's anyone left send them in exile to Siberia.
>
> But the Red bandits are wrong! Latvia will not be pillaged and its nation will not be wiped out. In its moment of danger the Latvian nation is not alone. Those who say that Germany will abandon the Latvian nation are wrong. The German Army will protect Latvia.
>
> Like in the past few weeks the German Army helped Finland† it will also help Latvia – until victory. We will all stand together, committed to fight to the end. Together we are giving the Bolsheviks the only possible answer. Now it's total war!
>
> The *Führer* has ordered me to mobilise all men in the Baltics, ready to fight or to work in this fight to save Latvia. General Bangerskis will look after the military. General Dankers is responsible for civilians.

---

* A reference to the previous Soviet occupation of 1940-41 with its executions and deportations.
† In its fight against the Soviet Union, which it ultimately lost.

All Latvia must become a united fighting nation. Whoever can't fight must work. Whoever you are – a scientist, a farmer, a civil servant, a worker: man or woman. If you have hands that can work you must devote them to your motherland in its moment of danger.[20]

Alongside Jeckeln's message was a column directed to the civilian population from General Dankers.

In the following days every man who can bear arms will be called into the Army to protect the borders of our land. Many women and men will be involved in building defensive trenches and ditches. This total mobilisation will affect all aspects of our life. In offices and businesses work activities will be reduced and everyone whose work is not essential to the economy will be freed for defence work.

Dig trenches and defence systems, build air defences, join the ranks at the front: participate in ensuring internal security. It can't be any other way![21]

The scale of the involvement of Tukums' society in the war effort was reflected on the inside pages. The paper carried a series of notices and messages from soldiers at the front – in fact, there was barely any content that wasn't war-related.

Messages and greetings from the front:

SS-Grenadiersturmm Oskars Rice greets friends and girlfriend at home in Strutele [near Jaunpils] and his parents in Irlava.

SS Legionnaire V. Labronovics greets his wife, his parents, friends and family at home.

SS Legionnaire A. Cīrulis, returning a second time to fight for the Fatherland sends greetings and love to parents, family and his girl in his homeland.

Kar E. Osi cordially greets birthday cousin Erna Pravin

At the bottom left of the page in a large sombre black-lined panel, a wife's grief for her much-loved husband was recorded.

1944: 16 July after a lot of suffering my beloved husband, police battalion Iron Cross cavalier Corporal FRICIS KIRŠTEINS
Deeply grieving wife
Quietly in love
My tears run for you
What I lost with you
My heart will never forget

Amid general notices of where to collect skimmed milk and an electric motor for sale, an announcement of the blackout times:

From 23rd July till 29th July blackout needs to be between 2110 – 0340.

FOOD VOUCHERS
Tukums Supply Office informs that you can exchange food voucher number 28 and one skimmed milk coupon for either one litre of skimmed milk or buttermilk.

At the top of the page, under the heading 'Tukums and District News' is this call for 16 year-olds to join up for military training.

The most serious stage of the war has arrived. Your brothers and fathers have been fighting against the Red Dragon. Don't stand by and watch! Join the fight against the Eastern beast.

I call upon all young people born in 1928 to join the military support cadets. It will not interfere with your studies – they will be part of your service. Studies will be supervised by a military manager.

You will be involved only in activities that will correspond with your level of development. Service will be only within Latvia and at least 40 kms from the front. You'll be supervised by medical doctors and insured.

All military service participants will receive a free uniform, food and lodging and a wage. You will have 28 days' leave a year and every five weeks you will have a 48-hour leave for visiting parents, excluding travel time.

Young people! Take on this responsibility and you will be serving your nation and your Motherland.

Signed: Tukums and District youth organisation manager.[22]

I turn the fading pages of the next newspaper, dated six weeks later. The situation had worsened. Jelgava had fallen to the Soviets and the Germans were preparing to abandon Riga. The newspaper carried a list of instructions headed 'Decree number 3'.

Tukums Ziņas 31st August
Everyone over the age of 15 living in the district of Tukums must re-register their passport or identity card before September 5th. For each of the six days to that date, addresses are listed which must register, between 8am and 1pm. After that date anyone who hasn't re-registered will be arrested.[23]

There was also a very direct message to deserters from the commander of the Latvian Legion, General Bangerskis.

Announcement from the General Inspector of the Latvian SS Legion
I call on all soldiers who left their military units without permission and did not return: also those who have strayed away from their units, because their units

have moved on they have not re-joined them, either deliberately or by accident. In general, anyone on an unauthorised absence from their unit is to immediately report to their nearest military headquarters. The same goes for those who haven't answered their call-up.

This is the last chance for anyone who deliberately or without understanding the consequences of their actions has not fulfilled their duty to their nation or their Motherland.

This is the last chance to return to the ranks of honourable soldiers.

Those who do not respond to this call will have missed their last chance for rehabilitation. In this decisive moment, when a nation fights for its life or death, standing aside or neglecting your duties is the most serious of offences.

General R. Bangerskis.

Persons mentioned in this call can report to Kronvalda Bulvāris 6, Riga, or Herman Goering iela 3, Tukums, on September 5 and 6 this year.[24]

Seventy years later, there's no mistaking the scale of what's at stake. This is total mobilisation, with even 16 year-olds being called up.

While Bangerskis appeals to deserters to return and fight for Latvia's life, the Nazis promise solidarity until the end - with dire consequences for those who shirk this patriotic duty.

'In its moment of danger the Latvian nation is not alone. We will all stand together, committed to fight to the end. Together we are giving the Bolsheviks the only possible answer. Now it's total war!'[25]

That evening I sit in a café and open up a map of significant military sites and memorials in Tukums produced by the local tourist office. It's one of the few maps I have found that is in English. More than once there is mention of these memorials having been blown up after Latvian independence. Soviet special forces were often considered the perpetrators of these attacks.

- Memorial stone near *Trubas*. The memorial stone near the former farm *Trubas* was unveiled in May 1970. Here the 121st Guards Regiment of the 10th Latvian Riflemen Corps of the 42nd Army (43rd Guard Division) on 9 May 1945 accepted the capitulation of the 19th SS Division and 24th Saxon infantry Division. Vāne parish, Kandava region.
As I understand it, that's Latvian surrendering to Latvian.

- Plāņi Manor: Dating back to 1459, Plāņi Manor was originally part of the von Stromberg family lands. Here in the master house of the manor on 8 May General von Schultz signed the capitulation of the 24th Infantry Division, ending the Kurzeme Fortification.
That's the manor house near the Zante war museum that Mr Brucis mentioned.

- Saulīši Mound. This is the final resting place of about 800 Latvian Legionnaires and German troops who died at the Laukmuiža Hospital. The memorial stone was set up in 1989 but was blown up. It was re-made and set up anew in 1990. Veclauki, Jaunpils.

- Monument to the Christmas Battles in Džūkste: The designer of the monument dedicated to the Latvian Legionnaires of the 19th Division who died in the 1944 Christmas battles is the sculptor Igors Dobičins. The architect is Rita Dobicina. It was first unveiled in 1990 but was blown up the same year. The remains were put back together and set up again.

- Memorial stone to the defenders of the Kurzeme Fortification [Courland Pocket]: The memorial stone is dedicated to the Kurzeme Fortification defenders, the Latvian Legionnaires, who despite being overpowered by the Soviet army tenfold, did not give up. Thanks to [them] about 300,000 Latvian refugees who were in Kurzeme at this time … had the chance to emigrate.

  The memorial stone was set up at the place where the farm *Rumbas* once stood. It was designed by the prominent Latvian sculptor Ojārs Feldbergs. On the Riga to Liepāja highway, before the turn to Lestene.[26]

I have heard of the wild battles over fortified farmhouses in the Courland Pocket, so I look up the history of *Rumbas* on a local council website.

Fierce battles between Legionnaires and the Red Army took place here between 23 and 31 December 1944 with the Legionnaires outnumbered ten to one. As ten Soviet divisions attacked with vast numbers of tanks, control of the farm *Rumbas* changed hands 19 times as the Red Army tried to split the front and break through to Ventspils. There were Latvians on either side: the 19th Division Latvian Legion fighting two divisions of the 130th Latvian Rifles. The website concludes:

> It was a tragic chapter in the history of the nation when foreign powers forced Latvian to fight Latvian. From August 1944 until the spring of 1945 the Red Army illegally mobilised and sent to the front in Courland 57,422 men who had managed to escape from the German Army. Thousands who fell in battle were buried in cemeteries, Soviet fighters remained lying in forests and countless fighters disappeared without trace.[27]

Where *Rumbas* used to be is marked today with a memorial of a large inscribed boulder – a common sight in this country. But it's becoming clear to me that the defence of Courland by every means possible – trench, tank, every single person and building pressed into service, including the old manor houses and even fortified farmhouses – is a sign of how desperate that fight was, and how the whole nation was consumed. And when the resistance of the Courland Pocket ended the ruins of *Rumbas* were swept away, the old farmsteads collectivised and anyone who didn't agree with the new system sent to Siberia. This would be a fight for the heart and soul of Latvia.

Notes

1   Tukums tourist information website: http://www.turisms.tukums.lv/index/vietas/4361572/9431259/3607788.
2   Lumans, p.65.
3   Ibid, p.72-75.
4   Ibid, pp.79-80.
5   The Jewish Museum in Latvia website http://www.jewishmuseum.lv/en/item/139-tukums.html.
6   M. Meler, *Jewish Latvia: Sites to Remember*, p.385.
7   A. Ozola, *Savējo stāsti, ne svešo*, p.41.
8   Emilija Benjamin website http://www.emilija-benjamin.com/ plus correspondence with family historian Herbert Linde, August 2015.
9   A. Ozola *Savejo Stasti, ne Sveso* p.41 and correspondence.
10 Emilija Benjamin website http://www.emilija-benjamin.com/ plus correspondence with family historian Herbert Linde, August 2015.
11 M. Meler, p.386.
12 Ibid, p.390, advice from Tukums museum director Agrita Ozola.
13 The Jewish Museum in Latvia website http://www.jewishmuseum.lv/en/item/139-tukums.html and Meler, p.390.
14 Lumans, p.335.
15 Interview with author, Tukums, August 2014.
16 Interview with author, Tukums, August 2014.
17 McAteer, *500 Days: The War in Eastern Europe, 1944-1945*, p.199.
18 Ibid, p.237.
19 Buttar, p.225.
20 *Tukums Ziņas* [Tukums News] from Saturday 20 July 1944 in Tukums museum archive.
21 Ibid.
22 Ibid.
23 *Tukums Ziņas* [Tukums News] from 31 August 1944 in Tukums museum archive.
24 Ibid.
25 Ibid.
26 Tukums and District Tourist brochure: http://www.turisms.tukums.lv/izdevumi/pdf/Celvedis_ENw.pdf.
27 Dobele Municipality website *Driving routes...* at http://www.dobele.lv/page/Turisms_ar_auto?action=description&t_id=267.

7

The Men Who Fought for Hitler

With clusters of historic and ornate houses around a picturesque market place, Kuldīga is one of Latvia's most beautiful towns. That's by day. By night my impression is of a confusing one-way system through poorly-lit streets lined with ancient wooden and stone houses, most of which are shuttered up or empty. It's like a one-way system designed in the 16th century. Which, of course, it probably is.

Eventually I find the turning I want and arrive outside the Metropole Hotel, an impressive building dating from 1910. The tourist information office is in an historic building on one side of the square a short distance away. There I find the regional tourist association chairman Artis Gustovskis, a tall, lean, wiry man with an energetic look in his eye.

'Come on,' he says cheerfully. 'It's just around the corner'.

We stride purposefully away across the square and take a left down the main shopping street until we reach a shoe shop. A passageway alongside leads to a flight of stairs, which we climb to the floor above. Through some double doors and overlooking the street is the office of the Kuldīga branch of *Daugavas Vanagi*, the association representing veterans who fought in the Latvian Legion. The organisation was born in the displacement camps of 1945 Germany: the name means 'Hawks of the Daugava'.

The red-white-red Latvian flag is in one corner of the room. Sitting at a table in the centre are three elderly men, clearly waiting for us. Two elderly ladies place plates of biscuits on the table as we enter.

Two of these men wore Nazi uniforms in the war. One of them won the Iron Cross in the Christmas Battles. The third was a partisan. The two ladies were children then. With Artis translating, I switch my tape recorder on.

The first to speak is Antons Leščanovs; taut, rigid, shaven-headed and clearly a very proud man. He is the holder of the Iron Cross. Born in March 1921 he was mobilised aged 22 when he was living in the southeastern village of Silajāņi, near Rēzekne. Trained in Riga he first saw action at the Volkhova Front outside Leningrad and also fought at the Velikaya River, the symbolic battle when the Latvian 15th and 19th divisions fought together for the first time on 16 March 1944, the moment remembered now as Legionnaires' Day. A sergeant in the Legion, he was wounded in fierce battles the following month. Sent back from the front for medical care, he was one of only eight men to survive from a unit of 160.

> I was a machine gunner. We had seven-man crews. One man fired the gun, one man changed the barrels and the rest fetched ammunition. The first two men

were the best shots and took turns firing the gun. If a gunner was killed they were replaced by one of the others.

When we were pushed back from Russia we retreated at night. In the daytime there was a battle, then it would go quiet. The Germans used that moment to escape, but we did it at night so we'd have the cover of darkness.

I was in the 19th Division of the German Army. I served with General Roland Kovtunenko at Nītaure.* We had standard issue German uniform with Latvian badges – tunic, helmet, with camouflage and in winter a snow uniform.

The Russians pushed us back to Riga. About the 11th of October we crossed the Daugava on a pontoon bridge and then German special forces teams blew it up. I was one of the last across. First we went to Sloka, then Tukums, then Dobele. This was the start of the *Kurzeme Katls* [the Courland Pocket period]. We fought to the very last moment because we had heard from other Latvians there were English and American forces coming, and they would save us. Nobody wanted another Russian occupation because to us it was clear that no-one would survive.[1]

Mr Leščanovs' first action in Courland was in October at Putnakrogs, little more now than a junction on the road between Jaunpils and Tukums. It's notable mostly because the Soviets lost 26 tanks there in the first engagement of the Courland Pocket.

Soldiers in my unit blew up five tanks at Putnakrogs. I was a machine gunner so my target was to get all the soldiers who were walking. The other guys took out the tanks. I took out the soldiers who were riding on them, especially if they were shooting. Sometimes the tanks would break through and the artillery in the back would shell them.

We had seven barrels for the machine gun and when one got so hot we couldn't use it we'd change it. We killed a lot of men in one day… we didn't count them … but the machine gun was rarely out of work. When it got hot it wasn't so accurate, so we just used to fire and sweep the line of men coming at us. They didn't stop. But we found out why.

He smiles wryly.

The Russians had a system – Russian soldiers told us this later. Behind the first wave were NKVD political officers who said: 'If you do not go we will shoot you'. So they had no choice. They had to go. And sometimes they would use schnapps and get drunk before they go and shout 'For victory'.

At Lestene one of our men deserted to the Russian side – we could almost see each other from the front lines – and the Russians played a popular Latvian song

---

* A bloody stand by Latvians at Nitaure and More against overwhelming odds in September 1944 to delay the Soviet advance on Riga.

on the loudspeaker and then made this man talk on the loudhailer. He knew everyone's family names.

So he started saying: 'Latvian boys, come over to the Russians. Nothing will happen to you. They will thank you and let you go free'. This officer was [supposed to be] Major Wolfson. But in fact he was already dead – and everybody knew it. Every person who went over to the Russians was shot.

Then we moved from Lestene to Blīdene, to another section of the front line, and I was wounded again, this time for the third time. In the face. So I went into the hospital in Puze. This was in March 1945.

A general came to the hospital and said 'Anyone who can move – to the front line. Anyone who can walk must go'. One doctor said 'Maybe they can walk, but what if they can't see?' And the general said 'Only if they're really sick can they stay at the hospital'.

We found ourselves transported on a narrow gauge railway back to Stende, moved to Kandava and then Zemite, where we were stopped by German gendarmerie, policemen. They kept us four days and another three Latvians turned up. The Germans wanted to send us to Remte because there was another headquarters there, so they sent us guarded by one policeman with a rifle.

All the Latvians were looking at each other and saying 'Why don't we just kill this guy and escape?' And that gendarme knew it. Every time they stopped for a smoke they discussed killing him, but didn't – just in case he shot one of them before they could overpower him. Eventually they said 'Don't do anything. Let God decide what happens, not us'.

When they got to Remte the gendarme handed them over and said 'Auf Weidersehn' and he looked so happy… like he'd known what they were thinking!

In May 1945 we were dug into positions in the front line at Gaiķi, in the forest in Remte, but there was no real fighting. Suddenly a Russian captain appeared. Someone shot him, but during the night we got new instructions. In the morning about 1100 or 1200 someone in the Russian positions put up a white flag on a house and started shouting: 'The war is over. Don't shoot!'

Seven Russians started to come towards us with a white flag, over to our side, and said: 'Where is your officer?' So our officer went over to the Russians and suddenly both officers on either side exclaimed: 'Oh, it's you!'

Both were Latvians. One was a Latvian in the German Army, the other was a Latvian in the Russian Army. And the ordinary soldiers were Latvians too.

Then we moved to Kabile – we still had our guns – and soldiers who lived nearby were slipping away and changing clothes. One man from Kandava said 'Let's go to my house and change clothes and maybe no one will recognise us'. So we went to near Abava. There was a big river and the water was very deep so we tried crossing on the bridge, but Russian security captured us there.

The first thing the Russians did was search you for valuables, and take what you had. There was a famous story about two Russians who killed each other fighting over something one of them had. The other wanted it because he thought it was more valuable, and they both ended up dead.

Having sat silently for some time now, Žanis Grīnbergs the former partisan leans forward. Born in 1926, he is younger than Mr Leščanovs. His wartime experience is very different.

I lived in Īvande, near Kuldīga. Schoolmates and friends of mine joined the Legion and they all died. Four boys from the village didn't join and one night in November 1944 the Germans came and rounded up all the men by force. This was not voluntary. They took them by train to Toma Street 19 in Liepāja.

It was a prison where they collected all those who escaped being mobilised. They were transferred from there to Liepāja Prison, where there was a proper jail. I was put in a cell, number 33.

In December 1944 there were lots of refugees and soldiers in Liepāja and they were all put on a ship heading for Germany: people who'd escaped from battles, who were fleeing from the Russians, who were refugees. They were all loaded onto the ship and so were we.

I had a friend who was a seaman. He said 'Let's escape from this ship'. So we climbed down into the hold where the cattle were kept. The ship was split into two parts – one part was like a prison to hold the men who hadn't volunteered for military service. The other side was for reliable civilians, people who could be trusted. From the hold we climbed up to the deck and found some stairs alongside the ship where there were no guards and no checkpoints. Crew were going up and down and people were loading cargo and so on, so we used those stairs to get off the ship. Liepāja was so full of people at that time – thousands and thousands of them, the streets were really crowded – that it was impossible to control everybody. So we used that as a cover to escape.

This friend had a sister living in Liepāja so we went to her house. There were *utis* [lice] all over us, so she made us sleep in the woodshed. Then we tried to move to Grobiņa but the railway was guarded by Germans. So we took a shovel from the sister's house and when the Germans asked who we were and where we were going we said 'We are workmen digging trenches for the defences'. And the Germans let us through!

The roads were full of people. Everyone was heading for Liepāja; everyone was panicking. So we went into the forest and walked to Īvande. It took us three days. When we got back to my house there was a Russian family living there from Novgorod called Prosins and a Latvian family from Smiltene called Klavins. They'd fled west from Smiltene after the Germans had pulled out but the Germans had mined the roads to slow down the Soviets. Many refugees stepped on the mines and horses were blown up too.

In May the Russians came to Īvande so everyone went into the forest. They were scared of the Russians, scared of the Germans. The Russians came through the forest rounding everyone up between the ages of 16 and 60 and asking who they were. They gathered everyone together in one place and then questioned them about who they were and where they had come from.

The Russians soldiers were very poor. They stole watches from the people they were rounding up. If someone they captured had good boots they would take them.

Many of the soldiers had more than one watch on their wrists – just like that picture of the Russians raising the Red Flag over the Reichstag when the soldier supporting the man with the flag had watches on both wrists.* They would take the horses saying: 'The Army needs them'. Then they would go to the next village and sell them for money.[2]

We take a break for coffee and cakes. I ask the ladies if they have any memories from that time. Gunita Freiburga was ten at the time, having grown up in Talsi.

There were special days when the German Army would get deliveries of food from home and at that time they received a lot of products like jams and chocolates. Usually they gave those chocolates to small kids. I got some and so did my little brother. We were very happy about that. When my parents went to the workers' ball, I stayed at home with the German soldiers but I was not afraid at all because they were very polite.

Then the Russians came. Their culture was not very advanced. They said they needed the stove so my parents said: 'OK, take it'. When the Russians came in they took everything, even cosmetics. If your father had supported the Germans, you couldn't get a job.[3]

Austra Sunina lived in Rende, near Ozolmuiža. She was two years older than Gunita.

I was very small, a girl. I remember the Germans going into the forests to check whether there were any Red partisans there. They were called *Sarkanā Bulta* [Red Arrow]. And there were deserters in the forest too.

I remember one moment from the 9th May very well. We didn't own our own home and on the 9th May the Red partisans came out of the forest with a red flag. They came into Ozolmuiža manor house and put the red flag on the second floor. They lived there for a long time after that. At the same time the neighbours had a funeral – they were in the graveyard nearby. When they came back from the graveyard the Red partisans had been through everything and stolen everything of value.

Right at the end of the war a German officer gave me some pictures and said: 'Little girl, please look after these pictures. I will come and get them when the war is over'. But he never came back and I have never found him.[4]

---

* Photographer Yevgeny Khaldei airbrushed the watches out before sending the picture to Kremlin censors because the soldier would have fallen foul of Stalin's 'no looting' rule.

What was it like, I ask the men as a group, fighting for the Germans against the Russians on their own land? With boys from their own village, their friends and classmates, joining the Army and being sent to the front?

Mr Leščanovs replies.

> There were boys leaving the village and joining the Army and after only a few hours at the front word was coming back that they were dead. They fought for Latvia – for Latvian freedom. They had no choice. At that time only Germany supported us, therefore they went into the German Army. American and British forces promised they would help, but … nothing'.

Mr Leščanovs is shouting and emphasising his points with powerful sweeps of his hand. He stops and stares at me. I hold my hands up and shake my head.

'I'm sorry', I say.

Then I begin to laugh at my powerlessness to turn back the clock and make things different. I am apologising for things that happened before I was born. They stare at me for a moment, then laugh too.

I am a British man sitting at a table laden with cakes and coffee, hospitality laid out for me to hear these stories from seventy years ago. These men were expecting the British to come and help them fight the Soviets, but they never came. A Latvian is translating so the British man gets the message. He does. I shake my head and shrug.

'I wish we could have helped'.

I know that the Nazi occupation of Paris distracted attention from the Soviets moving into Latvia; that Dunkirk meant we had to focus on our fight; that Churchill didn't insist on the restoration of Latvian independence at Yalta. Latvians think, with some justification, that the British sold them down the river. I wasn't even alive then. We find ourselves all laughing, realising the same thing. But how deeply they wish things could have been different.

Mr Leščanovs continues.

> Everybody wanted the same thing to happen as in the First World War, when the Americans and English helped us get independence.
>
> There was radio from America which reached Latvia. The partisans and working people were listening. 'We will get you free,' the Americans promised. But nothing happened. After the war Churchill said to Roosevelt: 'We didn't kill the right pig. We needed to kill the Red pig'.

I am aware that some may consider these men Nazi sympathisers. I feel I need to ask the two Legionnaires to clarify their positions.

'You were both fighting for Latvian independence?'

'Yes. Certainly'.

Both men nod. The more conservative tabloid British press has in recent years reported that because the Latvian men were fighting for Germany and some were in the SS, they were Nazi sympathisers. I have an opportunity to ask the very men who fought in those German uniforms what they feel about this. I ask Artis to translate my question carefully.

> This is a sensitive question but it is an issue in England. They have lost their friends and the people from the village, made many sacrifices fighting for Latvian independence – but they were wearing German uniforms. Now, sixty, seventy years later, people are saying they were Nazi sympathisers. How do they feel about that?

Mr Leščanovs waits for the translation, then shrugs.

> What can you do? What can you say about it? You cannot react. It's true, it's shocking – but what can we do? We're used to it. In Soviet times they called us fascists. They said Legionnaires killed the Jews but it was the Arājs Battalion, a special force, not connected with us. And if we're speaking about Arājs and his personality, then the story was that the Soviets killed his parents – so when the Germans came of course he went on their side. Because he wants revenge.

I ask another question about the motivation of these Latvian men. How much was the Year of Terror a factor for them in fighting against the Soviets?
Mr Leščanovs answers, suddenly quite agitated.

> The Russians came in here and put white flags everywhere and showed films and said: 'You must go to Siberia and work with an axe'. We laughed because Latvians were very modernised then – it was like England. And then some angry Russians said 'Now we see Latvian ladies walking in silk stockings. Soon you will not be'. The Russians took our food and sent big shipments to Russia on trucks because the Communists were poor. Some Russians thought it was like an exhibition here. 'It's so beautiful,' they said.

'How do you feel now the Soviets have gone?' I ask. Mr Leščanovs laughs.

> You can speak at least. You know that the NKVD won't catch you. In Soviet times you couldn't speak because you'd be thrown in prison immediately if you said anything about Russia.

I ask the men if they have any medals. They nod. Mr Grinbergs has a silver wound medal. Mr Leščanovs has the Iron Cross 2nd Class for his service in the Christmas Battles, plus the Close Combat Clasp.
I ask if he would describe the incident he got the close combat medal for. Suddenly things become a little confused. A strange look comes over him. He looks haunted and seems to be struggling with his answer. I hear a voice – it must be Artis – say:

> Most of the time they gave it when they got into the enemy's trenches ... hand-to-hand fighting, with the bayonet? Yes, in the Christmas Battles.

Mr Leščanovs has closed his eyes, seemingly summoning up the power to shake off the mist that's descended upon him. He utters a sentence quietly, which Artis translates.

It depended on who was faster – your life depended on that.

One of the women goes over to console him.

'Did you think you would ever see a free and independent Latvia?' I ask. He shouts out his answer, seemingly torn between his bloody experiences in the war, his hardships in the camps and his love of his nation.

Yes! Even in the labour camps in Siberia I still hoped that we would be free. Two and a half years I was there. We didn't get to eat for a week. There were no toilets, nothing. But if you don't eat, you don't need the toilet. We put salt in the water to take away our appetites so we didn't need to eat. Once every 24 hours we would get something to eat.

It has been an extraordinary experience meeting Mr Leščanovs. I sense that beneath his tough Sergeant's exterior, he is a man living with some terrible memories. As he puts his coat on to leave I shake his hand and clasp his shoulder.

'Thank you for sharing your memories with me, even if they are unhappy memories. I appreciate this very much'.

He looks back at me, stiffens and says:

'I hope I will get your book while I am still alive'.

Heads shake sympathetically as Mr Leščanovs leaves, at the thought of what he must have been through at the age of 21. We turn to the second soldier, Fricis Borisovs, who has waited patiently for his turn.

I'm from Kuldīga, from the village of Planīca. I was in both divisions, the 15th and the 19th. I was mobilised in August 1943 and sent first to Liepāja and then to Dresden for military training. I was a sapper, trained to lay mines and blow things up, especially bridges.

After about five months of training we went to the front line. I was shot through the arm by a sniper and sent back to hospital in Lübeck. I was there about three weeks and met some Latvians from Kurzeme. The doctor was sending soldiers who had recovered back to the front, so I said: 'I'm ready'. While we were having breakfast I heard there was a truck going to Kurzeme so I joined that group and when one of the men was missing – a man called Leimanis – I said: 'I'm him'.

We went to the port at Swinemünde.* It was full of big boats and people everywhere. Our boat had about 1,000 people on it. About 2am the Russians started to bomb the port.

---

* A city seaport on the Baltic in German-occupied Poland, now known as Świnoujście.

There were sirens going off, bombs dropping. Many people got off the boat and went into air raid shelters. I stayed on the boat. But then the English bombers came, and their bombing was very accurate, not like the Russians. All the ships were hit and put out of action, except ours. Many people were killed – many refugees. Of the 1,000 people who were on our ship, only 200 returned.

The next day the ship left for Liepāja and from there we got on a military train to Ventspils. It was so slow you could walk faster. After that we got a train to Tukums. I got back to Džūkste and was wounded in the shoulder by a piece of shrapnel. I was in the battle for an hour. I was sent to Kandava Hospital, then to Ventspils and I was being taken back to Liepāja when someone stopped the train and said 'The war is over'.

The Russians took over the hospital and started to treat the wounded. They wouldn't let me have any painkillers when they did an operation on my shoulder. Two nurses held me down while they did that.

We got to Liepāja and all the hospitals were full, so I was sent to Šiauliai Hospital [in Lithuania]. That's where I had another operation, again without anaesthetic. The Russians said 'No drugs for Germans'. I was still in my German uniform at this stage, being called a fascist by people. It was like a prison hospital because it had a fence around it with guards in watchtowers. We would pick flowers and pull the petals off going: 'We will get home, we won't get home. Will get home, won't get home'.

Doctors came to check out those who were healthy but sometimes the more seriously wounded died after being given injections by them. Every day people died that way. I was at the hospital until December 1945, hoping to get well enough to get out.

Then I was sent to a camp where they checked out my past, to see what I did in the war. They sent papers to my village to see what I did there before the war, to make sure I wasn't anything special, that I hadn't been killing Russians. A report came back saying that I was no harm and I was sent to Jelgava, still wearing the German uniform.

They sent me on a train and some Russian soldiers were at the train station and shouted: 'You fascist. What do you think you are doing?' Someone kicked me. A freight train came so I jumped on it to get away to the next station and wait for the next passenger train. But when that came it was full of Russian soldiers. I jumped off at the next stop – no idea where, but it was near Saldus. By then it was getting dark. I found what looked like a stable to sleep in but it was a coal store. I slept there anyway.

I had a Russian pass that allowed me to go home even though I had served in the German Army – I still had the uniform on – so the next morning I carried on heading for Kuldīga. A woman came by with a horse and cart so I asked her for a ride. She took me to the outskirts of Kuldīga and I walked the rest of the way. When I got home my mother was there, but because I was covered in coal dust she didn't know it was me! She only recognised me because of my voice.

I recovered from being very seriously wounded. In Kandava Hospital, the doctors thought I was going to die and asked me if I had any last words. But I've survived to this day.[5]

At the end of a long afternoon Artis and I say our thanks and retire to the Metropole Hotel for something to eat and a slow cold pint of strong dark Latvian ale known as *tumšais*.*

Notes

1 Interview with author, November 2014.
2 Interview with author, November 2014.
3 Interview with author, November 2014.
4 Interview with author, November 2014.
5 Interview with author, November 2014.

* The author returned to Kuldiga to launch this book two years after this meeting and, having checked Mr Leščanovs was still alive, presented him with a copy.

8

From Refugee to President

Twenty minutes north of Kuldīga I take a left into the forest as instructed, on my way to meet the President of Latvia, Vaira Vīķe-Freiberga. She is a child of the war, born in Riga in 1937 and at various stages in her life a displaced person, an émigré and then President for two terms, between 1999 and 2007. Her step-father, a lathe operator and volunteer fireman, was mobilised into the German Army in spring 1944 and wounded just as the Soviets closed in on Riga. He packed his family into a truck heading for Liepāja and they left Riga on 10 October 1944, three days before the city fell. Three months later, on 1st January 1945, they left Liepāja by boat for Germany.

Seventy years later I steer gingerly along a frozen track through first one forest and then another, looking for a red three-storey country house. This is where the former President spends her private time, a long way off the beaten track. Her husband Imants answers the door and makes me a cup of tea as we sit down to talk. I notice that she is recording the interview too.

> Everybody had this naive idea that the Latvians had to push back the Russians as long as possible to show that the annexation of 1940 was completely illegal and not done voluntarily.
>
> By fighting against the Russians, the message would be sent to the free world – particularly to the British who had helped us in the First World War – that the Latvians were not in agreement with the Soviet annexation and were fighting to the last man against the Russians.
>
> [The hope was] that as soon as the Germans had lost the war – which was increasingly clear to everybody – the Allies would restore order and free the three Baltic countries and Poland.
>
> Stalin had asked for military bases in Latvia even before the war had started and had then marched in with his army of 80,000 men in 1940. The government was overthrown, a puppet government was put in its place and shortly a referendum was organised under this military occupation which presumed to show the Latvians asking to be admitted to the Soviet Union.
>
> Everybody thought the world would know this was a sham; that people were forced to go and vote 'yes' in this referendum. My mother told how a militiaman came with a gun [to their apartment] and she said: 'I'm not going to vote in that referendum' and the militiaman said: 'Oh yes, Citizen. You are. We're going now, and you're going to vote'. That's how it happened. She voted for annexation at gunpoint. She wasn't ready to die at that moment and she put in her ballot.

She, like many other Latvians, was naively comforted by the thought that the whole world knew about it. They had no idea about the Secret Protocol of the Molotov-Ribbentrop Pact, nor about the attitude of the Western powers towards Russia, none of this.

Objective information of any sort was in short supply during the war. All people had was rumour and propaganda. Thus ordinary citizens had no idea about the Holocaust; just vague rumours that Jews were being rounded up and shot. But under both occupations all sorts of other people were rounded up and shot as well. The full scope of the horror unfolded only gradually.

I personally witnessed an incident when we were walking along with my Dad and two men wearing yellow Stars of David on their chests were coming from the opposite direction. Two German soldiers walking in front of us stopped the men and ordered them off the sidewalk and into the street. At that point my Dad said: 'If those are the new customs here, then we are going to step off the sidewalk as well'. And we did.

I remember as a child listening to the news on the [German-controlled] radio in the summer of 1944. 'The front line has been straightened again and our troops have been withdrawn by another 15kms in order to regroup'. 'Our troops' – that's how they were referred to on the radio, even though they had been put in uniform against the principles of the Geneva Convention. 'Our troops are fighting valiantly'.

They were indeed, they really were...because of this pitifully mistaken idea that their courage and desperation was sending a message to the free world.

And nowadays the Russians are using the situation during the German occupation as fodder for their propaganda, saying that these men were born fascists who defended the Germans to the last. These were the men that I remember marching off to the front, singing in Latvian: 'First we will beat the 'lousy ones', and then the bluish-grey ones'. This was an indirect reference to the First World War, when the fighting went backwards and forwards with the Bolsheviks and the renegade German troops. Back then the French and British had helped us, and little as it was, it did help at crucial moments. The Estonians came to help us then at the Battle of Cēsis and the Poles helped us here in this region [Kurzeme]. These memories had led to this feeling that surely the world understood our desire for independence, in spite of Latvian men being made to serve in both occupation armies during the Second World War.

During the war German propaganda had encouraged the idea that fighting to the death was a sign of Latvian patriotism and a signal of how much the soldiers cared for Latvian independence. Yet to this day, Mr Putin is using that ardour in battle as a sign that Latvians were sympathisers of Hitler and born fascists by nature. These men were being killed and maimed on the battlefield with a conviction that they were sending a completely different message to the world.

Had they known that sixty or seventy years later their courage would be misinterpreted and used as nasty propaganda against their country I don't know what they would have done. They wouldn't have believed it. It never crossed their minds that that would happen.

Latvians had had close to 700 years of hating the Germans, for heaven's sake, so how all of a sudden could they become Nazis and fascists?

Before we left Riga, the Germans were picking people up on the streets, putting them on boats and sending them to Germany because they were short of labour. So many men had been killed at the front. They issued you with a ship card which said 'You will be leaving on such and such a ship to go to Germany'. If you were stopped on the street by the Gestapo or the police and you didn't have a ship card, they would take you to a holding camp.

We had a neighbour in Riga who went out early one morning in his pyjamas for a bottle of milk and was picked up. His wife had a small child, did not speak any German and was in hysterics. My mother felt she had to do something to help. She spoke German so she took her own small baby in her arms and went out looking for the courtyard where the latest captives were being held. Once there she said to the guards: 'My husband went out this morning and was picked up in his pyjamas. I'm left here with a baby and we were leaving. Please let him come out so we can pack a few things and leave together'. Because she was pretty and young, the guard took pity on her and let her go and find him. When she saw the neighbour, she went up to him and whispered 'Pretend you're my husband and come with me!' And she walked him out of the place and back to his family. The family stayed in Riga but she got him out.

My parents, especially my mother, couldn't stand the Russians – well, the Communist system, actually – and she said: 'Whatever awaits us, it cannot be worse than the system we saw in 1940-41. We're going to leave'.

My grandparents were in Dunika, southeast of Liepāja, next to the Lithuanian border. We couldn't get through to my grandfather's farm because the Russians were already there. The front stayed on top of Dunika for nine months. Meanwhile, we stayed in Liepāja, where the food supplies were getting lower and lower. We had a period of hunger through the second half of October through November and December. Two and a half months.

Decades later a cousin told me what it had been like in Dunika. There was incessant shelling and killing and the locals were evacuated. When they returned there were piles of corpses everywhere. The ditches were full of dead German soldiers that the Russians refused to bury, as a sign to the locals of what losing the war means. My cousin said some local men dug a mass grave in the middle of the local cemetery and secretly moved the bodies there at night. After independence one of my cousins put a cross up at that place. There are Germans still going round looking for the remains of their relatives.

After the war, the Latvian men who escaped the filtration camps would congregate around natural leaders, former Latvian Army officers like my uncle, Edgars Vīķis. He was one of those who was involved in the Resistance, or 'the war after the war' until 1949. He came voluntarily out of the forest after his parents had been arrested and pardons had been promised. He spent a year in a cell on Death Row, then his sentence was commuted to 25 years in Siberia.

The awful thing about this Resistance movement in the Baltics is that some of these groups had received shortwave radio messages from Britain asking them to keep up armed resistance because the British would come and save them. They would come with parachutists and in boats like they did in Normandy. These messages of false hope actually stemmed from the British spies in MI6; Philby, Blunt and the whole bunch of them. Eventually the messages would say: 'The situation is getting hopeless. We don't think we can help you to continue fighting for your land. We will take you to Sweden in rubber boats in the night. Please gather in a certain spot where we will pick you up'. Instead the KGB would turn up and pick them all up ... so the British spies did some very nasty things to the Latvians.

From 1945 until 1949 Vaira lived in a Displaced Persons' camp in Germany, from the age of seven until 11. Then she spent six years in Morocco before going to Toronto in Canada aged 16, an experience that left her able to speak Latvian, German, English and French. She stayed in Canada until 1998 when she returned to Latvia to head the newly-created Latvian Institute. Eight months later she was elected President. She smiles at the memory of this remarkable twist: 'You might say that the stars were all in the right place for me'.

We move onto the wider topic of remembrance, and particularly how as President she tried to represent the suffering of Latvians who fought on either side of the Courland battles. Even remembering the veterans is not straightforward in Latvia. The Legionnaires celebrate one day, March 16th, as Legionnaires' Day, though this is controversial because of the Nazi links and involvement of some Legionnaires in the killing of Jews. The pro-Moscow supporters celebrate May 9th as Victory Day, gathering at the Victory Monument on the other side of the Daugava. Recent anniversaries have been marked by trouble between rival groups.

I try to convince people to celebrate November 11th [Lāčplēsis Day] as the date to remember Latvians who fought for our independence. Soldiers go where they are told, sometimes with a pistol to their head – the alternative is being shot or sent to a concentration camp. We should honour all soldiers who were honest and decent soldiers, who fulfilled their duties and didn't kill civilians and massacre populations.

Whatever uniform by mischance Latvians had to wear, we need to honour them and respect them and Lāčplēsis Day is the day to do it. Don't talk to me about 16th of March or the 9th of May. We do not need any other dates to remind us of our common humanity and the common fate of soldiers who get picked up, put on whatever uniform they're given, pick up a weapon and go and fight whether they like it or not. Like the Russian soldiers who got shot in the back if they didn't advance.

Is it possible, I ask, to create a single Latvia from a nation that's had such a split experience and where almost every family has been affected by loss and suffering?

I was hoping time would heal these wounds. Shortly after he was elected I met President Putin in private. He said he wasn't ready for an exchange of official visits. We had to meet at a ski resort in Austria, so I said 'Fine. I'm willing to show every sign of goodwill'.

We agreed in advance to see what we could do to improve relations and not to go into mutual recriminations. Once there, President Putin came with a whole list of complaints. To start with, he was bothered about our policy of not giving automatic citizenship to the Russian-speaking workforce that had been transplanted into Latvia during the years under Soviet occupation.

I explained that we couldn't give automatic citizenship to people who had arrived after a military invasion, during an illegal occupation and a forced annexation. In addition to the 80,000-strong army and their families, new cities and factories were built during the Soviet times just to bring a Russian-speaking population as a workforce to replace the Latvians deported in several mass deportations under Stalin.

They did everything they could in a process of Russification, particularly in Latvia, to create a Russian wedge in the Baltics. What Kaliningrad is for them now, the vision was to have Latvia as an enclave in the Baltics with the three harbours that don't freeze in the winter.* Latvia, after all, had been the most industrialised region in the Tsarist Empire in the period just before the October Revolution.

Putin kept telling me what a tragedy it was that these people who came here in Soviet times woke up one morning as foreigners in a strange land. Where before they had been full-fledged citizens, now they didn't have a passport and so on. And I said: 'Well, no-one has a Soviet passport any more so they are not alone in that'. Then he said: 'Now there's this border between Latvia and Russia and it's a terrible thing: people have to get visas to cross the border and families are divided.

I replied: 'Yes, Mr President, it's true. We have an awful lot of Latvians who got free rides across the border to the East over the years and some of them actually managed to come back alive. Strangely enough, they're happy to have a Latvian passport now and pay for their voyages, because now instead of the Gulags around Vladivostok, Omsk or Tomsk they can go to Paris or London or Berlin as free men. He didn't like that'.

I'm interested in hearing more about remembrance and reconciliation. 'How do people in Latvia reconcile the past?' I ask.

When my uncle came back from Siberia he was a remarkably serene and cheerful man, not bitter at all. Just feeling lucky to be alive, I suppose. With some of the Siberian survivors, true enough, I have felt a very oppressive atmosphere of bitterness and lasting pain, but there is no general feeling of *revanchism* [a desire

---

*   An ice-free port on the Baltic between Poland and Lithuania, Kaliningrad was once the capital of East Prussia and known as Königsberg. It became part of the Soviet Union at the end of the war. The German population was expelled and replaced by Russians. Source: BBC news profile 12 March 2015.

for revenge]. Those who fought in the war however would like to get recognition as fighters, rather than as criminals. Some of them have chosen the 16th of March as a commemorative date for their fallen comrades but I think that choice of date was a mistake, for it plays into the hands of Russian propaganda.

Latvians have accepted the Russians among them long ago. They were bringing them in by the thousand, you know. Yet Latvians are fully aware that in many ways these immigrants have enriched the country. Not least demographically – some 20% or more of all the marriages in the country are mixed marriages.

Latvians have survived wars, pestilence, invasions from every point on the compass, by being strong workers and having a strong work ethic. I think they did have a strong sense of solidarity – you couldn't survive without it – but also a strong sense of individual responsibility. And that's something the Communist Party attacked systematically and successfully.

What did she think of the Soviet system in Latvia?

The communist system was quite satisfactory to the *nomenklatura* – the elite and the chosen few of the times – but quite harmful to the Latvian nation. It was merciless in destroying lives and wiping out entire families. As with any ruling system there were Latvian collaborators. Again – one concrete example told to me by a neighbour of another uncle, Alvīne. A local Communist party bigwig, K., was an old friend of her brother's from his youth. This man was lame and ugly; not liked by the girls and not generally accepted by the boys. But he became a big cheese in the Communist Party and terrorised the whole village until the end of his days. He quite enjoyed his power over others, apparently.

These neighbours in Dunika were deported on 25 March 1949 and only half of them returned. The morning they were deported my informant's brother got up early to water his horses. It's an old Latvian tradition for young men to have one fine horse reserved just for riding. It was very early in the morning yet there was K. leading his best horse out of the stable and across the courtyard. Naturally he was astounded. 'What are you doing with my horse?' he asked.

K. turned to him and said: 'Where you are going, my friend, you won't be needing this horse anymore, so I am taking it'. Only then did her brother look across at the road and see the convoy of trucks coming to pick him up. K. had clearly been part of the committee making up the list of deportees and decided to get the good pickings before anyone else did. In a system like that it's survival of the fittest, but of the basest sort.[1]

I was promised an hour, and we've talked for longer than that. The President glances at her watch. I sense that it's time to move on.

Note

1   Interview with author, January 2015.

9

Winter Joins the Fight

A lull in the fighting after the first battle of Courland gave the defenders time for repairs and reinforcements. There was time for military commanders to consider the best tactics for the terrain, especially with the long, bitter Latvian winter approaching.

Until now Soviet infantry attacks came after artillery barrages designed to soften up defensive lines but the gunners were now firing patterns across the battlefield. This created corridors to allow the first line of troops to penetrate deeper into German defences than in conventional assaults.

As a result German defences were re-thought. They were laid out in primary, secondary and tertiary positions with road barriers, ambush locations and bunkers so that quarters could be created for the men. Civilians were pressed into the construction work and anyone capable of firing a weapon was pressed into combat – with orders not to yield a single metre of ground.[1]

Nazi generals knew the two major objectives of the Soviets: to capture Liepāja and cut off the supply and evacuation routes from Germany, and to pound the centre of the Courland bridgehead between Auce and Saldus to split the front into two and thus make it easier to destroy. They would then drive a wedge between Liepāja and Ventspils and split Courland into two zones, northeast and southwest.[2]

In the swamps and forests around Saldus defence in depth meant using the natural geography as a weapon in itself. Woods were cleared to allow unobstructed fields of fire. These areas were filled with mines, trip wires and explosive devices. Strongpoints concealing anti-tank guns were set up: the killing zones precisely targeted so artillery gunners had the exact co-ordinates to respond to any changes in Soviet battle tactics.

The German generals were aware that Hitler would not order an evacuation of Courland. He refused to consider the very idea of withdrawal even though the position was impossible. One reason for this was control of the Baltic Sea. Although the fortunes of the war had now turned decisively against Germany control of the ports of Liepāja and Ventspils meant there was still a way out for all the soldiers, staff officers and German civilians trying to get back to the Reich. Secondly, Swedish iron ore, a raw material vital to weapons production, was still being shipped to Germany. Thirdly, holding the Baltic ports would mean bases for the 'super U-boat' Hitler hoped would be his latest secret weapon.

A thousand designers and engineers worked on the new boats from August 1943 after more effective Allied anti-submarine tactics and detection techniques dramatically increased U-boat losses in the Atlantic. Navy chief Admiral Karl Dönitz planned a new generation of U-boats: bigger, faster and capable of remaining submerged for much longer – and he needed the Baltic to train his crews. Forty boats a month were promised from April 1944.

The Type 21 U-boat was 237 feet long with a crew of 57 and could maintain a submerged speed of 12-14 knots for ten hours or 18 knots for 90 minutes. This made approach and escape much faster. Their electric engines allowed for 'silent running' – thicker hull plating and better listening and location devices meant attacks were possible without having to rise to periscope depth.

The smaller Type 23 was intended for use off Britain and the Mediterranean as a flexible attack boat, small enough at 114 feet long to be transported by rail, able to cruise underwater at twelve and a half knots for an hour, armed with two torpedoes. Because of their electric engines, these U-boats were called 'electro-submarines'.[3]

In the autumn of 1943 Dönitz placed an order for 170 Type 21 and 140 Type 23 U-boats. They would be built in sections at eleven fitting yards on the coast and then assembled in Danzig, Bremen and Hamburg. Vast resources were pumped into the U-boat effort. Production was transferred to an enormous bombproof site on the river Weser near Bremen, large enough to take 13-14 submarines at one time with room for 24 sections under construction. It had a roof of reinforced concrete nearly 7 metres thick and walls 9 to 13 metres thick.

This would be the first of several gigantic Nazi Super U-boat factories with yet more advanced models being built, such as the Walter U-boats, designated Types 27 and 28. Capable of 28 knots underwater the Type 27 reached the training boat stage but the Atlantic-capable Type 28 didn't reach completion before the Nazi defeat.

Allied attacks on Germany itself caused serious delays and disrupted production of the U-boats. The Type 21 and 23 entered service in November 1944 but having been built without prototypes, engineers were kept busy solving technical faults and engine problems. Only five or six Type 23s put to sea and only two Type 21s went into action. *U-2511* spent four days at sea from 17 April 1945 but developed engine problems. *U-3008* left Wilhemshaven on 3 May 1945 just as Dönitz issued his order for all boats to cease attacks and return to base for the capitulation.[*4]

The new submarines did not yield a single Allied casualty despite tying up 40,000 production workers on the Type 21 project alone and using enough steel to build 5,000 tanks – which might have had a greater impact on the war.

It was up to the men in the trenches in Courland to hold the line against the Soviet attackers, and keep the Baltic ports open for the evacuation of hundreds of thousands of wounded men and as many soldiers and civilians as possible.[5]

Air support over Courland came from *Luftflotte* 1[†] which had 267 aircraft, including 80 ground attack aircraft, 63 fighters, 73 night fighters, 19 long-range and 32 short-range reconnaissance planes, operating from bases in Liepāja, Saldus, Tukums, Skrunda and Ventspils. There had been Estonian and Latvian Air Legions

---

*   *U-2540* was scuttled at the end of the war without seeing action. The boat was salvaged in 1957 and restored. It's now a floating museum ship at the German Maritime Museum at Bremerhaven.
†   1st Air Fleet.

operating as part of this wing but a series of desertions involving pilots flying their planes to Sweden led to them being disbanded. A small band of German pilots in Focke-Wulf 190s landed heavy blows on the waves of Soviet planes.

The premier unit was *Jagdgeschwader* 54 [54th Fighter Wing] known as 'the Green Hearts', whose war diary records 293 enemy planes destroyed in the first two battles of Courland. In two days of aerial battles over Liepāja during the third they accounted for another 100 Soviet aircraft. Eleven fighters were lost. During a subsequent Soviet air offensive the German pilots flew up to five sorties a day and shot down a further 60 aircraft. Flak batteries accounted for an astonishing 500 Soviet aircraft.[6]

JG-54 flew from bases at Liepāja, Grobiņa, Cīrava, Tukums, Skrunda, Ventspils and Sabile against an enemy that sometimes outnumbered them 10 to one. From 1 January 1945 to 8 May 1945 the squadron's pilots shot down 400 Soviet aircraft.[7]

The heavy Soviet bombing raids on Liepāja in late October 1944 that Vaira Vīķe-Freiberga and her family survived caused severe damage to residential and port areas and sank several ships. Then an enormous artillery barrage on the morning of 27th October was the prelude to a 400-tank attack between Auce and Dobele, the centre of the 170km front line.

The fighting was wild and frantic. Overwhelming numbers of Soviet tanks rolled through the German positions with infantry in support. Close combat tank-killer teams stopped the armour with *panzerfausts* as machine gun nests opened up on the advancing Red Army soldiers. More than 1,000 Soviet bombers and ground attack planes pulverised Liepāja and Auce, attacking railway stations, road junctions and troop columns.

Against them flew the fighters of JG-54, led by squadron commander Major Erich Rudorffer, who earned himself the nickname 'The Fighter of Libau'* for singlehandedly tackling a group of 60 aircraft preparing to attack German airfields. The story goes that Rudorffer took them on alone, downing nine planes in ten minutes and driving the rest off.[8]

JG-54 shot down 80 Soviet planes in three days between 27th and 29th October. Rudorffer ended the war with 222 kills from 1,000 missions, 302 of which resulted in combat. He was shot down 16 times and baled out on nine occasions. The seventh most deadly ace in aviation history, Rudorffer died in April 2016, aged 98.[9]

The intense Soviet pressure forced Auce to be abandoned and the constant reinforcement of the attack wave meant the Germans were vastly outnumbered. At Dinzdurbe a flak battery fought to the last man, knocking out nine Russian tanks before being silenced. Over several days German divisions in the centre fell back to prepared positions between Lake Lielauce and Zebrus Lake: difficult, swampy terrain that was possible to attack only in frontal assaults. A second attack on Priekule was cancelled and, on 3 November, the offensive was called off. The Germans had lost 44,000 men between 1 October and 7 November, with 3,128 wounded in four days between 31 October and 3 November.[10]

---

*   The German name for Liepāja.

The determined resistance kept open the lifeline through Liepāja. Every ship that arrived brought fresh soldiers, supplies and ammunition and enabled the Army, Luftwaffe and civil administration to keep functioning. In addition the resistance in Courland tied up considerable Red Army forces and resources that could otherwise have been used for the assault on Germany itself.

At this time persistent rain turned the ground into a greasy, slimy mass over which nothing could move without sinking. Troops were wet during the day and cold at night. They dug bunkers and lined them with wood to keep out of the mud.

Reinforcements arrived in the form of several thousand survivors of a battle for the Estonian island of Saaremaa [in English: Osel] off the coast of northern Courland.

Saaremaa was strategically important because it covered the Irben Straits, the sea lane from the Baltic Sea into the Gulf of Riga. The Germans had seized the island and others around it in *Operation Beowulf* in 1941. In October 1944 Soviet amphibious landings on the islands had pushed the German defenders back to the southernmost tip, the Sworbe peninsula. The Germans resisted for several weeks, bringing in the heavy ships of the German Navy – the *Lutzow, Prinz Eugen* and *Admiral Scheer* – to bombard the attackers.[11]

The loss of Sworbe would greatly increase the threat to German shipping into and out of the Baltic ports and the possibility of Soviet amphibious landings on the Courland coast. Resistance was stubborn but costly. In one of the largest ground support actions of the war, the German Navy suffered more than 2,000 casualties.[12]

After a week the Soviet pressure proved too much and on the evening of 23-24 November the surviving German defenders clambered into landing craft and motor-boats to be evacuated to Ventspils.[13]

After a pause to allow re-supply and reinforcements the Soviet pressure on the front line in Courland resumed. The Red Army had pushed the front line back far enough to be able to shell Liepāja and Skrunda from long range, softening up defences for a fresh tank offensive.

An intense artillery barrage began on 19 November pounding the entire sector between Saldus and Priekule. Hundreds of tanks rolled towards, forcing the Germans back 10kms. Red Army infantry pressed on through the woods despite appalling casualties.[14]

Gottlob Bidermann was one of the men resisting the attack.

> The Russians tore through the front in several locations, including the sector held by our division. Only with reinforcements from various units was the offensive halted near Saldus* several days later... immediately thereafter the rains began, and all movement, regardless of how insignificant, was conducted only with great effort. Along the line the terrain became a vast swampy morass to which even the Russians, with their motorised units, had to yield.

---

*   Known to the Germans as Frauenberg.

The line consisted mostly of shallow holes half-filled with water from melting snow and ice, in which *landsers* [infantry] alternated sentry duty while attempting to remain physically able to further resist the enemy. Re-supply, when at all possible, became sporadic due to the impassable roads and constant disruption from artillery barrages and the relentless strafing aircraft that appeared suddenly and without warning from the grey sky. The horses were now often collapsing from lack of nourishment and for the *landsers* in the earthworks, warm food had become a rare luxury.[15]

On the morning of 23 November Russian artillery fired more than 200,000 rounds in one sector alone between Krote and Skrunda.* Soviet armour broke the line for an infantry advance but German assault guns in the woods cut them down as the defenders retreated across the Koja river then blew the bridges.[16]

The second battle of Courland petered out into a shuffling of resources in preparation for the next. When temperatures dropped in December, movement around the front in Stedini and Pampāļi where Bidermann was located† was possible again – though that was equally true for the Soviets.

The earth froze to the consistency of stone. The muddy roads were once again passable and a forbidding atmosphere of expectation swept over the ragged army. The companies far in the front and the artillery observers reported the sound of heavy movements of vehicles coming from the enemy lines. Throughout the nights the grinding of tank tracks was clearly audible.

Our artillery remained powerless to fire on targets of opportunity as munitions had become scarce and were carefully rationed. Bands of fighter planes and squadrons of bombers displaying the five-pointed star on their fuselage and wings flew over us at random. With impunity they made daily excursions during these clear, frost-laden December days on their way to bomb the supply harbours of Liepāja and Ventspils in attempts to disrupt our tenuous lifelines.[17]

The next confrontation in Courland would be the Christmas Battles, where countryman fought countryman, brother fought brother and the pain inflicted on Latvians by this conflict struck ever deeper at the heart of the nation.

Notes

1   Kurowski, p.90.
2   Ibid, p.89.
3   Grier, p.171.
4   Ibid, p.179.
5   Ibid, p.182.

*   An area just south of the A9 west of Saldus.
†   To the south between Skrunda and Saldus.

6   Kurowski, p.275.
7   Ibid, pp.279–289.
8   Ibid, p.135.
9   Lepage, *An Illustrated Dictionary of the Third Reich*, p.44.
10 Kurowski, p.137.
11 M. Murfett, *Naval Warfare 1919-45: An Operational History of the Volatile War at Sea* p.345.
12 Grier, p.74.
13 Ibid, p.69.
14 Kurowski, pp.143-144.
15 Bidermann, p.257.
16 Kurowski, p.144.
17 Bidermann, p.259.

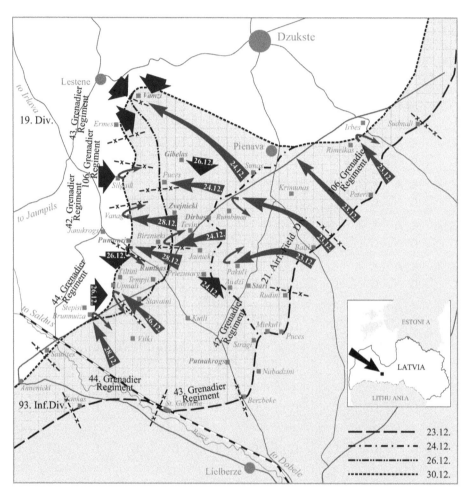

Map 2 The Christmas Battles, December 1944.

10

The Christmas Battles

The countryside around Lestene and Džūkste is undeveloped and uncelebrated. There are few memorials to the savage conflict fought here. In the Christmas Battles of 1944 Latvian faced Latvian across the battlefield, fighting in the uniforms of the Soviet Union or Nazi Germany.

A generation of Latvians died here. Countless thousands of Germans, Russians and men of other nationalities from across Europe and the USSR died with them. It was an international battlefield of death.

Flat swampy fields surround Džūkste and Lestene, with clumps of trees gathered at intervals. Sand roads lead to neighbouring villages. The fields have been ploughed and are the consistency of heavy clay. A lorry loaded with logs passes me. Fog hangs in the air. I can almost feel the ache and weight of sadness in this damp atmosphere. I sense a melancholy here that I've felt before on the battlefields of the Western Front. A poster on a bus stop noticeboard is advertising a service of remembrance for Lāčplēsis Day, with a quote from the writer Ojārs Zanders.

No matter how far away the ghosts are
They still love their country
The ghosts who are the furthest away
People's love of their country doesn't end.[1]

Then through the wisps of fog I see the white stone tower of Lestene Church. The entire building bears deep scars from bullets and shells. Great gouges are visible in the stonework. The area around the tower window is pockmarked with bullet strikes and the impact of shells. The main window at the back of the church is still bricked up and the repairs to the brickwork are extensive. The artillery and machine gun damage to the back wall makes it look like a giant hand has thrown great dollops of plaster at it, splattering across its surface in patches big and small.

This church has taken one hell of a battering. In some ways it is symbolic of the pounding and punishment taken by Latvians over the corresponding period, from which the nation is only just emerging. Recently fitted with a cheerful red roof, Lestene Church is slowly regaining its dignity. A fundraising campaign is underway to raise the money to pay for its restoration, but the blows it has suffered have been profound and fundamental. Those who come here do so for a reason.

There has been a stone church in Lestene since 1670, a focal point for the community and place of worship. Its simple, almost stark exterior belied the treasures inside. At the end of the 17th and beginning of the 18th centuries, architecture and decorative art flourished in Courland and estate owners competed among themselves to build the most lavish and ornate churches.

The shipyards of Ventspils were home to very skilled carpenters and woodcarvers, who found their services much in demand. One of the greatest names in Baroque period woodcarving was Nicolaus Söffrens who spent five years between 1704 and 1709 adorning Lestene Church with a carved pulpit, confessional, pews and patrons' box. He fashioned a magnificent wooden case for an organ built by the most outstanding organ-maker of the period, Cornelius Rahneus. Carved figures moved as it was played; King David conducted, angels fluttered their wings and tapped on drums and above, a great eagle flapped its wings. There were magnificent Corinthian columns, rosettes and angels' heads.[2]

On 21st December 1944 that would all change. The third battle of Courland began at 6am on a winter's morning. Close to Christmas, temperatures were dropping to minus 15C. Eight hundred Soviet artillery guns, mortars and rockets launched an enormous wave of fire on the positions of Grenadier Regiment 438 near Stedini, southwest of Saldus.

The scale of the attack was colossal. Artillery barrages fired 60,000 shells in the morning alone. Soviet ground attack planes flew 2,491 sorties on the first day, 1,800 on the second day and 2,415 on the third.[3]

Soviet troops took the area around Lake Lielauce and pressed on towards Džūkste, Irbes and Pienava. The landscape north of Dobele, east around Zebrus Lake, Pampāļi and across the forests east to west was transformed into scenes from hell, as described by gunnery captain Gottlieb Bidermann.

> An incredible firestorm rained down on the trenches. Machine gun nests, earth-works, bunkers and reinforced fire positions along our front collapsed in clouds of dust and smoke. The earth trembled, roared, heaved and tossed. The bunkers collapsed; the trenches were levelled. The treetops were splintered, entire trees sailed into the sky, shells struck the reinforced bunkers and completely enveloped our surroundings. Minutes became an eternity.
>
> The first wounded appeared, stumbling and staggering aimlessly, often without helmets, uniforms covered with blood. Those unable to walk arrived in shelter-quarters* carried by *landsers* straining against the load. The wounded screamed in agony and thrashed wildly on the ground as they awaited the care of the medical officer.[4]

Legionnaire Pēteris Stabulnieks was at the front, waiting for that attack.

> Christmas time came and there was freshly brewed ale for everybody. Even vodka came in great proportions. We knew the Russians were preparing a huge attack. We kept thinking 'At least let us celebrate the festivity and do the attacking later'.

---

*   Waterproof sheets used as protection from rain as trench covers, shawls and wraps.

Every morning we heard how the Russians organised training, from early morning until late evening. They were training Latvians; we could hear Latvian songs and commands.

Then on the first day of the festivity, in the early morning, an artillery barrage started from our left side. The attack had begun. The first squadrons of bomber planes showed up and started bombarding the roads behind us as well as our artillery positions. They flew right over our heads. The attack lasted a whole day and twice the Russians kept hitting our right side where 44 Battalion were, but we beat them back.

In the evening supplies arrived: bread, some kind of biscuits and desserts as well as some gifts – we did not know where to put it all. Beer and vodka were forbidden. We could not afford to get drunk. In the evening we had to retreat as the Russians had advanced quite far and we were in danger of being surrounded.[5]

Even in the night the Russians wouldn't leave us alone. Several times they tried to attack us but we managed to overcome them every time. The Russians attacked us with large forces supported by all their guns but they moved forward very slowly. Very heavy battles occurred. Positions changed hands between defenders and attackers, often with hand-to-hand fighting for the most important areas. Both sides lost lots of casualties.[6]

The fighting was concentrated in two areas from the western edge of the forests at Jūrmala across to Skrunda. The eastern area ran from the southeastern tip of Zebrus Lake in a bulge southeast of Lestene and Džūkste and north of Dobele. The western area was south of the modern A9 between Skrunda and Saldus in the forests around Pampāļi and Zanenieki. Battle commanders navigated by farmhouses, which were often massively fortified. Some key names from the Christmas Battles are still marked on Latvian maps today. Orient them by rivers and roads and they will reveal that where the most intense battles were, little remains today.

The modern A9 runs right alongside the battlefield where Latvians faced each other on opposing sides, just south of the area between Lestene and Džūkste, at Sudmali and Krimūnas. Here the Red Army's Latvian 130th Riflemen fought the 106th Grenadiers of the Latvian Legion. The 106th Grenadiers took heavy casualties as they resisted a strong assault by tanks, losing more than 60 per cent of their men.

The 130th Latvian Riflemen Corps brought together the 43rd Guards and the 308th Riflemen, units of Latvian soldiers who survived the purge after the Soviet occupation and then the defensive fighting at Staraya Russa and the Velikaya River.[7]

When the Red Army crossed into Latvia in June 1944, large numbers of Latvian men in the east were swept up in the Soviet advance through Latgale and Vidzeme* and pressed into uniform. They were commanded by Major General Detlavs Brantkalns, a Latvian communist who had fought for the Bolsheviks, survived Stalin's purges and

---

*   The two eastern regions which with Courland and Zemgale make up modern Latvia.

taken command of the 43rd Guards at Staraya Russa, facing some of the men telling their stories for this book.[8]

Between 80,000 and 100,000 Latvians fought in the Red Army in the Second World War, with 50,000 killed. Some were Latvian Army soldiers evacuated ahead of the Nazi invasion in 1941 who served with distinction in the Battle of Moscow and at Demyansk and Leningrad. Others were mobilized into the Red Army during the liberation of Latvia from June 1944 onwards.[9]

It was here that 25 year-old Legionnaire Roberts Ancāns won a Knight's Cross for his bravery. On 24 December 1944 a renewed Red Army offensive pushed the Latvian 19th Division back 8kms leading to the capture of *Zvejnieki* and *Paugibelas*, two fortified hotspots that were the focus of repeated intense clashes. In that assault a stronghold at Dirbas, about 5kms southeast of Džūkste was surrounded, trapping 180 men of the SS Close Combat Training School, commanded by Ancāns, who was from Talsi and an *Obersturmführer* in the *Waffen-SS.**

From a defensive point of view the situation was desperate. The Soviet attacks had almost reached Army HQ at Lestene and another Latvian stronghold at Stari had been cut off for 24 hours.[10]

As night fell the fighting was dramatic and desperate. Eight Soviet tanks outflanked a Latvian artillery regiment and attacked it from the rear. The battery returned fire and destroyed four tanks but lost three of its guns. The surviving crews knocked out the four remaining Soviet tanks with *Panzerfaust* rockets, bringing their total kills for the day to 13.[11]

As December 25th dawned Ancāns and his men were still holding out at Dirbas. Russian attacks continued through the centre and right of the front throughout the day with the Red Army gaining ground, then losing it, then re-gaining it. This is how one Latvian artilleryman spent Christmas Day 1944.

> At 10am the bombardment begins, something I could never have imagined. For three hours artillery shells of different calibre are constantly exploding. There are no separate explosions, just a perpetual dreadful rumble. We hide in pits we scrape out. All the shells explode in the trees and the ground is being hacked by shrapnel. When most of trees in the forest have been hacked down, shells begin to explode on the ground. There is no point hiding in the bunker – the shells go through that too.
>
> I stay in my pit and wait for a kindly hit to send me to my forefathers. One shell splinter hits my back, rips my coat, goes through a fur waistcoat and a knitted shirt but does not wound me! My pistol! It gets hit too! And there is little left of it, bent and broken. A third splinter goes from my elbow to my hand, ripping open my sleeve, but the skin is only scratched. Another shell explosion

---

*   A senior assault leader, equivalent to the British rank of lieutenant.

buries me in sand, leaving only my head sticking out. At least the shrapnel is not hitting me now."[12]

As evening fell the decision was taken to pull the 19th Latvians out of the front line. They had taken a pounding all day. Orders were sent to Ancāns and his surviving men to abandon the position at Dirbas, where by now just 35 men remained alive. Ancāns himself was wounded. The survivors gathered the wounded men, including Ancāns, and managed to break through the encirclement back to the safety of their own lines.[†]

At this point in the battle, reports came in from positions around Džūkste that soldiers had been seen coming from Red Army positions on the battlefield wearing German uniforms.[13]

The Legionnaire Pēteris Stabulnieks gave this account.

One of our groups of soldiers were located in a forestry building and some Russians were hidden 50 metres away in a school. One night, some Russians disguised as our soldiers had snuck past the lookout positions and got behind the men at the forestry building. These [our] men thought they were on our side as they spoke in Latvian. Nine men were in a bunker, one was next to the bunker, three were on lookout and two were in the forestry building. The man next to the bunker was shot and killed and those inside the bunker saw no other option and surrendered. The Russians had so many prisoners they didn't even bother going anywhere else and instead they escaped. This was the first time they managed to take so many prisoners in this manner.[14]

In the next attack, on December 26th, the Soviets outnumbered the defenders six to one as fierce battles raged around the marshes, particularly for higher ground, which changed hands several times. By the evening the Russians had forced a 2km wide gap in the front.[15]

Another Latvian, NCO Žanis Ansons, would distinguish himself at this point. Taking eight men armed with hand grenades and machine guns he worked his way behind Soviet positions on a hill then attacked from the rear, successfully re-taking the hill. For this he, like Roberts Ancāns, was awarded the Knight's Cross, the first Latvian NCO to receive the decoration.[‡16]

---

*   The author of these memories was captured by Russians and sentenced to 10 years for shooting at the Red Army.
†   For his bravery at Dirbas, Legionnaire Roberts Ancāns was awarded the Knight's Cross, one of Nazi Germany's highest military honours. Wounded just as the war entered its final days, he was evacuated to Germany and surrendered to the Allies, later emigrating to America, where he died in 1982, aged 62.
‡   Žanis Ansons survived the war but chose to go into the forests rather than surrender. He was captured by the Soviets in December 1945 and deported, serving ten years in Siberia and returning in 1955. He died in 1968 and was buried in a country cemetery outside Kandava.

The fighting was savage in that small sector of front between Lestene and Džūkste. Fierce tank battles erupted as the Soviets piled the pressure on the defences at Džūkste. Pienava, just a short distance away, was attacked by 30 tanks. Another 43 rolled toward Rozukaln, a little further south. But the defences held. Morning attacks on December 27th were repulsed and the Soviets lost the chance to encircle the 42nd Grenadiers at *Zvejnieki* when they bombed their own positions.

Undeterred, Soviet generals ordered another attack on 28 December and this time the Red Army broke the line. Desperate defending pushed them back but with huge loss of life: only eleven men survived from one company. Counter attacks by the Latvian 19th Fusiliers the next day recaptured the lost ground and the front lines were reinforced in front of Lestene.[17]

After one final assault on December 31st with temperatures down to minus 20C, the Russians abandoned their attacks having made few actual territorial gains and suffered unbelievable casualties. Nazi losses totalled 27,134 killed, wounded or missing.[18]

Limited German and Latvian counter-attacks took place in early January to straighten the front line and clear an area of deep forest. The attacks met stiff resistance and farmhouses and strongpoints changed hands several times until the 19th Latvians took and held *Gibelas*. Pēteris Stabulnieks was involved in those attacks.

After a few days pause, on the morning of 5 January 1945 we started a large scale artillery bombardment against the Russians. We fired from every barrel. Over our heads towards the Russian position flew thousands of tonnes of steel. Everything ahead of us was completely covered in smoke, the air was filled with howling from every kind of calibre bullets and bombs. Ahead of us rose huge lines of fire. Trees, stones, human remains, all hurling through the air. After some hours the bombardment moved further behind the Russian positions.

Now the infantry moved forward, together with tanks and cannons. We moved through what used to be marshland. After the bombardment, barely a tree remained.

Scattered everywhere were fallen Russian soldiers. Now we saw the consequences of the tonnes of steel that were launched at this site of destruction. There were soldiers who died from the pressure alone as no scars were visible. With black, puffed faces they lay like trees in a forest after a storm. Many of them were Latvians, and those who were alive stood their ground like real soldiers are supposed to.

I remember one Latvian boy. The rest were dead, some had escaped, but he had remained in his position – alone – when we surprised him. He had run out of ammunition and was in a hopeless situation. We called to him – 'Surrender' – but he wouldn't give up. He pulled the pin out of a grenade and blew himself to bits, injuring one of our men too. He was only a kid, just 18 years of age as we discovered from his documents. But he was a true hero.[19]

We were relocated to a new area near the Zebrus Lake. For the first time I saw so many casualties. All were Latvians. It was hard to walk at night as we got tangled amongst the dead bodies. It was a real Latvian cemetery. The Germans we swapped shifts with were telling us how the Russians mowed them down with machine guns. The first wave went with guns – they were shot down. The second wave went with no guns and had to collect them from the fallen; they were shot down … and so on until everybody was dead. Those who had seen certain death ahead had tried to escape but were shot down by their own soldiers.[20]

The Latvian Legion deputy chief Artūrs Silgailis noted:

> During the nine days of combat 46 Russian infantry and several armoured divisions had suffered complete destruction, all for the price of capturing some tens of square kilometres of terrain. The 19th Latvian Division alone had knocked out 10 specially trained infantry divisions and one armoured Corps. Among the prisoners and the dead were Latvians from Vidzeme the Russians had hurriedly conscripted after the German retreat to Kurzeme.[21]

Latvian historians regard Lestene Church as once the most spectacular historic religious building in the Latvian countryside. Almost to the very end of World War II everything had survived in its original form. But then came disaster.

In February 1945 Soviet artillery spotters sneaked into the church tower and used the vantage point to bring shells on their enemy nearby. When they were discovered the tower was shelled until they were silenced. Through half a century of Soviet occupation, when it was used as a grain store, Lestene Church stood as a ruin, the tower and church without roofs; a forlorn reminder not only of what happened here but also of the Latvian nation's powerlessness to repair the damage and move on.

Following the second independence an organisation was founded to gather the Latvian war dead together in one cemetery. Their graves were scattered across Courland and in some instances during the Soviet period had not been treated with the respect they deserved. An area of farmland alongside Lestene Church was marked out and a competition held for a suitable design, which was won by architect Edvīns Vecumnieks and sculptor Arta Dumpe.

In 2000 the foundation stone of the cemetery was laid and Dumpe's vast statue to the fallen *Homeland Mother Latvia* was winched into place.

Construction work finished in 2003 and the cemetery opened, but even more than a decade later names are still being added to the lists of those who lost their lives in the war.

Lestene *Brāļu Kapi* [Brothers' Cemetery] is a solemn, dignified place, full of space and room to reflect at the graves of the fallen. It is a place of rest rather than a place where personal stories are told.

More than a thousand Latvian legionnaires who fell in the Second World War are buried here. The walls surrounding the cemetery are lined with the names of more than 17,000 victims of war, including the national partisans who fought against the post-war Soviet regime. They are not all Latvian, either.

Among the seemingly endless lists of the dead are Estonians, Lithuanians and even Germans, deserters who realised there was little future for them either in Germany or in Soviet-controlled Latvia – and so chose defiance.

> Anelunas Jonas, Lietuva 1916 – 12.12.49.
> Arfmann Dietrich 1921 – 11.49.
> Jozef Bruder 1923 – 27.5.48.
> Dandzig Herbert 22.10.45.
> Horst Friedel d 1947.
> Willi Fischer 15.07.49.
> 'Heini' – Deutschland 8.6.48.
> Hubert Werner 28.7.48.
> Anton Koll 22.10.45.[22]

The war in Courland did not end with the capitulation, and the partisan war is even more complicated than the conventional war. But the end result is the same: lots of dead people, most of them Latvian. Courland is a vast graveyard.

Notes

1   Poster in Lestene quoting Ojārs Zanders, writer and literary historian b.1931.
2   Latvian Coins website at http://www.latc.lv/en/collector-coins-of-bank-of-latvia/oh-holy-lestene/.
3   Kurowski, p.152.
4   Bidermann, p.262.
5   Gribuska, pp.53-54.
6   Ibid, p.54.
7   McAteer, p.299.
8   Occupation Museum website: http://www.occupation.lv/#!/en/eksponats/05VI.3.
9   Latvian History website https://latvianhistory.com/2013/06/28/ accessed 20 June 2016, quoting *Divas Puses* by Uldis Neiburgs (2011).
10 Silgailis, p.137.
11 Ibid.
12 Lācis, *Kurzeme (1944-1945): Latviesu Gara un Patveruma Cietoksnis [Courland stronghold 1944-1945]*, p.77.
13 Kurowski, p.156.
14 Gribuska, pp.56-57.
15 McAteer, p.300.
16 Silgailis, p.138.
17 Silgailis, p.139.
18 McAteer, p.300.
19 Gribuska, pp.54-55.
20 Gribuska, pp.55-56.
21 Silgailis, p.143.
22 Author's visit to Lestene Cemetery.

11

A Morning with the Bomb Squad

The Army bomb disposal squad EOD 54* has its headquarters just behind Saldus town centre. I'm let through the gates and greeted in the yard by Captain Oscars Lejnieks and First Lieutenant Aigars Pūce, both bomb disposal veterans.

We step into the main building and climb the stairs into the kitchen. It's warm and feels well used, as though men spend a lot of their time here. The three of us make coffee the Latvian way; three spoonfuls of ground coffee into a mug then add boiling water. The Latvians add three spoonfuls of sugar, a national tradition dating back to Ulmanis's time, but I can't take it that sweet.† I add a half-spoon then we sit down around the wooden table, stirring our coffee and waiting for the grounds to sink.

I politely decline their offer of a bowl of wild boar and mushroom soup and instead we nibble biscuits from a plate on the table. I produce a bag of Latvian *Serenade* chocolates and spread them out in front of us, dividing them into three piles.

The phone barely stops ringing throughout the morning I am with them. Seventy years after the war that alone tells its own story about the amount of ammunition fired in this small stretch of land. Some days these men come face-to-face with death several times a day. They do it with good humour and determination: the symbol of their EOD company is of a shell split in half.

There are three companies of thirty men each, based in Ogre, Rēzekne and Saldus. They are on standby 24 hours a day and deal with 1,200 calls a year.

On average they get four call-outs a day per company from people who have found UXBs. The whole of Latvia is literally littered with old bombs, shells and bullets.

First Lieutenant Pūce is 38 and has worked his way up through the ranks.‡ Oscars Lejnieks is five years his junior, and a Captain. Both have family history shaped dramatically by war, and by the Courland Pocket particularly. Oscars is the first to speak.

> My father was 10 years old when the war started. I never saw my grandfather. I was born in 1981 and he died in 1956. I don't know much about him because my father didn't tell me much. He fought in both the first and second world war, both times for the Germans. In the Second World War he was captured by

---

*   Explosive Ordnance Disposal.
†   It was said that Latvia's first Prime Minister Karlis Ulmanis took three sugars in coffee, one for each of the country's three sugar beet factories.
‡   A Latvian First Lieutenant is one rank higher than in the UK.

American soldiers near Berlin. The US soldiers sent him back to the Soviets, and then the Soviets decided he should go to Siberia as punishment.

A lot of the Latvians in Germany at the end of the war [the 15th Division] decided that it would be better to be captured by the Americans rather than the Soviets. The guys who were handed back to the Soviets and sent to Siberia … they didn't live so well. Living conditions were completely different.

In the Soviet time people were pushed to forget those things, to forget about an independent Latvia. But when we got the second independence that changed. Now lots of people are trying to find where their relatives and grandparents are buried.

Many people were sent to Siberia and many died there. A lot came back and lived normally, of course. My cousin's wife was born in Siberia. Now she's around 50 – not old – but she has a lot of health problems.

There's been a fair amount of activity in the background while we've been talking. Soldiers have been striding purposefully up and down the corridor outside. I wondered why Captain Lejnieks' phone kept ringing and he kept stepping outside. Now I realise why. Aigars explains.

At the moment there is an operation going on near Liepāja, in a town called Durbe. Four live artillery shells have been found by a road working team. The call-out team is surveying the site to see if there are any more. And the team in Ogre is out as well. It's like this every day… three or four calls a day for each team. The record is sixteen calls in one day. That was here. It just comes and comes, working till dark.

Through the window I see a sandpit. That's where they detonate small arms rounds. Bigger UXBs often need more specialist treatment. Mostly here they tackle unexploded Second World War bombs and munitions though, since Latvia joined NATO, they are also expert now at making safe IEDs from the modern conflicts in Iraq and Afghanistan. Aigars drains his mug and begins his story.

My father never saw his father. My grandfather was killed by Russian secret police who were clearing the front line after a battle. He was killed by the NKVD filtration force at the end of February 1945 and my father was born on 13 March 1945. My grandmother never talked about it. Perhaps it was easier that way – not so painful. My grandfather was in the *Aizsargi*, the Home Guard. I think that's one of the reasons he was killed.*

---

*   Latvian veterans say that in post-combat clearances of the dead and injured, wounded soldiers with SS badges were often executed by NKVD men on the spot: the *Aizsargi* were considered a part of the Nazi power structure and so received short shrift too.

A lot of my grandmother's sisters and brothers were sent to Siberia. It's the same story as Oscars. One day the Soviets would come to your house, force you into a truck and put you on a train to Siberia.

Oscars shakes his head.

This happened a lot in those times. In Soviet times we weren't allowed to remember these things. We should think normally, and remember those times, and do everything we can to make sure that those times don't come back. In fact that's one of the main reasons many of these guys serving now are in the Army... to prevent that happening again.[1]

We are interrupted again by the phone ringing. Details are coming in of another munitions find, this time of a single but huge 183mm shell in Liepāja town centre, weighing about 80kg. If that went off it would blow a crater three metres wide with a blast lethal for 150 metres in all directions, throwing out shrapnel fragments capable of killing at distances of up to 300 metres and more. Oscars and Aigars don't seem unnecessarily bothered, so we keep talking.

'It's 25 years after independence,' I say. 'You've served through that period and you're the Majors and the Generals of the future. How much damage did the Soviet times do to the Latvian national mentality and its confidence... knowing where everything was. Grandfather, father, mother, children gone... there are big holes in Latvian society, aren't there?'

Oscars nods in agreement.

I believe it's an influence, definitely. My father always taught me that we should remember those times. My father was born in 1931 during the first independence. Then he saw the first Soviet time, then the Nazi time, then the second Soviet occupation. He served in the Soviet Army when he was 18 during the 1950s. All Latvians want to be good soldiers. They tried to make him join the Soviet Army as a professional but he wouldn't.

And then – a long time later – came the second independence. He was one of the first to join the National Guard when we got independence. He joined immediately. Thousands and thousands of men did the same. They had waited the whole lives for that moment. When it came, they did their patriotic duty to defend Latvia.

Now Aigars is nodding. 'My father did the same. They wanted to defend Latvia'.[2]

The phone rings again. I decide I've taken up enough of their time and they should be free to deal with all these situations but before I go they introduce me to one of their team who is a 'Digger'.

Tall, powerfully built and physically strong, Dmitrijs Mežeckis is an energetic member of EOD 54. He's from the nearby town of Brocēni and is a member of *Legenda* like Andris Lelis in Riga. The EOD encourages its soldiers to help *Legenda*, not least to ensure the safe disposal of any munitions found alongside a dead soldier – bullets, hand grenades, machine guns, anti-tank RPG *Panzerfausts*. When I ask why he does this work, Dmitrijs smiles.

> It's my hobby. Soldiers should rest in a brothers' cemetery, not scattered about in forests and under trees. They should be buried with military honours. It's a respect thing. To the west of here, about 15kms from Liepāja there is a forest where it's possible to find fallen soldiers still lying on the ground. One day I was walking through there and I saw a boot sticking out of the ground. I opened up the trench and there was the body of a soldier. Of course the animals had found him too but we got him out.
>
> I have found 30 soldiers, split between Russians and Germans. Around 15 of each, over about 15 years. I feel happy if I find a soldier; even happier if I find medals with the body or identification, because then we can identify the man and send the medals to his family.
>
> Russian soldiers were buried without any identification, just in their uniform. They didn't have dogtags round their neck, they had their details on a piece of paper in a tube – and of course soldiers are superstitious. The word went round that the tube was unlucky, and if you kept that tube, you would die.
>
> So Soviet soldiers would throw away these unlucky tubes – and the ones that we find without the tubes can't be identified. Soldiers who'd been awarded medals and were then killed can be identified though, because the medal has their number on it and they can be traced through the archives.
>
> Last year we found a soldier about 15kms south of Saldus. We were able to identify him because he had a comb in his tunic with his name on, and we found out something about him. He was from Kazakhstan and under age for the military. He faked his papers when he was 17 and a half so he could join up. But he fell here in Latvia. This year his relatives came here. His brother's son came because his brother was so old and we organised a burial. Kazakh people are very strict about where they are buried, like in a family plot in their homeland, so it was very good that we could do that.
>
> You're helping families solve the mystery of what happened to their loved ones. If you don't see the body you are never really sure what happened. Finding a body enables people to let go, to rest: to finally stop searching, stop wondering.[3]

And with that he heads off to load a truck with equipment needed at that most recent call.

The death toll from the six Courland battles is staggering. At least half a million men were casualties of combat, the vast majority of them from the Red Army. The scale of Soviet casualties is mind-numbing: estimates are that the Red Army lost about 400,000 men killed or wounded in the Courland battles. They were men from Russia, Georgia, Ukraine, Uzbekistan, Kazakhstan – all the Soviet republics – as well as Latvians, both volunteers and those who were pressed into service. Of 1.5 million men involved in the Baltic campaign from 14 September to 24 November 1944 alone, 61,000 were killed and 218,000 were wounded.[4]

German casualties in Courland throughout the Pocket period were 150,000 men, the heaviest losses being in the Third – Christmas – Battle.[5]

In 1996, fifty years after the war ended and following the second period of independence, Germany signed an agreement with the Latvian Republic over caring for the graves of war dead.

A large area of land at Saldus was given free of charge to the Germans so they could bury their dead in one place. When the Saldus Friedhof German cemetery was consecrated in 1999 more than 14,000 dead from battles in Saldus, Liepāja, Kuldīga, Tukums, Ventspils, Talsi, Dobele, Jelgava and Bauska had been re-buried there. That figure has now reached 25,000 and is expected to pass 30,000 by the time the task is completed.

Notes

1   Oscars Lejnieks, interview with author, November 2014.
2   Aigars Pūce, interview with author, November 2014.
3   Dmitrijs Mežeckis, interview with author, translated by Oscars Lejnieks, November 2014.
4   Glantz and House, p.299.
5   Grier, p.84.

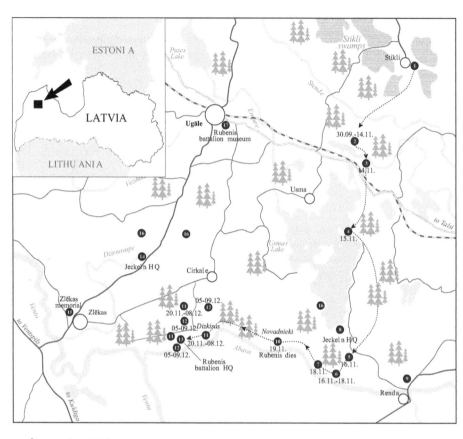

········>····   Rubenis battalion route

1.   The German crackdown begins at Kurelis's HQ at Stikli
2.   Rubenis's units rest in this area between 30.09 to 14.11
3.   Rubenis retreats from here after first engagement
'4.   Rubenis's first resting point, 15.11
5.   Battalion rests at Upatu forester's house
6.   The battalion camps out at the Perkonu house from 16.11-18.11
7.   Rubenis is wounded here on 18.11
8.   Jeckeln's HQ in this area is at Lejasmeki
9.   The wounded men in the battalion are treated at a doctor's here
10.   Novadnieki, where Rubenis dies on 19.11
11.   Rubenis battalion rests in this area around Zlekas, in the houses Dizkiri, Zilumi, Sildruvas, Veveri, Grauzi, Murnieki,
       between 20.11 and 8.12. These houses were targeted by the Nazis for reprisals for the help they gave the men
12.   Places of most serious fighting between 05.12 and 09.12
13.   Sildruvas was the HQ for the battalion in the Zlekas period
14.   Jeckeln's base in the Zlekas period was Ruzeli
15.   Burial place for the fallen Rubenis men and the civilians killed by the Germans
16.   The sites of the camps of the men who survived after the battalion split
17.   The Rubenis battalion museum today.

Map 3 The Battles of the Rubenis Battalion, 1944.

12

Bunkers in the Snow

I'm making good time along the Ugāle to Talsi road, driving fast in my hire car, enjoying the open road, the fresh clear air and natural beauty of the region around Usma Lake.

This is an area where people come to camp, to swim, to fish – to enjoy the outdoors at its best: campfires, beautiful sunsets, lovely walks and so on. I have been here several times already for holidays without realising exactly what happened around the shores of Usma Lake. Now I am about to find out.

This is the story of the Rubenis Battalion, a group of Latvian soldiers turned partisans who fought to the death against the Nazis. It ends with one of the most shocking and savage episodes of Latvia's war, the brutal and sadistic killing of 160 civilians by Nazi death squads as revenge for supporting those fighters.

Almost too quickly I have passed a brown tourism sign by the side of the road pointing into the forest which says 'Roberts Rubenis *apmetne* [camp]'. I turn the car round, turn off the main road and take to the forest tracks.

Life in the wartime forests was a complicated and dangerous existence. Villagers, refugees and deserters alike sought sanctuary among the trees and a mindboggling number of partisan groups roamed there, with deadly weapons and a complex series of loyalties.

Some partisan groups were actually Soviet special forces. Red Army commandos parachuted into Courland from as early as 1942 to organise local Communists into fighting groups and operate behind Nazi lines. There were as many as 800 Moscow-backed 'partisans' in the forests between 1942 and 1945 in 47 different units. About half those were Red Army commandos, with around 300 escaped PoWs and 145 local sympathisers.[1]

The best known of the pro-Soviet 'teams' was *Sarkanā Bulta* [Red Arrow]. Formed on 31 October 1944, they operated in the area around Usma Lake, Zlēkas and Renda, boasting nearly 300 men at the height of their strength. Around a quarter were men refusing to serve in the Latvian Legion alongside Soviet PoWs who had escaped from work details or camps. There were also 'volunteer' workers pressed into Nazi labour teams known as *Hiwis** who chose driving, cooking or other rear area activities in preference to prison camp. Many decided to slip away when it became clear the Germans were going to lose the war.[2]

---

* From *Hilfwilliger*, the German word for volunteer.

113

Lesser groups ranged in strength from 80 to 100+ men, usually 30 to 60 per team, which harassed and disrupted operations in the German rear. By the autumn of 1944 the level of partisan activity across the whole of northern Courland was causing major problems for the German Army.[*3]

In Spring 1944 German military intelligence approached a retired Latvian General, Jānis Kurelis, about raising a group of irregulars that could carry on partisan warfare behind Red Army lines. The *Kurelieši*[†] were intended to be Germany's answer to the Soviet partisans. Supposed to target and eliminate the pro-Soviet fighters, this group of Latvians grew into quite a strong force. However the leaders of the *Kurelieši* were ardent nationalists linked to the Latvian Central Committee,[‡] a group of politicians and public figures demanding that Germany restore Latvian independence.

Kurelis made his chief of staff Kristaps Upelnieks, a patriot who had avoided joining the Legion. Initially made up of *Aizsargi* Home Guard in Riga, their numbers had risen to 1,200 by late July 1944.[4]

On 23 September, as the Red Army closed in on Riga, 150 *Kurelieši* re-located to northern Courland, picking up vast numbers of deserters from the German-controlled Legion who were attracted by its nationalistic aims and lack of German command. The strength of the *Kurelieši* in October 1944 had swollen to around 3,000 – though some estimates put it higher.[5]

What prompted a German crackdown was a sudden and dramatic increase in the number of desertions from the Legion's 19th Division in early November 1944 following speculation that the division was to be transferred to fight in Germany. The Latvians had signed up to defend their own land, not Germany, and increasing numbers began to slip away and head for the forests around Ugāle and northern Talsi to join the *Kurelieši*.

The commander of Army Group North, Ferdinand Schörner, moved quickly to stop desertions. He assured the Latvians they would stay and fight on their own soil and that Germany would not abandon them. This of course was what they wanted to hear. Some deserters returned, new recruits joined up, and the apparent morale crisis passed.[6]

Alfrēds Puķīte was among the soldiers on the receiving end of Soviet attempts to undermine morale in the front lines in Courland.

> We men from Vidzeme, Latgale and Zemgale [regions to the east] had heavy hearts when we arrived in Kurzeme [Courland]. After heavy battles in the east we had lost our father's homes. We did not know anything about the fate of our relatives and we had lost any hope of winning the war.
>
> Men from Kurzeme wanted to get home to see their families. They hadn't seen them for more than a year. So there were cases of desertion on both sides of the front.

---

[*]   For a comprehensive overview of partisan groups in Northern Kurzeme, see Table 1, p. 121.
[†]   English meaning: Kurelis's men.
[‡]   In Latvian the *Latvijas Centrala Padome*, or LCP.

Desertion to the East was facilitated by a cunning method from the Russians. On quiet nights loudspeakers were used to play Latvian folk songs to the sector where Latvians were known to be. There were invitations to go home, popular soldiers' songs, even sisters and fiancées pleading for the men to come home. Just like in the Greek story about Odysseus.

From converts* they got unit soldiers' names and addresses. They found their family members. They sent pleas for certain soldiers to come home. Sometimes they made threats against a soldier's relatives if he didn't convert to the Russian side. Soldiers were urged to ignore officers' orders and to defect at night. In situations like this, we began to shoot but the melodies we heard hurt our hearts. Not surprisingly, some men disappeared.[7]

Because the Latvian men were on their own land and many had families nearby, the desertions were not always intended to be for good: more, as Puķīte explains, a question of popping home.

Most of the cases of deserting, if that is what it should be called, were planned without the knowledge of higher officers in order to visit relatives behind the front and to collect provisions.

Roberts 'Robciks' Sprogis† was one of those who went deep into the rear, where his father's brother had a country house. After a few weeks he came back with a heavy cart and a couple of calves tied to it, successfully avoiding German gendarmes.[8]

I trundle through the forest on a snow-covered track for several kilometres with the window down, taking in the freshness and the sights and sounds around me. The forest is so close that if I stopped and took two steps away from the car I'd be in among the trees. It's great, and so natural and fresh.

This is classic Latvian tourism for me: driving through a forest in the middle of nowhere without a clue where I'm going, no signs anywhere, just keeping going. There's a certain amount of trust and good faith involved. I reach a Give Way sign after several more kilometres of dense pine and then see a tiny, tiny sign which takes me down an even smaller forest track. This leads eventually to the Rubenis hideout. I park the car and climb out into the fresh snow.

The bunker is genuinely impressive, especially in the snow which conceals it even more. It's dug into the forest floor, built from wooden logs nine high with a log roof covered with turf. Spruce and fir trees surround a clearing where the occupants may have stretched out and perhaps cooked. It's a reconstruction but it's really good. I didn't even see it at first.

---

*   The name given to those who deserted from the Latvian Legion to the Soviet side.

†   The youngest brother of Captain E. Sprogis, later a member of the New York branch of the veterans' group *Daugavas Vanagi*.

The original bunker here was used as a base for the Rubenis men in October 1944 just prior to their showdown with the Germans. Rubenis was a lieutenant in the *Kurelieši* operating in the Usma Lake region against the Red partisans.

Kurelis was only supposed to take certain people into his ranks – the Germans had specified that deserters were to be sent back to them. But in autumn 1944, as desertion rates from the Legion increased, so the ranks of the *Kurelieši* swelled and, with nationalist ambitions, they became a significant threat.

SS Obergruppenführer Friedrich Jeckeln, the chief of police in Courland, asked Kurelis directly to stop accepting deserters, but neither he nor Rubenis would agree. So Jeckeln sent his troops to surround Kurelis's headquarters at Stikli and ordered the 600 *Kurelieši* to surrender. Several men resisted and were killed but the majority laid down their weapons. Upelnieks was tried by a military court and quickly executed. Kurelis was sent to Danzig, survived the war and died in Chicago in 1954.[9]

Of the remaining *Kurelieši*, 454 deserters were sent to the Stutthof concentration camp in Germany while the rest were dispersed among German forces, most to the 15th Division which was re-grouping in West Prussia.[10]

The same day Jeckeln moved against Rubenis at Usma Lake, but Rubenis had prepared defences against the expected attack – trenches, strongpoints, bunkers.

What followed was a series of fierce battles between the 400-strong Rubenis Battalion and Jeckeln's security forces. The battles lasted from 14 November until 9 December, when, having lost 160 dead including their leader, the remnants of the Rubenis group slipped away to fight another day. But those living in the forests accused of helping the partisans would pay with their lives.

The story of the Rubenis Battalion and the subsequent Nazi reprisal at Zlēkas is a tale of bravery and butchery that ends, as is usual, with lots of Latvian blood being spilled.

A sign alongside this bunker offers these thoughts on the *Kurelieši*, the men who joined what is considered – by some – to be a struggle for Latvian independence.

> Their fight [the *Kurelieši*, but in particular the Rubenis battalion] has been the most lasting and important in the history of the national resistance movement in Latvia.
>
> As the military power of the Central Council of Latvia they were supported by a broad range of civilians, fighting for the idea of renewed independent status for the Republic of Latvia.[11]

This sign rather jars with the views of some historians who consider the *Kurelieši* a brief footnote to history when seen against an anti-Soviet partisan struggle lasting eight years from 1945 to 1953. Now, they say, the *Kurelieši* are being celebrated as more important than they were.

With the *Kurelieši* neutralised, Jeckeln trained another commando group for operations against Red partisans, the *Meža Kaķi,* or Wild Cats. This was a specially selected, tightly-controlled counter-insurgency group trained in Germany by the legendary SS commando officer Otto Skorzeny which began operations in late 1944.

With the German capitulation some Wild Cats fought on as part of the national partisan movement, known as *Meža Brāļi*, or Forest Brothers.[12]

I turn my car round in the clearing and steer carefully along the snowy tracks back to the main road. There I set a course for Kuldīga where I am to meet a man who knows about this period in great detail.

Half an hour later I rumble along a cobbled road across a bridge at a spot that has become a symbol of Kuldīga, the Ventas Rumba waterfall. It's the most popular tourist attraction in Latvia, and it's not hard to see why: it's a charming spot.

The water roars across the falls under the seven arches of a red brick bridge hung with black metal lanterns decorated with fish. They are symbols of the generosity of nature here – there are vast amounts of fish in the river. In April and October the fish try to jump the waterfall to get up river to their spawning grounds. The fishermen simply put their baskets in the way and the fish deliver themselves.

I park in a shopping centre at the far end of the town and cross the street to a block of Soviet-era flats typical of any town in Latvia. Here I meet Artis Gustovskis from the tourist board who has kindly offered to translate for me. We're meeting Herberts Knēts, a former history teacher and director of the town's secondary school. Artis was one of his students. He's pleased to see him and offers us tea and cakes as we settle down. Naturally, we accept.

A map of Courland is fastened to Mr Knēts' bookcase. He puts his tea down and walks over to it, pointing.

In this area, south of Usma Lake, around Cirkale and Ezeri a Red Partisan group was operating called *Sarkanā Bulta* [Red Arrow], a very famous group. They said the Zlēkas tragedy was due to their activity, but they had nothing to do with it. It was all down to the Rubenis battalion and Kurelis.

There were very tough battles around Renda between the Germans and the Rubenis battalion in autumn 1944. Rubenis was ready for a real war. The Germans thought it would be easy, like with Kurelis. When the Germans started to surround Rubenis he fought them from prepared defences.

Many men were killed when they attacked, including the German commander. They called off the attack and tried to negotiate a surrender but Rubenis was smart. He said: 'Give me a day to think about it and maybe tomorrow we will put our weapons down'.

That night he took his 400 men and made a secret move to a location around Renda to another place he had prepared as a defensive site. At the end of the 1990s I met a man in Kuldīga who had been a tracker for Rubenis and guided him through the forests. He showed me all the places.

Jeckeln set up a secret face-to-face meeting in Renda with Rubenis. He said to him: 'Put down your weapons. We will kill you all if you don't surrender'.

On the 18th November 1944 – Independence day – Jeckeln sent planes to bomb the area Rubenis was holding and sent a very big force against him. Rubenis' men fought very bravely and beat the Germans back. There were about 40 dead on either side: Rubenis was badly wounded in the stomach.

Then his men attacked Jeckeln's headquarters and forced him out of it. Jeckeln sent planes to bomb them and they pulled out. Rubenis and his remaining men moved to a secret hideout deep in the forest on the Abava river, with no roads or people around. This was a forester's cottage called *Novadnieki*. Rubenis died there.

Jeckeln had a headquarters at a house called *Lielmeki* by Usma Lake. He put all the forces in the area on standby to look out for Rubenis and his men.

There was a German Army construction battalion in the area around *Novadnieki*. They were armed, but they were mostly Latvians. When they heard Rubenis was in the area they refused to fight against him and even went to meet him, shaking hands.

But not everyone in the battalion was Latvian. The men who had refused to fight against Rubenis fled into the forest. They knew more German troops were coming and would kill them. And when the Germans came they followed the Latvians into the forest and did indeed kill them; about 20 of them.

The remainder of the Rubenis battalion moved along the right bank of the Abava river to two houses, *Zīlumi* and *Vēveri*, where they rested. Before long the Germans found them; around the beginning of December 1944. On about the 4th or 5th they started a big offensive to finish them off.

The partisans were surrounded. The battles were fierce but once again the Rubenis men managed to slip through the net into a very dense forest, perfect for hiding. Big equipment could not get into there, there were no roads, it was only possible to go on foot, so they managed to escape again. Then the Rubenis men came across a small group of German officers relaxing by the Abava river, smoking and so on. They ambushed them, killing them all, including the commandant of the camp at Salaspils.[*] But of course this gave away their position.

By this time Rubenis and the senior men were all dead. The survivors didn't know what to do so they decided to split up. One team went across the river and went west, another team went north to Puze Lake; one went towards Ēdole. They'd killed about 300 German officers and soldiers as they chased them across the area. Jeckeln even called some frontline troops back to help with the fight. The German Army was very angry about this and decided to get revenge. Local

---

[*] A labour camp east of Riga with a reputation as a 'death' camp where many Jews and prisoners were killed and medical experiments conducted on children. Soviet-era figures put the death toll here at 100,000, but new research by Latvian historians argues this has been inflated by propaganda. They say a more accurate figure is a maximum of 2,000 dead among 21,000 prisoners there between May 1942 and September 1944, 1,000 of whom were Jewish. The book concludes between 250 – 650 children died from malnutrition or illness and were not subject to medical experiments, as the Soviet story held. As many as 4,000 inmates were transferred to camps in Poland and Germany where many will have died. Source: Summary, *Beyond this Gate Moans the Earth* by Kārlis Kangeris, Uldis Neiburgs and Rudīte Vīksne. (Lauku Avize, 2016)

people had supported the partisans – there was even a song written about the co-operation between them.[13]

'What happened to the people in the houses in the forest?' I ask.

'One minute,' he says, and disappears into his back room.

He returns with a thick file of papers, which he opens at a divider marked 'Zlēkas'. Inside are pages and pages of handwritten notes, copied from the Soviet-era archives in Ventspils. There are notes detailing exactly who was in each house and what happened to them.

German revenge squads were sent into the forest after the Rubenis men slipped away. They killed infants, youngsters, teenagers and grandparents to extract a price for the deaths of comrades killed by the partisans. And then they burned all the houses, sometimes with the people inside. It's unspeakable brutality. I feel like I've had enough killing for one day.

'Maybe Zlēkas is one for tomorrow if we can come back?' I ask.

Mr Knēts nods. 'I will get my files out,' he says, smiling.

I look at Artis, who also nods.

'Great,' I say. 'Well, perhaps we could talk now a little about what happened to you in the war?'

At the time of our interview, Mr Knēts is 87. He was born in 1927 near Puze Lake in the district of Ventspils, to the southeast of the city. He was 17 at the time of the Courland Pocket and was mobilised as Air Force support staff to serve in the Luftwaffe. His brother Alfreds was three years older and was drafted into the Army, seeing action as a radio operator with the 15th Division in the fierce battles at the Velikaya River in Russia. He was wounded, and after recovering in hospital he was awarded the Iron Cross. When in spring 1944 he was allowed home on leave he took the opportunity to go into the forest with a group of men who didn't want to fight in any army. But they were betrayed in March 1945, arrested and held in Ventspils prison until the capitulation. Mr Knēts takes up the story.

> Everyone the German Army put in prison was released. In the first filtration of 13 May 1945 the Reds came to the house and took both my brother and I to a filtration camp, like all men from the Ventspils district. We were taken to the Zūras Agricultural School where all the men were checked out: their documents, their history, what they did in the war – everything. I remember the columns of men marching from Spāre, Ugāle, Dzirciems, near where I lived.
>
> When they took us from the house they told us to take enough food for ten days. When we got to Puze Lake we slept overnight in a pub, *Grīžukrogs*.
>
> Before we got to Ventspils we stopped for a toilet break and a headcount and one man was missing. At that moment an old man was driving past with his horse. The officer stopped him and said: 'You must get in this column. One man is missing'. That was the system of the Red Army. You could not say to the big General that one man was missing because you would be killed. So they took the old man to make up the numbers.

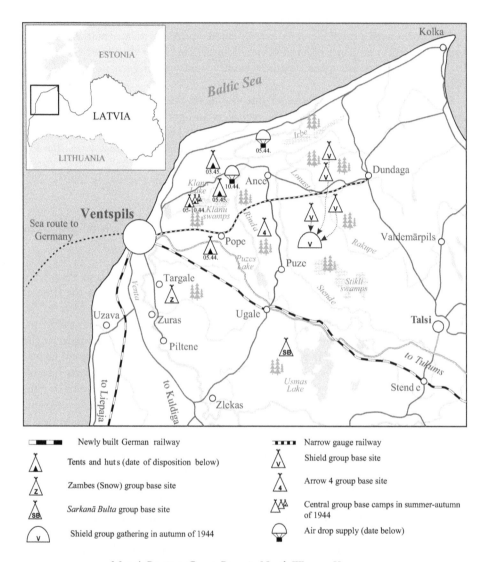

Map 4 Partisan Group Bases in North Western Kurzeme.

Table 1 Red partisan groups and pro-Soviet groups fighting in Kurzeme (1942 – 45)

Number	Unit name	Operations begin	Operations finish	Operating in	Total number	Soviet fighters	Local citizens	PoWs	Displaced People	Avoiding Legion	Comments
1	Macpana unit	Summer 1944	26.02.45 unit defeated	Aizpute, Kuldiga counties	Summer 1944 150 men. 09.01.45 only 80	7	About 40	3 groups, total about 80	Not known	About 23	
2	Zuras Forest unit	Autumn 1944	08.05.45	Piltene, Zura, Targale areas	08.05.45 89 men	Cooperated with some groups	11	34	38	6	
3	*Sarkanā Bulta* – Red Arrow	31.10.44	08.05.45	Renda, Usma Lake, Zlekas area	08.05.45 293 men	Until 12.44 worked together with the Spartacus group	23	138	46	83? And 3 German deserters	
4	Popes Bulta – Popes Arrow	Summer 1944	08.05.45	Pope, Ance areas	Early 1945 108 men	1	18	About 30	About 30	22	
5	Popes-Ances 'Shield'	Summer 1945	Ceased to exist early 1945	Ance, Pope area	Dec '44 60 men		About 20	About 20	About 10	About 10	
6	Kapustina unit	Autumn 1944	08.05.45	Kabile, Renda area	About 60	15	11	23	About 11		
7	K. Salmina 'Snow' unit	Autumn 1944	01.01.45	Targale area	34 men		22			10 + 2 German deserters	
8	Soviet fighting groups	Dazadi 1942 - 45	Throughout 1942 - 45	47 different fighting units in Kurzeme	801 men	343	145	313	Not known		
All of Kurzeme				Kurzeme	1595	366 23%	280 18%	638 41%	125 8%	159 10%	17

Source: Herberts Knēts

We stayed there about a week and a half for the filtration. They started with the young ones. If you were clean, they let you go free; usually at dawn, before sunrise. They let me go like that and I hiked home through the forest.

I went free but my brother was taken, because he'd fought in the 15th Division. He was sent to the White Sea to work on the Belomor Canal and didn't come home till 1946, 1947, then he was sent back to Riga to work in the Mežaparks in a phosphorus factory. I didn't really see him again until 1990 – it's a long story. A lot of people who had served in the punishment camps, the Soviets didn't leave them alone afterwards. Again and again they made problems for them and their families.

My brother chose to go and live in Latgale, deep in the forest, in a small village where no-one bothered him. From time to time we met somewhere but it was not easy, and not often. The Soviet political government watched everyone to see who they were meeting, and meeting someone like that caused concern: maybe you were a spy. Then he got married and lived closer to Tukums, but he died in 1992.

The partisan team around Zūras was led by Vasili Retchko, a Russian who lived in Moscow. I met him after the war, because I was a historian. He invited me to go to Moscow to interview him. He loved spirit alcohol very much and he told me many stories, so I poured him more drink and he told me the lot.

Retchko was brought from Russia to Courland as a prisoner of the Germans. There were about 40 of them who escaped into the Zūras forest in 1944. They didn't have any guns at first. At the same time in the same area another team was forming, the Zambis group; Latvians who had escaped from the Legion, the German Army. There were about 34 men in the Zambis team at this time, including a few German deserters. At the beginning everyone came together but conflicts developed between them. One group had guns, the other didn't; one was Latvian, the other Russian. So they split into two camps and lived separately but in fact very close to each other – only about 800 metres between the two. I knew exactly where it was because I lived nearby.

Retchko wanted guns but the Latvians wouldn't give them any so Retchko joined forces with a Russian parachutist group led by Malaschenko, who was very popular with local people despite having been sent by Moscow. Retchko sent some of Malaschenko's people to try and talk to the Zambis Latvians about joining forces, because they had guns – but they refused.

On the morning of 1st of Jan 1945 I heard a lot of shooting about six or seven kilometres from my house. The Zambis group were wiped out by a unit of German commandos who had been tipped off that there were German deserters in that forest. They were betrayed. Retchko and the parachutist group went to help but although it was only 1km away all the Zambis men were killed.

Retchko later united all the small groups of partisans in the forest – six or seven men in each – and his group was very powerful at the end of the war.

When the news came through that the war was over all the partisans came out of the forest. They gathered in one place to vote for a leader to be in charge of all the partisans – and that man was Malaschenko.

He had lots of authority with local people, he was brave and honest and he was a commando too, so he was respected by the other commandos. He was just a simple sergeant but there was an officer who outranked him. One night Malaschenko came back to his base and found all the guards asleep, very drunk. And he said: 'What's going on? What are you doing? This is terrible'.

The senior lieutenant took offence at being insulted by this mere sergeant and shot him. A gunfight broke out between Malaschenko's men and the lieutenant's men and several were killed, but not the lieutenant. When the fight was over, the dead men were buried and that was that.

Vilis Samsons, the education minister of Soviet Latvia,* gave me access to the archives and said: 'Take what you want. If you need something, just ask me'.

I copied out everything that was written by the partisan leaders. But all my documents were taken away by the special state organisation investigating all the wars and totalitarianism [whose researchers promised to return them].

I gave them as little as possible, but they still took them.

'Did you get them back?' I ask.

He shakes his head. 'No, I didn't'.

Then he grins.

'But I'd made copies!'[14]

We roar with laughter and congratulate Mr Knēts on his foresight, then leave him to enjoy what's left of his evening. Tomorrow we will continue, when the subject will be Zlēkas.

Notes

1   Herbert Knēts, personal archive.
2   Buttar, p.300.
3   Herbert Knēts, (see table, illustrated).
4   Lumans, p.367.
5   Lumans, p.368.
6   Silgailis, p.134.
7   Lācis, p.82.
8   Lācis, p.82.
9   E. Jekabsons, U. Neiburgs, *Kurelieši Commanders* at http://latvjustrelnieki.lv/lv/ljudi-98761/kurelis-janis-106019/komandir-kurilieshej-106033.
10 Lumans, p.369.
11 Information board at Rubenis bunker, Ugāle.
12 Lumans, p.370.
13 Herbert Knēts, interview with author, January 2015.
14 Herbert Knēts, interview with author, January 2015.

*   A wartime partisan leader and war historian whose books were read by generations of Latvian schoolchildren in the 1960s and 1970s.

13

The Silent Stones of Zlēkas

We are due back with Mr Knēts after lunch so I have time to look at Zlēkas for myself. The actual village of Zlēkas is about half a kilometre from the main road between Kuldīga and Ventspils but it is literally a small settlement in the middle of nowhere. There are two old buildings. One is a grocery store, the other is the local administration office. The rest of the town is modern Soviet blocks from various periods; some from the 1960s, some from the 1980s, with garages behind. In front of the flats, and the focal point of the village, is a turning circle for buses with a noticeboard.

To my left is a well-preserved white Lutheran Church. This dates from 1645 and was known as 'Zlēkas Cathedral' because of the quality of its wood-carved interior, a feature for which, as previously discussed, the churches of Courland were famous.

Nowhere is there any indication of what happened in Zlēkas during the war – in any language. There's a sign on the road indicating a war memorial 'hill' but I find it more by good luck than design.

This is a mound about half a kilometre away from the village, a right turn off the main road on the other side of a wood. A path leads up to it. A black stone obelisk stands at the top of the mound. It bears a sombre announcement in Latvian that this monument 'commemorates the 160 people murdered at Zlēkas between 8th and 9th December 1944'.

Boulders have been placed in a circle around the crest of the mound, each bearing the names of some of those people. Some stones have lots of names on them, indicating the murder of entire families. I brush the snow off to read them.

Supe: Jānis, Lidija, Anna.
   Then another name. Matvejs 1898 – 1945. Did he survive?
   I move to a second grave marked with a bigger stone. I brush the snow away to reveal the family name: Jēkabsons.
   This is Valts; 1897 to 9.12.44. Milda Jēkabsons, 1909 to 9.12.44, Gunārs - 1907 to 1944, Marta: 1931 to 1944. She was 13.
   The next name brings me up short. Imants Jēkabsons – he was three? And then the next. Uldis Jēkabsons. Born in 1944. So this is a baby?
   Surely it can't be a baby.
   The next stone has a single name. Gulbe Anna. Killed on 9.12.44.
   Here are three names on a stone. Meija Edgars: 1923 to 9.12.1944. He was 21, the son of Andrejs. Bedrītis Valdis, son of Jānis, 1922 to 9.12.44 and Sesko, Antons: 1925 to that same date in 1944. He was 19.

Edgars, Valdis and Antons. 21, 22 and 19 years old. Whether they were friends or not they are united in death, forever.

Another stone next to that, a tall one. There are lots of names here.

Krišanovskis, Wilhelms: 1909 to 9.12.1944. Krišanovska, Līze: 1864 to 1944. She was 80. Līvija Ķērsta, 1898 to 1944: she was 46. Andžs Šulcs, 1896 to 1944: that makes him 48. Baltiņš Francis, 1910 to 1944. That could be several families living on a farmstead.

So we have a baby and a three year-old, a group of teenagers and several entire families, including an 80 year-old.[1]

After ending the resistance of the Rubenis Battalion the Nazi police chief Jeckeln told his men to go into that area of the forest, round up everyone they could find who may have helped them - and kill them. That would send a message to the civilian population that he was absolutely ruthless. The massacre included the murder of everyone living at the two houses that had offered shelter to the Rubenis men, *Vēveri* and *Zīlumi*.

It's 70 years since the war ended and 25 years since the Soviets left and still there are candles here, so someone somewhere remembers. Even though it's such a savage, sadistic chapter, I've never heard about Zlēkas before. I've been to Audriņi, the Latvian Lidice, and I've walked with the ghosts in the Litene forest where the Army officers were massacred – the Latvian Katyn - but Zlēkas is new to me.

I will come to understand over time that most Latvians of a certain age do know about Zlēkas but don't talk about it unless prompted. What I won't understand is the lack of information for an audience beyond the shores of Latvia. Putting up some signs in English would be a start. How can Latvians expect the world to understand the suffering and torture they've been through if they keep these stories to themselves?

I brush the snow off another memorial stone, feeling depressed at the cruelty humans are capable of.

Šķēle Vilis: born 1892, died 9.12.44. This is Dad, 52.

Šķēle Charlotta: Maybe this is Mum. No dates of birth but I can guess the date of death.

Šķēle Fricis: 1929 to 9.12.44. A 19 year-old son.

Šķēle Tekla: 1927 to 1944. Fricis' younger sister.*

Šķēle Ansis: 1869 to 1944. A 75 year-old, probably Grandad.

Anna Karga: 1864 to 1944: An 80 year-old woman, possibly Grandma.

Five members of the same family shot. Two pensioners. I take photographs to show Mr Knēts and to remind me of these sad, solitary headstones.

I feel rather – disappointed... unsatisfied perhaps – that there is no information board to explain the context of this solemn obelisk and circle of boulders in the middle of the Latvian countryside. There are no pictures, no information - in

---

*   Listed later as Teofilda.

any language - about the slaughter of these innocent people. The truth about what happened to them is awful.

I walk slowly to my car and head back to Mr Knēts' flat in Kuldīga. Artis is on hand again to translate. Mr Knēts has his files ready.

> I can show you the list of every house where people were killed. I took the list from official documents. We have a special book about all the happenings in Soviet times and especially about the Zlēkas tragedy. The authors are Red Communist writers* but there are documents.
>
> On this page is the announcement by the police [of what] they found from 7th to 10th December 1944 at the house *Vēveri*. Everybody was killed and then everything [was] burned. This is an official announcement of Ventspils District Police Department – local policemen. It might be a Communist book but it contains many documents which are facts.
>
> These are the houses where there were actions by General Jeckeln and the German Army. People were killed, burned alive and so on. These are reprisals for local people supporting the partisans. I visited the Ventspils archive many times to get this information and have written out all the details about every particular house.[2]

He opens his file and lays out sheets of handwritten notes. Line after line tells a story of awful butchery.

Killed at *Vecsāti* 8.12.44

1. Matvejs Supe: a forester. On 8.12.44 he was shot and wounded by drunk Germans and survived. Was shot after the war by partisans.
2. Anna Supe: His wife. Shot and mutilated.
3. Vitolds Supe: His son. Shot.
4. Lidija Supe: His daughter. Shot
5. Matīss Supe: Shot.
6. Isabella Koklača: Matvejs' sister-in-law. Survived.[†]
7. Viktors Koclačs: Shot. Isabella's father.
8. Bārbala Korklača: Isabella's mother.
9. Staņislavs Sarva, 1902 to 1944: Shot.
10. Paulīna Sarva: Viktors' sister. Shot.
11. Antons Sarva, son of Staņislavs and Paulīna, 1904 to 1944: Shot.
12. Jānis Koklačs: son of Viktors, 1909 to 1944: Shot.

---

* Soviet-era accounts are considered unreliable because of propaganda and political bias.
† She was staying with the family waiting for war to end hoping to survive. Somehow she did.

Killed at *Vēveri* 9.12.44

1. Anna Šaute: Shot.
2. Minna Šaute: (born 1881) Shot.
3. Ansis Pretics: (born 1879) Shot.

Killed at *Zīlumi* 9.12.44

1. Teofilda Šķēle, daughter of Vilis: (born 1927) Shot.
2. Fricis Šķēle, son of Vilis: (born 1929) Shot. These are sister and brother buried in the Šķēle family grave at Zlēkas.
3. Paraskoja Bogdanova: (born 1929) Shot.
4. Anna Kaģis: (born 1864) Shot.
5. Stepanida Bogdanova: (born 1864) Shot.
6. Ķersta Līviņš, daughter of Ernests: (born 1888) Shot.
7. Wilhelms Krišanovskis, son of Ernests: (born 1909) Shot.
8. Ansis Petrinš: (born 1869) Shot.
9. Ilze Krišanovska, daughter of Jānis: (born 1864) Shot - she was 80.

Killed in the house *Grauži*

1. Austra Leite: 9.12.44. Badly wounded but survived. She was in a group that was taken to the forest to be shot, near the house. Girl.
2. Valija Leite: She was shot together with her daughter Gizelda. She was the wife of Fricis.
3. Fricis Leitis: He survived because he was hiding from mobilisation to the Legion and living in a hiding place above the cattleshed.
4. Gizelda Leite: daughter of Fricis – shot. Small girl.
5. Herberts Leitis: He was killed in a barn which was then burned. He was 18 months old.
6. Harijs, also Haralds, Leitis: He died in the barn as well.
7. Renāte Leite: (b.1938) Six year-old daughter of Žanis. She was shot at the house. According to Fricis Leitis she was raped and then locked in a burning barn.
8. Lizete Jēkabsone: (b.1884) She was killed in the barn. Aged 60.
9. Zenta Ķeizars: (b.1936) Killed in the barn. Aged eight.
10. Erna Ķeizars: (b.1911) Killed in the barn.
11. Fricis Radziņš: (b.1863) Killed in the barn. Aged 81.
12. Ieva Vēze, daughter of Ernests: Killed in the barn.
13. Oļģerts Leitis: (b.1937) Killed in the barn. Aged seven.
14. Velta Tādenberga: Killed in the barn.
15. Līze Tādenberga: Killed in the barn.
16. Matīss Ķeizars: When they were being taken to be shot he pushed one of the Germans, who fell down. He ran away and survived.[3]

Killed at *Dižķiri* 9.12.44

1. Anna Stendere: (b. 03.02.1889) Locked in a barn, shot and burned.
2. Elizabete Stendere, daughter of Ansis: (b. 26.07.1925) As above. Aged 19.
3. Vilis Šķēle: (b.11.8.92) Same.
4. Šarlote Šķēle: (b.1903) Same.
5. Ansis Šķēle, son of Kārlis: (b.1869) Shot at the house.
6. Melānija Šojatskoja: (b.1882) Shot at the house.
7. Gunārs Jēkabsons, son of Valts: (b.1937) Shot at the house. Aged seven.
8. Valts Jēkabsons, son of Augusts: (b.1897) Shot.
9. Uldis Jēkabsons, son of Vilis: (b.1944) Shot. An infant.
10. Milda Jēkabsone, daughter of Ansis: (b.1909) Shot.
11. Marta Jēkabsone, daughter of Vilis: (b.1931) Shot. Aged 13.
12. Imants Jēkabsons, son of Vilis: (b.1941) Shot. Aged three.
13. Adelīna Vēzis: (b.1894) Shot and burned in the barn.
14. Andrejs Vēzis, son of Ernests: (b.1879) Shot and burned in the barn.
15. Aina Vēzis, daughter of Andrejs: (b.1934) Shot and burned in the barn. Aged 10.
16. Krišs Vēzis, son of Andrejs: (b.1928) As above. Aged 16.
17. Arvīds Vēzis, son of Andrejs: (b.1928) As above.
18. Andrejs Vēzis, son of Ernests: (b.1879) As above.*

Killed at *Mūrnieki* 9.12.44

1. Fricis Freibergs: Shot.
2. Hilda Rego, daughter of Matvejs: (b.1900) Shot.
3. Roberts Rego, son of Matvejs: (b.1930) Shot. Aged 14.
4. Alberts Rego, son of Matvejs: (b.1943). A toddler. Shot.

I finish photographing the documents and Artis and I breathe heavy sighs of relief. But Mr Knēts is not finished yet.

> I participated as a historian in Soviet times in the building of the monument. Most of the people were burned and there was nothing left of them, in fact. The house *Verlagi* was a headquarters of police. They made an open-air court and near the house they killed them. There was a graveyard for more than 20 people there. Those bodies were moved to the Zlēkas monument.

'So Zlēkas is a series of individual reprisals against civilians across the region?' I ask.

> Yes. They went into each house and killed everybody. Women, children, elderly. If they met people on the road, they would kill them too. They were a death squad: a revenge squad. For example, the 16 people killed in *Grauži*. Some

---

*   Author's note: This entry is possibly a repetition of detail above.

Soviet troops move forward during fierce street fighting in Jelgava,
July to August 1944. (Courtesy of the Jelgava Museum)

German troops advance past a Soviet Josef Stalin tank knocked out during fighting for Jelgava
July to August 1944. (Courtesy of the Jelgava Museum)

German troops in street fighting in Jelgava, July to August 1944. The medal flashes on the soldier in the foreground show he has served throughout the Russian campaign. He has the Iron Cross Second Class and the 'Order of the Frozen Flesh' *Ostfront* Medal, awarded to those who served on the Eastern Front between November 1941 and April 1942. (Courtesy of the Jelgava Museum)

Jelgava Palace in ruins after the fierce fighting for control of the city.
(Courtesy of the Jelgava Museum)

The Zante war museum run by Ilgvars Brucis houses a collection of weapons, ammunition and military equipment gathered from the battlefields nearby. This is just a small part of a collection of shells taken from the fields. (Author)

A field hospital operating table at Zante war museum, with leg brace for amputees. (Author)

Legionnaires of the 43rd Grenadier Regiment, 19th Division in the snow. Photograph taken in late 1944, probably posed. The Latvians are using a Russian DP-28 light machine gun and a German stick grenade. The gun could fire 550 rounds a minute: each drum held 47 rounds. It was a workhorse of the Red Army from the early 1930s until the late 1960s and has even been found used in Libya, Afghanistan and Syria as late as 2012. (Courtesy of the Occupation Museum, Riga)

Interviews for *Blood in the Forest* in Kuldīga, with (left to right) Antons Leščanovs, Fricis Borisovs and Žanis Grinbergs. Artis Gustovskis and Austra Sunina are to the right of the picture. (Author)

Courland Pocket refugee and later Latvian President Vaira Vīķe-Freiberga. (Picture: supplied)

Legionnaire and Iron Cross holder Antons Leščanovs. (Author)

The scene of devastation at Liepāja's railway sidings after an ammunition train exploded during the bombing of the city on 09.10.44. Picture by German Army photographer K.Wenzelburger taken the following morning. (From *Lokomotiven ziehen in den Krieg* by Hansjurgen Wenzel, published by Verlag Josef Otto Slezak, 1977, and reproduced with kind permission of Verlag Slezak)

When war came to Courland: Olimpija Liepaja footballers celebrate with their coach Otto Fischer, who led them to three league titles 1936 - 1939 but was murdered by the Nazis in 1941 because he was Jewish. Picture courtesy of Ilana Ivanova. Full story: Appendix 1.

The fledgling Latvian air force: members of the 5th Flying Course of the Liepāja-Grobina Aviation School by the aircraft Bücker 131 in August 1944. From left: Konrads Caune, Olgerts Capass, flight instructor Sgt Jānis Rudzītis, Edmunds Cirvelis, Artis Strelis. (With grateful thanks to the personal archive of Edvīns Brūvelis and the Occupation Museum, Riga)

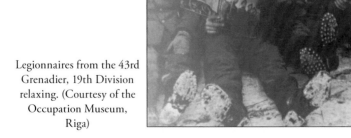

Legionnaires from the 43rd Grenadier, 19th Division relaxing. (Courtesy of the Occupation Museum, Riga)

Lestene Church and Lestene *Brāļu Kapi* [brothers' cemetery], a national cemetery for gathering fallen Legionnaires and partisans from the Second World War and the subsequent partisan war. Arta Dumpe's statue *Homeland Mother Latvia* is far right. (Author)

Vast amounts of wartime shells are still found in Latvia, keeping the EOD [Army explosive ordnance disposal squad] busy all year round. Left to right: Aigars Pūce, Oscars Lejnieks. (Author)

The German war cemetery at Saldus Friedhof, a central resting place for soldiers killed across Courland. (Author)

The reconstructed bunker in the forest which the Rubenis Battalion used as a base in October 1944 before their showdown with Jeckeln's forces that led to the massacre at Zlēkas. (Author)

Stones commemorating the victims of the massacre at Zlēkas at the memorial outside the village. (Author)

Historian Herberts Knēts was a boy during the Courland Pocket period and has gathered a valuable archive from Soviet-era records. (Author)

A postcard sent from Liepāja in 1939 to a friend in Ventspils, just before the first occupation by the Soviet Union and subsequent 'Year of Terror'. (Courtesy of the Liepāja Museum)

Devastation in Liepāja at the end of the war. German prisoners are used to clear rubble and repair buildings. (Courtesy of the Liepāja Museum)

The interior of the Café Bonitz in Liepāja, a well-known pre-war refreshment stop in the city for many years. (Courtesy of the Liepāja Museum)

The fishing boat *Centība* [*Endeavour*], with refugees from Courland on their way across the Baltic Sea to Gotland, 10 November 1944. At the front of the boat is a small Latvian flag. The headscarf worn by the woman in the foreground is now on display at the Occupation Museum. (Courtesy of the Occupation Museum, Riga)

A cross marking the
graves of Latvian and
German war casualties
in a field outside
Dundaga, with Aina
Pūliņa. (Author)

Līvija and Leonhards Stanga,
interviewed by the author in
December 2014. Leonhards
was both Legionnaire and
partisan, and married Līvija on
his return from Siberia. With
thanks to Agrita Ozola at the
Tukums Museum. (Author)

The Soviet cemetery at Priekule near Liepāja, the last resting place of 23,000 soldiers. Priekule bore the brunt of Red Army assaults to reach the vital port of Liepāja. (Author)

Mārtiņš Cerins with a shell casing found on the ground during a visit to woods to the east of Priekule, scene of fierce fighting between Soviet and German forces. (Author)

Left: Jānis Blums reads from his diary during his interview for this book, Skrunda, December 2014. (Author) Right: As a Legionnaire, aged 18: 'I was only a skinny lad'. (Courtesy of Jānis Blums. With thanks to Artis Gustovskis)

The soldiers' graveyard at *Brāļu Kapi* Tuski near Pilsblīdene. (Author)

The ruined church at Zvārde, still used as a place of worship by local people to this day. Their graveyard was used for target practice by Soviet bombers during the occupation. With thanks to Roberts Sipenieks (left) and brother Rūdolfs. (Author)

Bunka Church, where the Soviet Army accepted the surrender of the German Army, bringing the Second World War to an end. The quote by poet Eizhen Veveris reads: 'Only the memory of victory remains. Too much blood was shed for it'. (Author)

The monument to the Soviet Warriors at Dobele *Brāļu Kapi* [brothers' cemetery] which was built over a memorial to Latvian independence fighters. (Author)

The dreaded Stūra Māja 'Corner House' KGB headquarters at the corner of Brivibas and Stabu iela in Riga. Many Latvians entering by the corner door were not seen again. The building has been repainted in its original grey and the upper floors converted into apartments. The KGB Museum is on the ground and lower ground floors. (Author)

The execution room at the Stūra Māja. Opponents of the Soviet regime were murdered here and their bodies dumped in graves in the forests. A visit here by Leonhards Stanga spurred him to take up arms against the Soviets. With thanks to Aija Alba. (Author)

Left: The grave of Michael Zank at the Saldus Friedhof. (Author) Right: A photograph of Michael Zank taken before he left for Courland. (Courtesy of Klaus-Georg Schmidt)

were refugees not connected with the area. But they were registered as staying there. Everyone was killed, except for Matīss Ķeizars who was in the stables. He managed to escape, and told the story afterwards.

The newspaper announcement mentions the five houses by name.

Grauži – 16 people killed

Dižķīri – 18 people were staying

Mūrnieki – 4 people

Zīlumi – 9 people

Vēveri – 3 people killed

It started at *Vecsāti*. Twelve people died from that house. There's a story to that.

Artis and I take a sip of coffee and brace ourselves for what is coming.

The Germans came in the morning to have a look round, led by a doctor. They asked people to make them lunch to make them relax and not think anything was going to happen. Everyone was full of lunch so they waited until evening, then rang a bell.

The first chosen to die was Matvejs Supe. He was trusted by the *Sarkanā Bulta* partisans, a sort of a spy. It was already getting dark when they took the first people – Matvejs and his son Vitolds - to the forest line where they were going to kill them. That was about 100 metres away from the houses.

Vitolds was killed but Matvejs was wounded and fell down. When the Germans brought the next people Matvejs had run off.

He escaped, found the *Sarkanā Bulta* partisans and worked for them in the forest until the war ended. But in 1946 he was caught by the National Partisans, who knew what he'd done in the war with *Sarkanā Bulta* – and they killed him.

A similar thing happened with Austra Leite. She was shot and only wounded, then escaped when the Germans went for the next group. She was famous as a *kolhoz* worker after the war but of course she's dead now.

As well as his painstaking work copying out the gruesome details of what happened at Zlēkas, Mr Knēts has also examined the monuments relating to the war in Kuldīga. He applied his detective skills one afternoon in the archives and came up with an interesting discovery relating to the reputations of Soviet war heroes.

I made an inventory of the monuments relating to the war in Kuldīga. Many nowadays don't know anything about the people they are remembering there. I found out that there were 73 important people in the Ventspils district who made a special contribution to the war.

Mostly on these monuments it's written 'for their brave contribution during the war...' including a famous partisan leader, Semjonovs... but no-one knows what these contributions are.

From secret reports in the archives – secret Soviet-time reports – I found that 25 of them drank themselves to death with spirit alcohol. They didn't die in the fight for the freedom of the Soviet Union. They drank themselves to death, then they [the Soviet authorities] built a monument saying how brave they were.

He looks up, first at me and then at Artis, who is sitting alongside me translating.

'Believe me, it's true,' he says. 'I have the documents'.

He stands up and goes to his back room. Artis and I look at each other, incredulous. Artis is particularly surprised. He grew up in this town with the legends of brave Soviet heroes. Now it seems that history isn't what it seems. Mr Knēts returns with some more files.

'Are you ready?" he says. 'Some of this is quite shocking. I have a lot of information I got from the council offices, from the official archives. A lot of official records have some very valuable information'.

This is one episode from 1945. It's a true story about my neighbours which happened on 7 August 1945, in the evening. The Red Army had taken the German Army prisoners and put them all in one place near Puze Lake to sleep overnight. One Red Army officer went into a house where the Zīle family lived. He was a cavalry officer. He walked into the house and said to the family: 'Make me dinner'.

After he had eaten the dinner he killed everyone and robbed the house before leaving. Emriķis Baumgards was the father of the family. He was killed. Minna Baumgarte, aged 56, was his wife. She made the dinner. She was killed. There was Mirdza Zīle, the daughter, aged 24, who had a three year-old son. She was raped and then killed. The three year-old boy hid under the couch and survived. I taught him later.

Mirdza's husband, a tailor called Alberts Zīle, was working in Ventspils at the time. He came back and found everyone dead.

There was a military court and an inquiry was set up into this killing. Alberts was called to give evidence. He was a tailor so he knew about sewing secret pockets into jackets and so on. When he arrived he saw one of the officers on the inquiry panel was wearing a smoking jacket. He recognised it. It was his jacket that had been taken from the house on the day of the killings.

'Hey! That's my jacket,' he said.

'No it's not. How is that possible? You're a liar. How can it be?' the officer said.

'It's very possible,' said Albert. 'There'll be a secret pocket just there on the inside with my name in it...'

And there was. The tribunal was adjourned, shut down and nothing more was said. The house is still there, but with another family living there.[4]

'Do you have strong nerves?' asks Mr Knēts. 'Because the next story will be a powerful tragedy'.

On the 13th May 1945 there were three families living in a house called *Cīruļi*; the owner and his family and two families who were refugees from Latgale. Red

Army soldiers came to the house and said: 'We will stay overnight here'. This is the story told by the house owner.

Late in the evening he heard a big argument in another part of the house and then shooting. He escaped from the house with his wife. The arguing and shooting carried on all night. The next day the Red Army soldiers made up the horses for driving, put a lot of stuff onto the wagon that had been taken from the house and then drove off. The owner went into the house and found everybody dead.

Mr Knēts shows me a list of names typed up in a report. It's a list of the dead, copied from the records in the archives.

Izidors Barkāns: (b.1901)
Sofija Barkāne: (b.1901) Raped and killed.
Heinrihs Barkāns: (b.1901)

Mr Knēts hands me another sheet of paper. 'I hope you have a strong stomach', he says. I look at the page.

Jānis Andžāns: (b.1922) Killed.
Adele Andžāne: (b.1922) Raped and killed.
Jānis Andžāns: (b.1942) A three year-old boy whose throat was cut so violently his head was cut off.

'But why?' I ask. 'Why do that?'
   Mr Knēts shrugs and shakes his head.

A lot of Red Army officers liked to steal stuff and take it back to Russia. They didn't like it if people saw them do it or if they knew about it.

There was one farmer in Īvande who refused to let two Red Army officers kill his pigs and take them. So they shot him and took the pigs. I have their names, everything. They did that many times.

Colonel Krišs Ķūķis (1874-1945) was Latvia's most famous National Partisan leader in Kurzeme. He was killed by the *Sarkanā Bulta*. I have a secret official document written by a leader of *Sarkanā Bulta*. No-one else has that.

He shows it to me. It's headlined:

4-5 May in Pope area. List of people killed by *Red Arrow*.

He waves more papers, all covered in closely-measured script, and paraphrases the wickedness they document.

Another killing place on the day of victory, 12-13 May. Very small children, three years old. The Red Army just killed them. Another house where a small girl was killed; 11 years old. There were a lot of places like that.

I have information about a famous Red partisan leader, a man called Macpāns. In March 1945 he went to the house called *Māli* with a big group and started to rob it. The owner of the house, Māls Andžs, was killed. When the partisans had finished they left a sign saying: 'That's for the heroic actions of your son'. The son had been one of the first volunteers into the German Army and was a First Lieutenant. He'd escaped the massacre of the officers at Litene, volunteered to fight the Soviets and won the Iron Cross fighting for the German Army.

Mr Knēts is shuffling through his file of papers, a seemingly never-ending collection of tragedies.

Here's another story that's never been told. There's a village called Aizvīķi in Liepaja district. In 1941 soldiers of the Latvian Army were killed a few days before the war here started. They were killed in a terrible way. There's another story from Padure village, from wetlands near there. The Red Army made a special killing place in a bottomless swamp. They threw the bodies in and they were never seen again. There were many places like that.[5]

Some considerable time later I emerge from Mr Knēts' flat for the second time in less than 24 hours feeling absolutely dazed. The savagery and awfulness of what happened in those forests has rather knocked me sideways. Things like this don't happen in England. Not now, anyway.

At least I know now what happened to the people whose names are carved on that circle of gravestones. Their fate is unbearably awful. Rounded up, raped, shot, burned? I don't think Latvian history has done their suffering justice. I doubt that anyone who perpetrated this crime ever felt the grip of justice on their collar. At least Jeckeln did, hanged in Riga in 1946. But you can only hang a sadistic murderer once.

Now I know the awful truth of what happened in the forest at Zlēkas I feel a need to go back there and look again with … well, greater understanding, I guess.

I drive back towards Zlēkas. There's a pull-in for cars just before the turn for the monument. It offers a view over a lake which – were it not frozen – would lap the shores of the forests where these atrocities occurred. The air is clean and fresh, the sky is clear, blue and dry; the surroundings are beautiful. To the right houses are dotted in the woods and there's a farm by the lake's edge, with jagged sheets of ice breaking up around the trees growing in the shallower water.

I drive over to the forest. My map shows a tiny road marked through it which must be a logging track. I am curious to see where this might lead me.

It's a track leading into dense virgin forest; a single track with a ditch on either side which leads deeper and deeper into the forest until I reach a sign that makes my blood run cold. *Dižkīri'* – wasn't that one of the houses where the murders took place?

I drive on until the road becomes a pitted, muddy track, frozen hard and covered in sheets of ice over water with deep ruts where a tractor has passed. There are big humps in the middle of the track and a turn-off. I scrape the bottom of my rental car's engine as I negotiate the bumps and take the turning until eventually I decide it's not worth the risk of either damaging the car or slipping off the track and getting stuck.

I stop and get out. There are small footprints in the snow but no sign of anyone around. It's silent. This is literally just a path cut through the forest wide enough for a car or a truck. I think I can see a clearing ahead with a house and some swings ... but I get the feeling that I should quit while I'm ahead. My journey into the dark secrets of the war in Latvia has gone just about as far as it can for one day, and the light is beginning to fade.

I'm not going any further.

There's no room to turn round on the track without going into the ditch, so I reverse slowly back to the junction with the bigger road and swing the car round gingerly.

Although the forest has been beautiful I'm glad to get out intact. I breathe a sigh of relief when my tyres make contact with a proper road surface again. On my way home I stop at a bridge over the Venta river. The water is low and the banks rise gradually to farming fields extending for kilometres in each direction, absolutely flat. The farms are big here: small clumps of humanity and machinery on brown fields almost as far as the eye can see, with a church spire poking up on the horizon. It all seems very calm and peaceful.

Yet not far from here was the house where Jeckeln gave the order for his killers to go into the forest to extract a price in blood for the 300 comrades they lost in the battles with the Rubenis partisans.

Who would think these trees would hide such unspeakable secrets?

Notes

1. Memorial stones at Zlēkas.
2. Author interview with Herbert Knēts, November 2014.
3. Herbert Knēts, personal archive.
4. Herbert Knēts, personal archive.
5. Herbert Knēts, personal archive.

14

Liepāja and its Troubled History

I have arrived in Liepāja, the largest city in Courland and third largest in Latvia after Riga and Daugavpils. It's a place that has been in turn a vast trading port, a secret strategic naval base and somewhere to escape from the turmoil of Eastern Europe. It was a bustling harbour at the crossroads of Eastern and Middle Europe but also one of the places in its more recent past where the Holocaust began. The pictures of Jewish women about to be murdered up the coast from here in 1941 have become synonymous with the sadism and brutality of the Holocaust. I will encounter all these periods in my brief stay.

The scars left on Liepāja's history by its Nazi and Soviet occupiers during and after the Second World War are deep and painful. It was once one of the 'Jewels of the Baltic' with art nouveau architecture of a standard to rival Riga. The trouble is that all Liepāja's best years are behind it – about 150 years in the past.

Liepāja, like Ventspils further north, owes a great deal to the trading ambitions of the Duke of Courland. He ordered the Liva River dredged of sand and widened to create a canal, so Liepāja developed into a flourishing trading port along its banks.

When in 1795 Courland became a province of the Russian Empire, Liepāja developed into an export centre for grain, wood, linen and oil. It was the warm water port that Russian leaders dreamt of: a year-round trading harbour that didn't freeze over. By 1900, linked by rail to all the cities of the empire, seven per cent of Russian exports were passing through its docks.[1]

A huge exodus of Eastern European Jews seeking an escape from the pogroms and persecution of the early 20th century passed through Liepāja bound for new lives in America on a daily transatlantic liner service to New York and Halifax in Canada which started in 1906.

Hundreds of thousands of migrants sailed to America this way: 40,000 in the first year alone. Demand was so great that for 18 years between 1906 and 1924 Liepāja and New York were linked by a direct service.[2]

The city revelled in its pre-war reputation as a busy, bustling point on the crossroads between Russia, Prussia, Poland and Scandinavia. The trams rattled along the High Street past the wonderful art nouveau buildings of *Graudu iela* [Corn Street] and visitors – especially Germans – thronged to the well-tended gardens of the *Rosenplatz* [Rose Square].

The tea and cakes at the Café Bonitz a short walk away were known far and wide through Middle Europe. The Jewish dentists, artists and musicians were highly rated and much sought after. The more successful among them put their money into spacious homes just off the busy town centre, along a street called

Vītolu iela [Willow Street]. There was a beautiful beach, a promenade and a well-connected port.

During World War I Liepāja was occupied by the German Army. After the war, during the independence struggle against the Bolsheviks and the Baltic German Bermontian in 1919 Liepāja briefly became the capital of Latvia when the interim government fled the Bolshevik assault on Rīga, returning only six months later.[3]

At the start of *Operation Barbarossa* Nazi forces bombed the city and quickly routed the Red Army defenders. Within days Nazi death squads began searching out and murdering Jews; some on the beach at Liepāja, many thousands at the sand dunes a few kilometres out of the city at Šķēde.

The Soviet advance into Latvia in summer 1944 caused a flood of refugees west. Around 250,000 people headed for Liepāja to board boats for Germany, doubling the civilian population in Courland. Many who had collaborated with the Germans were desperate to save their skins and on 30 September General Jeckeln announced the evacuation of all Latvians, willing or not, to Germany.

Much rested on the defences at Liepāja and the thirty German divisions holding the front line against the Red Army. If the Soviets could break through and take the port they would cut the supply lifeline to the Reich. If the Germans and Latvians could keep the attackers at bay there was still hope.

The Soviets unleashed an unimaginable onslaught against Liepāja: artillery barrages, bombing raids from the air to sink the supply ships from Germany and knock out the port, full frontal assaults intended to break through the defences further east at Priekule and Grobiņa. Try as they might – and the 23,000 graves in Priekule cemetery are testament to just how hard they tried – the Red Army could not break through the German defences.

By May 1945, after six months of intense shelling and bombing Liepāja was a shattered city. The Soviets sealed it off after the capitulation and Liepāja became a secret naval base. Even local people needed passes to move around.

The post-war reconstruction did little to enhance its credentials as a tourist destination. Soviet town planners lowered joyless pre-fabricated apartment blocks devoid of personality onto the ruins. Grim, grey, unhappy-looking public buildings replaced graceful if shattered art nouveau. It's a shame because Liepāja was a very nice place. You just have to look quite hard to find it.

For decades after the war one of the sights around town was the conning tower of the Soviet submarine *L3*. The submarine in the film *The Hunt for Red October* is named after its captain Vladimir Konovalov.

Under his command *L3* sank the German ship *Goya* on 16 April 1945, a casualty of *Operation Hannibal*, the evacuation of troops and civilians from the Courland ports and the Polish Corridor from mid-January to May 1945 as the Red Army advanced.

In this time 350,000 soldiers and between 800,000 and 900,000 civilians were evacuated to Germany or German-occupied Denmark as 500 ships dodged British air attacks and Soviet submarines.

The *Goya* was carrying at least 6,000 civilians and military personnel. Its sinking is one of the worst maritime disasters ever: only around 170 people survived *L3*'s torpedo attack off the coast of Pomerania.[4]

Konovalov was made a Hero of the Soviet Union for his war service and ended his career commanding the Baltic submarine fleet. When the Soviets left Latvia they took the *L3*'s conning tower with them. It's now on display at Moscow's Museum of the Great Patriotic War.

The worst casualty of *Operation Hannibal* was the *Wilhelm Gustloff*, a former cruise liner launched by Hitler himself and used for holidays by the *Strength Through Joy* organisation. Initially used in the war as a floating barracks for submariners training in the Baltic it was pressed into service to help with the *Operation Hannibal* evacuation operation. Its sinking on 30 January 1945 by the Soviet submarine *S-13* is the largest loss of life in maritime history, with 9,400 people on board. Among them were 5,000 children, 918 officers, 373 female naval auxiliaries and 162 wounded soldiers who were either killed by the explosion of the torpedoes, drowned or died of hypothermia in the freezing waters of the Baltic off Gdynia (then Gotenhafen) en route to Kiel.[5]

Just 11 days later the same submarine torpedoed another ship in *Operation Hannibal*, the former passenger liner *SS Steuben*, sending between 3,500 and 4,000 people to their deaths in the Bay of Danzig, including 2,800 wounded soldiers, 270 Kriegsmarine doctors, nurses and medical staff and 800 refugees.[6]

Among those for whom Liepāja was a lifeline was future President Vaira Vīķe-Freiberga. Her parents had tried to get a place on one of the fishing boats secretly leaving the Baltic coast for Sweden. But by the end of December 1944 there were very few fishermen willing to risk the voyage and they were asking for payment in gold, which her parents did not have.

On 1 January 1945, aged seven, she stood on the deck of a ship in Liepāja harbour waiting for it to slip its moorings and take her away from a nightmare. Her mother cradled a young baby – her younger sister – who would die shortly afterwards in a Displacement camp.

> The refugees were on deck and it was cold. The wind was blowing and the spray was coming. It was dark and very scary. Every now and again a siren would go off because of a submarine alert.
>
> One could go in the hold to get out of the weather but that was by the engines, smelled of oil and was hot. When I went in there I felt sick so I went back on deck.
>
> At the beginning of the voyage one woman on deck who was wearing an expensive fur coat was making a fuss asking for privileges because of who she was and who her husband had been. One man in the crowd said to her 'Madam, we are all equal now. We are refugees and we are nothing. You and what your husband used to be are worth nothing'.[7]

In Liepāja city museum on a Saturday afternoon 70 years later I sit with Rita Krūmiņa, the Head of Collections, looking through photographs of Liepāja both during the war and before it. The first pictures we look at show a street with piles of rubble on either side.

'That is Vītolu iela [Willow Street] where many of the Jews lived,' says Rita.

'It was badly bombed, as you can see. These pictures date from 1941 when the Germans invaded. The story goes that Vītolu iela was deliberately targeted by Nazi bombers because many Jews lived there'.

The next collection dates from 1945, at the end of the war. There don't seem to be any pictures between 1941 and 1945. There are groups of men repairing railway lines and piles of rubble on street corners. I recognise Rose Square and the main street, *Liela iela*, where the tramlines still run today. I have just walked across there to get to the museum.

Rita opens another envelope and lays out more photographs.

'These are the pre-war pictures,' she says.

The contrast couldn't be greater. The first card is of a tram turning onto a street full of shops bustling with people, opposite a tidy well-kept garden square. Another card, this time colour-tinted, shows the same scene from 1904. I recognise the church spire: I'm staying in the modern hotel that now stands in front of it.

'That's where the Liva Hotel is now,' Rita says, as I nod in recognition. 'Those buildings across the road were destroyed and the University was built on the block the tram is going past. It's very different now'.

It's completely different … it's a different world. These pictures show people relaxing, shopping, trading. There are no cars. Men are wearing hats. There are flowerbeds, herbaceous borders and bushes in Rose Square. It looks like a charming place to pass half an hour chatting with friends.

This collection of turn of the century postcards of Liepāja – or Libau as it was known to the Germans – has survived because people posted them to their friends.

I turn one card over. It's addressed to Fraulein Elsa Dumpoff in Riga, postmarked 7 October 1900. The postcard's printed in Russian. In those days Latvia was part of the Russian Empire.

The next postcard I pick up was sent nearly forty years later to Ms Almiņa Lukševica at 2 Gaismais Street, Ventspils on 14 December 1939 – just a few months before the Russians moved in. It's an end of an era postcard if ever there was one.

'Hello Almiņa,' the sender writes in pencil. 'I'm sorry that I did not reply sooner. I didn't have time'. The rest of the message is too difficult to read.

But the back of the card tells a story in itself. The stamp in the right hand corner celebrates the 20th anniversary of the Latvian Republic, 1918-1938, with a picture of the Commander in Chief of the Latvian armed forces, Jānis Balodis, in the centre. Behind him is Riga's famous railway bridge with soldiers stationed on it and military airplanes flying above, symbolising the battle for Latvian independence which he masterminded.

It's a ten Santimi stamp, a special issue, designed to draw the world's attention to the fact that Latvia was celebrating twenty years of independence. Seven and a half million were issued, available from 0900 on 18th November 1938: Independence Day.[8]

The celebrations would be short-lived. Less than a year later, in October 1939, the Latvians had been forced to sign the Treaty of Mutual Assistance which allowed 30,000 Red Army troops into Latvia as a buffer against Hitler's expansion east.[9]

By the time the card arrived at 2 Gaismais Street, Ventspils – a house that's still there – Latvians were preparing for what would be their last Christmas as an independent nation for fifty years.

Six months after that, in June 1940, 200,000 Red Army troops crossed the border from Lithuania. By early afternoon the tanks were in Riga. The *Baigais Gads* – the Year of Terror – was about to begin.[10]

Balodis, a national hero and First World War veteran, was arrested and bundled onto a train to Siberia. He would be a prisoner for the next 15 years, returning only in 1956. Ulmanis was deported too and died in Krasnovodsk jail in Turkmenistan in September 1942.[11]

Among the postcards in Rita's collection are views of what looks like a high class café stretching across a corner block of the Old Town with balconies and fine stonework. The interior is dotted with tables covered with white cloths and a serving counter laden with cakes, cake trays and teapots.

It seems a blast from the past; such a bustling, busy place where people had the time to eat cakes and drink tea and coffee in such plush surroundings.

The postcards show a billiard room, a sumptuously appointed smoking room furnished with enormous palms and chandeliers and both a summer and winter garden – a haven from the stresses and strains of turn of the century life.

Modern Liepāja seems – sadly – so unlikely to have such a sanctuary.

'That's Café Bonitz,' says Rita. 'That was the best tea rooms in Liepāja before the war. Now it's boarded up. It's been boarded up for years'.

With painted ceilings, comfortable sofas and counters groaning with cakes, Woldemar Bonitz's café on the corner of Graudu iela and Valdemara iela was one of the gems of the city between 1890 and 1914. Bonitz was such a successful confectioner in Liepāja he commissioned splendid new art nouveau premises on one of the city's finest roads, then known by its German name of *Kornstrasse*. His cafe was built by the famed architect Paul Max Bertchy, Liepāja's head architect from 1871 till 1902, who played a vital role in creating the distinctive architectural 'face' of the city at the end of the 19th century.

The menu at Café Bonitz offered 'Tarts, sweet biscuits, layer cake, *Fantastiestucke*, creams, sweet dishes, jellies, ices, Marzipan and a selection of drinks: hot chocolate, cocoa, French fruit, juices, lemonade extract'.[12]

Café Bonitz was a focal point for the city during times of great social upheaval – the 1905 Bolshevik revolution, the 1906 pogroms, the mass migration of Eastern European Jews to America, a world war and the overthrow of the Russian Tsar in the Bolshevik revolution. The tea and cakes in the golden age of the Café Bonitz offered a haven from all this. A visitor to the café in 1900 sent a postcard of the exterior to a friend with the message:

'I am really impressed by this Café Bonitz. Knowing this I will now visit Libau more often. It puts Riga to shame that it doesn't have something similar'.[13]

The war brought trouble for Woldemar, a Russian citizen with German family roots. He was arrested and sent first to Kirov in Russia before being exiled to Samara, but returned to see out his final days in Liepāja.

In August 1921 Woldemar leased the Café Bonitz to some former apprentices, announcing in the local newspaper that 'they will continue to run his business in the same professional and workmanlike manner as he did for the past 40 years'.[14]

Four years later the Café Bonitz closed, to be replaced by the Grand Café Kuwald.

Woldemar Bonitz was so well known and so much part of the town's life that on his 75th birthday in 1927 the local newspaper wished him a happy birthday:

> Woldemar Bonitz, the founder and owner of the cosy Kaffee Bonitz, which was widely known before the war, but which like many other sites of Libau that were worth a visit disappeared as a result of the aftermath of the war, celebrates his 75th birthday today. We wish Mr. Bonitz, president of the choral society for many years and co-founder of the Philharmonie, many happy years to come.[15]

He lived for another six years, passing away in Liepāja on 11 December 1933.[16]

Rita has kindly offered to act as translator in a meeting with the editor of the local newspaper, Andžils Remess, a native of the city and sports journalist for many years at *Kurzeme Vards*, whose mother was a regular at Café Bonitz.

> Liepāja was a beautiful city. All of it was destroyed during the war. The bombing is one of my most powerful memories of that time. As a boy I remember the air raid sirens. I learned how to make that sound. One day I saw a few ladies walking past in the street so I made the noise of the air raid siren and they ran for the shelters! It was so funny ... but I got told off for it.
>
> In 1944 when the skies were clear then you knew there would be bombing that night. You went to sleep in your clothes as you knew you would have to go to the shelter. When the skies were grey there were no bombers. There was bombing all the time. We got used to it and by the end it was nothing special. The first thing that hit you when you came out of the shelters was the smell of burning. When you're a kid you're not really afraid. You get used to it and you think that's how life is.
>
> One time some people were having a party and a bomb hit the house and killed them all. They were all found dead in the room trying to shield themselves from the bomb. One person at the party was blown out of the window by the blast and survived – all he had was a broken leg. That was the only time I saw a dead body. We saw them lying dead in the ruined building.

I ask Mr Remess about conditions when so many refugees flooded into the city trying to get boats out. How did people manage, I wondered?

> When the Red Army came in from the East 300,000 people came to get away from the Russians. The city was absolutely crowded. The port was full of horses and carts. People were waiting for weeks standing in line, sleeping in the carts behind the horses, waiting to get on the boat.

There were organisations helping and people who donated money and food to help them. Many citizens of Liepāja took refugees to their apartment. We had a pretty big flat and took people in for a few nights. They slept on the floor and the tables – sometimes eight to ten people at a time.

We sang a lot. It helped us get through it. There was a need for it. Everyone was singing – the Legionnaires were singing the old folk songs, *schlager* songs, the popular songs.* Even the people who left on the ferries were singing the National Anthem as they left. You couldn't sing – it was banned under the German times. You couldn't display the Latvian flag either. It was against the law.

Mr Remess's father owned a timber yard and employed people which – by Soviet standards of 1940-41 – made him bourgeois, a qualification for automatic deportation. I ask him whether his family ever tried to flee Latvia, especially as they lived in a city with direct boats to Germany?

We tried to get away from Latvia four times but we never made it. At the end of August, beginning of September 1944 we had tickets and boarding passes for a boat out – just me and my mother. My dad and grandma would stay. But I said 'If Dad and Grandma aren't going, I'm not going either'.

The idea was that we'd go for six months or a year, the war would end and then we'd come back. But I didn't want to go. The taxi was outside ready to leave, and I hid so they couldn't find me. I hid in the garden because I didn't want to go. Eventually they found me and we went to the ferry but the boat was full.

The second time lots of families got together and tried to leave through Klaipėda. Lots of people were doing that. But the Red Army came and blocked the way. The third time was in the summer when we tried to get on a train from Priekule to Königsberg. We had tickets and a place to stay, but this time we decided to stay because of my mum. She said: 'We have crops in the field and meat and milk: what is there in Germany? Nothing'.

And so we decided that we should stay. At least we had food and a place to live.

From October 1944 Latvians were able to go to Germany on one of the big boats, 400 people at a time. That was our last try. The ferry we were supposed to sail on was bombed. It was a boat usually used as a coal ferry roped up alongside the quay just around the corner from here. It was loaded with flour and we were sitting on the bags in the hold. The boat was waiting for night so it would be safer but when darkness fell the bombers came. The boat was hit, twice. There were explosions and I remember being unable to breathe because of all the dust. The ship started to list so we broke a window and climbed up the stairs, kids

*   *Schlager* songs are popular melodies, usually sentimental, nostalgic songs accompanied by accordion.

first, to get off this sinking ship. The next morning we went to see what had happened but the ferry had sunk. This happened in the canal by the Fontaine Hotel. All the warehouses along the quayside were burning. You couldn't cross the bridge because it was on fire.

Mr Remess's family retreated to a house by the lake outside the city to await the end of the war. When it came, the abandoned and destroyed war equipment became a playground for children.

We saw the Germans marched away as prisoners of war, going off to the camps. The Russians took all their watches. Some Germans threw the watches to us kids as they left, or buried them in the ground.

There was a German listening post 100 metres from our house. We'd see them listening for planes with headphones on. At the end of the war when the Germans left we went to their positions and were playing with the headphones, pretending to drive the truck. Everything was left: guns, uniforms, belts, medals … we were putting the Iron Cross to our chest and trying it on.

In school breaks we walked through the damaged streets. There were tanks, wrecked aeroplanes and damaged cars gathered to be taken to the metal works to be broken up.* The streets were full of wrecked vehicles.

We were told: 'Never pick up a pencil from the street, or a packet of cigarettes. Never pick anything up from the ground because it could be a bomb or a booby trap'. Lots of children were injured. They had legs or arms blown off.

Some Russian soldiers came to our home. One stayed outside while another came inside. He searched through all the rooms and drawers and closets, took all the silver, anything with some kind of worth. They didn't explain anything and left.

A few minutes later more soldiers came. Grandma and Mother asked what they were doing: 'A few minutes earlier you came and robbed us of everything we had, and now you're here again'. These soldiers went to the car and drove away. Ten minutes later they came back with all the stuff the first soldiers had taken and gave it back to us. So there weren't only robbers, there were good ones as well'.

I ask Mr Remess if he ever saw soldiers take their anger out on people or if there was sexual violence against the women. Mr Remess nods, but the conversation becomes a little stilted at this point. I press him to explain a little.

I know of only once, but in the city there was talk that women were raped. The officer came and asked for it, so my mum and I left the house for an hour or so and only then came back. The officer said he needs it, he needs the woman. She

---

* *Liepāja Metallurgs*, which sponsored one of the best-known Latvian football teams of modern times.

was a runaway, a refugee. I don't know how it happened, but Mum said: 'Let's go.' And the officer took one of the women who stayed there…

I have another difficult question for Mr Remess. Although he was a boy then, was he aware of what was happening to the Jewish population, which was rounded up and shot by the Nazis? He points to an area on the city map we have spread out in front of us. It's on the other side of the hotel I'm staying at, literally a street away.

That's where the ghetto was: Dārza Street to Bāriņu Street and to the lake. There was a gate to the ghetto on the corner of those roads. We didn't know about the Holocaust. No-one talked about the situation with the Jews at all but next to our home there was a family who were hiding Jews all the time, all through the war. No-one talked about it – only after the war.

Before 1940 we didn't even think that Jewish people were different. They were just like us. We had very many Jewish doctors – famous doctors. Everyone wanted to be seen by them: they were the people you wanted to go to. They were very good merchants, musicians, artists. There were a lot of really good Latvian sportsmen and women. In table tennis, chess, very good boxers – Latvian champions.

The football team was legendary: Olimpija Liepāja. They won the League seven times between 1920 and 1939. Their trainer Otto Fischer was shot at Šķēde in 1941. The players tried to rescue him. There was only one Jewish player – the rest were Latvians. But no-one listened to the players. They were saying 'Don't shoot him. He's a great coach. You don't know what you're doing'. But they shot him.'[17]

That evening I walk the city streets to get a feel for the turbulent history that's been played out here. I cross Liela iela from the Liva Hotel and walk down Graudu iela admiring the art nouveau buildings. There's Café Bonitz, boarded up and apparently being turned into a shopping centre. A little further on is Vītolu iela where the well-off Jewish residents lived.

The street has a strange atmosphere. The road is wide but there are rows of five-storey apartment houses all along, set back from the road. So in one sense it feels deserted and in another it's very cramped. There's a large communal car park outside each block and then lots of flats on top of each other; hundreds of people living side by side. That's not how Latvians say they like to live. Not only did the Soviets impose their collectivist ideology on this country, they also forced its people to live collectively – something of an alien concept.

I feel a little intimidated walking down Vītolu iela. It's quite spooky. It's 8pm on a Saturday night and there is no-one about. Or rather, there are just one or two people:

*   For the full story of Olimpija Liepāja – the 'Barcelona of the Baltics' – and their coach Otto Fischer, see Appendix I.

a woman walking home from work and a man with a woolly hat on taking his dog out for a call of nature.

I turn into the street running parallel, Republikas iela. I'm told the architecture on this street is amazing and well preserved and this is what Vītolu iela used to be like. It's a street of big old brick buildings, some of which are clearly flats now, but again, there's absolutely no-one around. There are almost no lights on in the flats and there's one car parked on the entire length of the street.

A Saturday evening stroll through the heart of Latvia's third largest city is turning out quieter than a Christmas morning, and so dark it's like walking through a blackout. It's weird. It's like the city belongs to the ghosts.

I cross back over the main street and walk around the pedestrianised shopping streets near the market. A plaque on a three-storey stone building in Tirgoņu iela [Merchant Street] catches my eye.

> In this building Roberts and Johanna Seduls hid 11 Jews between 1943 and 1945, thereby saving their lives.

A second quote below it reads:

> That's why the name Roberts Seduls will remain in our memory, and be inscribed with golden letters in Liepāja Jews' history.

That quote comes from Kalman Linkimer, one of those eleven Jews. He also dodged the initial execution of Liepāja Jews and the massacre at Šķēde beach in 1941.

What the quote doesn't say is that in hiding those Jews Roberts Seduls would not only keep them alive but also ensure that the world would have proof of the horrors of the Holocaust.

Among the families Seduls hid in the secret compartment in the basement of this building was David Zivcon, an electrician sent to do repairs at an SS officer's apartment. He had found films there which he copied and then buried for safe keeping. The photographs on the films showed the executions of Jews on the beach at Šķēde,

As liberation grew nearer the air raids on Liepāja increased, and in March 1945 Seduls was killed. His wife Anna took over the operation to hide the Jews and when the war ended two months later Zivcon, his wife and daughter, Linkimer and two friends and two other families emerged from 500 days in a cellar. Zivcon went to the hiding place where he had left the photographs of the massacre and handed them over to the Soviet authorities, which used them as evidence at the Nuremberg trials.

Linkimer's wartime diary, written in Yiddish, was translated into English and formed the basis for a book. The cost of translation was paid for by Edward Anders, a Jew from Liepāja who survived the 1941 extermination as a 15 year old by claiming to be an Aryan foundling. His mother survived too and they escaped first to Germany in 1944 and then to the US in 1949. His father and 24 other relatives perished in Latvia. Anders was instrumental in the setting up of the archive of Latvian Holocaust victims and was one of the prime movers behind the monument to those who died at Šķēde.[18]

I walk back to my hotel deep in thought. Tomorrow I will visit those dunes where so much blood was spilt so cruelly.

Notes

1   Liepāja city website at http://www.Liepāja .lv/page/936.
2   Special Economic Zone website: http://www.Liepāja-sez.lv/en/Liepāja-port/history/.
3   Liepāja city history at http://www.Liepāja.lv/page/936.
4   Koburger, *Steel Ships, Iron Crosses, and Refugees*, p.71.
5   Zabecki, *Germany at War: 400 Years of Military History*, p.1465.
6   Koburger, p.71 and Williams, chapter 6.
7   Interview with author.
8   Latvian Stamps website at http://www.latvianstamps.com/front215.asp.
9   Lumans, p.79.
10 Ibid, pp.92-93.
11 Buttar, p.44.
12 Source: Bonitz family website; http://www.bonitz-forum.de/index_en.htm; conversation with Joachen Bonitz.
13 Transcript of postcard in city archive during author's visit, August 2014.
14 Periodika archive (http://www.periodika.lv).
15 *Libausche Zeitung*, 1 October 1927.
16 *Rigasche Rundschau*, Nr. 292, 22nd December 1933: Baltic List of deaths: Woldemar Bonitz, 82 years, died 11th December in Libau.
17 Interview with author.
18 Edward Anders biography at http://www.liepajajews.org/biogr.htm.

15

Karosta Prison and the Dunes at Šķēde

The number one tourist attraction in Liepāja is the Karosta Prison, a grim, cold and thoroughly disheartening 18th Century jail on the other side of the Trade Canal. It's a small corner of a vast and once secret War Port* built by Tsar Alexander III, a vast sprawl of now-disused barracks, fortifications and even a Russian Orthodox Cathedral capable of holding 1,500 people. For a century prisoners have been held at the jail awaiting their fate – sometimes freedom, sometimes another prison, sometimes a burst of gunfire in the woods opposite.

Tours of Karosta prison are run by historian Juris Raķis, a tall and very forceful man who cares passionately about Latvia. Much of his collection of war memorabilia and photographs has been used in exhibitions at the Liepāja Occupation Museum. He has opened up Karosta early on a Sunday morning so we can talk. His friend Einars is on hand to translate.

> In 1944 Soviet troops came to Latvia. On the radio, the Soviets played the Latvian national anthem. It's for propaganda. In Riga there was a march through the city by victorious troops with the Latvian anthem playing and in the windows there were red-white-red flags and everyone was happy.
>
> But after the march they took the records and threw them away. After the parade these two Latvian corps marched in military style towards Tukums. The story goes in my family from an uncle from Madona [in the east] that the parade kept going towards Tukums and then turned off and went directly to a military camp. And the camp was guarded by the NKVD! [KGB].
>
> Because who knows? These guys are maybe freedom fighters fighting for Latvia. So the units were broken up and used as work battalions without weapons. Of course a lot of the men in the Latvian battalions weren't just Latvians, either. There were Russians, Georgians, Jews, Ukrainians … approximately one third of the unit wasn't Latvian'.

In several years prior to my visit, memorial services for Legionnaires have been marked by disturbances involving accusations that the Latvians fighting in the Legion were

---

*   In Latvian *Kara Osta*.

Nazis. That also led to some of the anniversaries descending into political slanging matches. I ask for his thoughts. He snorts.

> For seven hundred years Latvia lived under the Teutonic Order and for Latvians, Germans and Germany are Enemy Number One ... for 700 years! Even though we were part of Tsarist Russia from the 18th century, the people running Latvia – all the business, all the laws – were the Germans. So that's why they were Enemy Number One.
>
> And then we have Enemy Number Two, the Soviet Union. They come in 1940 and we have The Terrible Year. It's enemy number one, then enemy number two. Same enemies. Enemy number one: Soviet Union. Enemy number two: Nazi Germany.
>
> Many, many thousands of people fight under the Nazi German flag against the Soviet Union. After enemy number one is destroyed they want to destroy number two. That's where we got the song [from the War of Independence]: 'First we're going to beat the guys in the east, then we're going to beat the guys to the west.'
>
> Today Russians propaganda says 'The Latvian Legion were Nazi troops'. But they weren't Nazi troops. They wanted freedom. They didn't have Nazi Party documents. In Great Britain there was a Nazi Party – Oswald Mosley. But no-one in Latvia was in the Nazi Party.

Einars nods.

> They weren't told they would fight for Nazi Germany, but they were told they would fight against the Soviets. Joining the Legion was about the only way they could do that.
>
> Let's say in your book you say the Latvian 15th and 19th Divisions were good and they were fighting for an independent Latvia. I believe the Russian and German Embassies will call you and say 'You are glorifying Nazis'. The *Kurelieši* partisans are not considered Nazis. But the two Latvian divisions really did fight and fought a lot but they were denounced as Nazis.

Mr Raķis puts both his hands out, as if weighing the crimes of each regime.

> You can't say the [Nazi] death camps are bad and the [Soviet] gulags are fine. They're equally bad. It's not a pleasant part of history for the Soviet Union. It's easier for the Soviet period for them [the Legionnaires] to be Nazis, enemies, spies, terrorists or whatever.
>
> An 80, 90 year-old Red Army soldier to me is a hero. Those battles were tough. He's a soldier, not the security service. Not the NKVD, not the Gestapo. 16th March is a day to remember the men who died on the battlefields – normal soldiers – and for their families and relatives.
>
> There were many Latvians serving in the Red Army – thousands – fighting against the Latvians in the German Army. In my family there were two brothers

here in Courland serving on opposite sides. One brother in German uniform, one brother in Soviet uniform. It's a big tragedy for Latvia.

My family is originally from Madona in Vidzeme, in the east. In 1940 my grandfather had six children and a farm, a factory, a car, a tractor and a big family. When the Soviets came in 1940 they took everything. My family came to Courland to get away. One brother was 20 years old, another was three years younger. The 20 year-old was mobilised into the Soviet Army, then the other was mobilised into the German Army. They were on opposite sides at Džūkste.

One brother shouts: 'You come to me'. The brother on the other side says 'You come to me' – but it's not possible. They didn't see each other for 45 years. One brother went to Australia and didn't return until after independence.

I mention to Mr Raķis a story I'd heard that Latvians in the Legion wrapped the red-white-red national flag around themselves under their uniform. I'd yet to find a Legionnaire who had done that or who had even heard of someone doing that. Perhaps it was a patriotic story put around by mythmakers?

He nods, and pulls his cigarettes out of his pocket.

'The flag around the body: it's a dream of independent Latvia. Sometimes the problem comes as to how we reach that dream'.

He gestures at the heavy prison door with his cigarette, indicating that he is going outside for a smoke.

'Now it's nearly time to open the doors, yes?'[1]

A short drive from Karosta Prison is the beach at Šķēde, one of the sites of mass butchery of Jewish men, women and children by the Latvian murder squad the *Arājs Kommando* between Monday 15 December and Wednesday 17 December 1941.

At Šķēde today there is a gravel path lined with white posts leading towards the sea and a monument in the shape of a menorah, the seven-branched candlestick that has become a symbol of Judaism.

Each of the posts along the path is dedicated to a Latvian who helped save Jews from being murdered during the Holocaust. Those Latvians are known as 'Righteous Among the Nations' – non-Jews who risked their lives and the lives of their relatives in saving Jewish people. It's a special award by Yad Vashem, Israel's official memorial to victims of the Holocaust. Of the 135 non-Jews who have been awarded this title, 26 of them came from Liepāja.

'Those who save one life, save the whole world' reads the inscription on a stone slab at the start of the path. It records the grim details of what happened here: 3,640 Jews machine-gunned on the beach, including 1,000 children. A further 2,000 Soviet prisoners of war killed, along with 1,000 Latvian civilians: those who resisted the Nazi occupation or helped the Jews and the prisoners.

There are the Zivcon pictures too on an information board: pitiful scenes of women about to die stripped to their underwear, trying to protect themselves, utterly vulnerable and defenceless. The sheer sadism of the killing is hard to process. The killers machine-gunned defenceless, often naked women and children standing on a ledge dug into sand dunes so their bodies fell into a mass grave. Then they lined up the next victims to a marker on the ledge so they fell into an area alongside them. One man worked as a 'kicker' on the ledge, kicking, rolling or shoving anyone who didn't fall conveniently into their own grave.*

The massacres attracted crowds of German soldiers. The gunmen refreshed themselves from a milkcan full of rum placed nearby and changed shifts after each team had shot 10 groups of 20 people on the ledge.[2]

Here I am 70 years later, standing on the same sand. This is a beautiful place, a lovely golden beach looking out to sea with woods nearby … the kind of place usually associated with happy childhood memories. But instead this sea view is the last thing thousands of unfortunate people would see.

On my way back to town to collect my bags and head up the coast I call in at the offices of Liepāja's Jewish Heritage Foundation. I climb the stairs to the second floor and am offered tea and cakes – to my amazement – by the daughter of David Zivcon. Her name is Ilana Ivanova.

> I was born Ilana Zivcon in Liepāja on 13 October 1946. I am alive thanks to the Righteous Gentiles, the Sedols[†] family, who saved the lives of my mother and father. We have a special tradition: we support them, we help them always, all the 11 people, their families and their children.
>
> There were eleven Jews in the shelter, and two little girls, the daughters of Sedols, living in the apartment near the market at Tirgoņu iela 22 [Merchant Street]. They tried to avoid asking questions: 'Why is Father buying so much bread. Why is he bringing things to repair?' There were many questions. They are both alive still. One is a retired teacher, the other worked at the sugar factory, and we are very close. Every year we celebrate Christmas with them. We make coffee, we buy small gifts.
>
> I feel we are facing a situation today when the children of the new generation know very little or nothing about the Second World War or the Holocaust. There's a terrible mixture of historical events and a tendency to re-write history – and this is the greatest crime that we can commit.
>
> Germany did it. They never denied it. The Jews don't need any excuses. The only thing we need is that people, nations, countries remember this terrible example in the history of the 20th Century to avoid any possibility that one nation could be exterminated because they were of another religion.
>
> I was about seven or eight when I noticed at home the negatives of the photographs of the shooting at Šķēde. I saw naked people standing near the shore. My father never spoke about the war. Mum didn't talk much. We spoke German at home – there's a paradox. I asked my father about the pictures. 'That's the war,

* For further information on Šķēde and the scale of the Holocaust in Latvia a good starting point is the online Yad Vashem site (www.yadvashem.org). There are a number of authoritative books in the bibliography, especially Ezergailis.
† Also spelt Seduls.

and you must know what it is,' he said. Then the negatives disappeared. I always wondered why: I always felt that something was wrong about that.

We discuss Ilana's sense of identity: a girl born in Latvia, Jewish, schooled in Russia, able to speak four languages. Where does she belong?

I consider myself Latvian. I am real Courland Jewish elite – eight generations. My ancestors have been here since the 16th century although I was educated in St Petersburg. I speak fluent Russian. It's no problem for me to speak any of four other languages – German, Latvian, English and Yiddish. This is what made many of the Latvians collaborate with the Nazis.

That, and they thought Hitler would bring independence to Latvia. That's despite the fact that there's no evidence anywhere of Hitler saying he would do that. And what kind of independence struggle is shooting defenceless women, children and old men on a beach?

Liepāja was a fantastic city before the war. In terms of tolerance, in terms of understanding each other. It was integrated: Jews, Poles, Lithuanians, Latvians, Germans. Everyone respected each other's holidays. There were 15 Jewish schools, a Jewish theatre. Famous people performed there. The town was beautiful – it looked like a little town in Switzerland.

But first the Latvians were stopped from supplying raw materials to Jewish shops, so there was no business. Then the Jews weren't allowed to walk on the pavements and had to wear the yellow square.* Tolerance was destroyed. Today there are seven Latvian-born Jewish families living in Liepāja. The others are incomers, some sent here in Soviet times to work at the steel factory. Russian Jews, mostly.

When we celebrate the end of the war we celebrate victory over fascism. We consider the Soviets liberated the Jews. They came here in 1940 and deported people and then they came back in 1945. I fully understand why people call the Soviet time an occupation, but it was a peaceful occupation. No-one was killed. They built factories, hospitals, schools. But there is no respect to anything connected to Russia and Russians.

How can I judge when they liberated my family? But when people talk about what the Nazis did, they say 'Jews were killed'. They don't say 'the people of my country were killed'. As if we were not citizens. Why?

This is how I feel, and I share it for one reason. I want my grandchildren to live in Liepāja in peace and tolerance. We must learn to live together'.[3]

Ilana is a direct connection to the Holocaust and her words are heartfelt and sincere. Talking to her adds to my feeling that the Nazis injected a hatred of Jews into Latvia that may or may not have been there before, but it has certainly separated 'Jews' from other Latvians.

---

* Everywhere else it was a yellow triangle.

Perhaps the Nazis offered an outlet for the natural sadism in some people and an opportunity to behave in a cruel and inhuman way. I'm curious about how an educated, cosmopolitan woman with such a personal connection to the Holocaust and who commits much of her time to commemorating it might define herself. Is there a flag she might declare loyalty to, perhaps? She thinks about this for a moment then gives her answer.

> I am 100 per cent Latvian, but I am a person of Europe, of the world. I speak Russian, German, Latvian, English and Yiddish. It would be two flags: Latvia and Israel.

My final question before I leave relates to happier times, to the Café Bonitz. Was it really such a feature of Liepāja life? Ilana smiles.

> Oh yes. It was a very luxurious café. My mother went there. It was very beautiful and people liked to drink chocolate there.
> There was a famous doctor in Liepāja and his son used to go with his nanny to the Café Bonitz. He liked the chocolate and he always had a small anchovy sandwich, specially made for him. Even though anchovies and hot chocolate don't go together they made it for him. The men used to go there and play billiards. Women weren't allowed in there.

As I'm leaving Ilana gets a small box out of her desk and pulls out some photographs. 'Otto Fischer', she says almost absent-mindedly, leafing through the pictures.

> My mum knew him. He was a small man, well dressed in elegant suits. My mum trained at the Stadia Olimpija at the same time as him.
> We are making a project together with the Austrian Embassy. Yes, the football team went a few times to the Nazis to ask them not to shoot him. That's Fischer in the suit.

She points at the picture of a small man in a suit surrounded by footballers. Everyone looks happy. No wonder. This is the Barcelona of the time, the team Fischer coached three times to the League championship. I photograph the pictures for reference, amazed at Ilana Ivanova's connection to the past.

Notes

1   Interview with Juris Raķis.
2   Meler, pp.208-216.
3   Interview with Ilana Ivanova, January 2015.

16

The Baltic Coast – North to Ventspils

The drive from Liepāja up the Baltic coast in the late afternoon November sun was magical. Setting slowly to my left and with an open road ahead the journey north was a rare moment of motoring pleasure, with wisps of mist gathering where forests trimmed the fields.

I'm on my way to Ventspils following the coastline so many soldiers travelled in the defence of Courland and where, in the later stages of the war, the underground nationalist resistance movement the LCP [*Latvijas Centrālā Padome*, or Latvian Central Council] started evacuating the intelligentsia by boat to the small Swedish island of Gotland, 140 kms across the Baltic.

With Soviet victory inevitable, from mid-1944 to the spring of 1945 many Latvians preferred to take their chances at sea than face a second occupation by the USSR. Politicians, writers, musicians – anyone who could play a part in a Latvian resistance abroad – set out in crowded motorboats and fishing boats for Gotland and then neutral Sweden.

They took significant risks. Many of the boats were not suitable for open sea and they had to run a gauntlet of German patrols, sea mines, Soviet planes and naval ships, often without enough food, fuel or proper navigation equipment. Because of the secrecy involved no-one is really sure how many tried but roughly 4,500 Latvians made it to safety, ferried by around thirty different sea captains.

The Latvian Central Council was a political coalition seeking an independent, democratic and west-leaning Latvia. It was led by Konstantīns Čakste, son of the first Latvian president Jānis Čakste, who brought together leaders of the four major pre-war parliamentary factions; the Social Democrats, the Democratic Centre, the Latgalian Christian Farmers' Association and the Agrarian Union, which had been led by the former President Ulmanis. He had suspended the constitution and given himself emergency powers in 1934, ruling like an autocrat,* so the Agrarian Union was required to renounce this period of his rule unequivocally.[1]

In March 1944 the Council presented a declaration to the Self-Administration running Latvia under German control signed by 189 prominent Latvian politicians, public figures and artists, calling for the restoration of a democratic and independent Latvia. This was intended as evidence to the world that Latvians were opposed to the

---

* Governing by decree, without parliament, others use the term 'dictator'.

German occupation and wanted independence restored. Copies were smuggled to Sweden and to American diplomats abroad.

The most prominent signatories immediately became targets of a German crackdown. Čakste was sent to the notorious Stutthof concentration camp near Gdansk, where he died. In September 1944 52 signatories to the declaration were captured attempting to flee to Sweden by boat.[2]

Undeterred, the boats slipped away from the shores of Courland at the dead at night. Those who made it were issued with 'foreigner' passports by Sweden and allowed to settle. In 1945 there were 4,418 Latvians over the age of 16 registered in Sweden.[3]

I break my journey briefly at Pāvilosta, once home to the Baltic coast fishing fleet and a wartime German harbour, so well-defended and guarded that Latvians were deterred from making a dash to freedom from here. Nowadays it seems to have slipped back into being a pretty but unremarkable port on the western coast with a small museum, a restaurant and little else.

There's been a harbour in this area since the Middle Ages, but that was six kilometres inland at Saka. The Swedes closed it after the war with Poland in 1660 and it wasn't until the mid-19th century that the coastal trade was revived by a local Baron, Otto von Lilienfeld. He built the harbour in its present location in honour of his brother Paul, the governor of Courland, re-naming it Paul's Harbour, or Pāvilosta.

Until 1890 there were just ten fishermen's houses here, but that expanded over the next 20 years to become home to a fleet of more than 100 fishing boats operating during the First World War. There the town's history goes more or less dead.[4]

But there are dark stories from the Second World War in Pāvilosta that have slipped from local memory, commemorated only by signs at the roadside marked 'To the victims of Fascism'. This bald statement scarcely does justice to the horror those unfortunate and un-named people endured.

The Jewish populations of Pāvilosta, Jūrkalne and Saka were wiped out by the Nazis on 4 December 1941 having been force-marched to a place of execution at Grini, near Saka. They were forced to dig their own graves and then shot. The massacre was carried out by policemen from Liepāja and members of the local Self-Defence Squad.

One schoolboy was taken from his classes to be killed. The local doctor, Dr Lowenstein, asked his executioners to shoot his daughter first so she would not have to see her parents die. They did. Another Latvian man asked the soldiers to kill him as well as his Jewish wife. They refused. He went back to Pāvilosta to tell the town what had happened.[5]

In the oral history archives in Riga is an interview with a woman who grew up in Pāvilosta, Lydia Doronina. She was 16 in 1941. Her family narrowly escaped deportation by the Soviets after being tipped off that the authorities were after them.

> You know, the most horrific, the most terrible experiences were during these two totalitarian regimes. Shortly after the Germans had arrived all Pāvilosta's Jews, with whom we had been so friendly, grown up alongside and lived with, were

arrested. I hadn't even thought that they are Jews and I am Latvian or…about any ethnicity at all.

At school I sat with Minnīte Swarzman and in summer they came to help us with the hay. I was friends with her. Suddenly they are all taken to Saka parish and made to dig pits and shot at the side of the pit and all of them were killed. I was following them when they were taken away. I had a very strange feeling, I still remember it; a very strange feeling. The Germans pulled us away, we who were following our schoolmates, they dragged us away by the hand, and said: 'You are not allowed to go any further'.[6]

I swing the car round, head out of Pāvilosta and continue my journey along the coast. The sun has slipped a little lower from this blue, almost cloudless sky, casting a beautiful golden glow across the fields. A gentle bluey-grey fog is gathering at the edge of the forest, licking at the rolls of hay, enveloping the occasional cow munching grass.

The road runs close to the coast now. Signs tell me I've reached the outskirts of Jūrkalne. A road forks to the left and there is a parking area so I stop and follow a track through a wood of pine trees down a sandy slope to the sea.

As I reach the bottom of the slope an idyllic sight greets me.

The pine trees finish at the edge of steep sand dunes more than 10 metres high in some places, like bluffs. They lead down to a beach of soft, golden sand. There is a whole community of fishermen here, each with their rods in the sea. Some are on sandbanks, others are in little pitches in their own nest of rods. In the late afternoon sun several couples are strolling along the sand by the sea.

I imagine that seventy years ago nervous escapees would hide among the pine trees until nightfall, then carry their boat to the sea, push off and try and get away without the alarm being raised. With guards raking the sand every night and patrolling along here, it would be difficult to do this undetected. But then again, with the trees coming right to the beach and no streetlights, it might be possible to get within five metres of the chance of freedom. On a moonless night, or in fog, you might just have a chance.

The crossings were organised by Leonīds Siliņš, secretary of the LCC's foreign delegation, and signed off by General Verners Tepfers, representative for Courland. The journey was free for refugees, underwritten by the USA Refugee Council and the Sweden Defence Headquarters, but the secret services of the USA, Britain and Sweden were keen to hear the latest information about German troop movements and forces in Courland. Encouraged by hopes of a British intervention, the LCC developed an intelligence and military network across Kurzeme. The close contact with British intelligence was less than secure, as in the immediate post-war period the KGB comprehensively penetrated MI6 through the Latvian network in Sweden.*

---

* The author's second book on Latvia's turbulent history, *Up Against the Wall: the KGB and Latvia* (Helion, 2019), develops this story in more detail.

With the involvement of the British, American and Swedish Secret Services, the KGB and boatloads of Latvian political escapees running the gauntlet of both Nazi and Russian boats off the coast, the plot is thickening at an alarming rate.

I pull into a café to read the memories of Boris Mangolds, who first worked as a radio operator for the LCC underground which arranged the boats to Sweden, then made the dangerous journey himself.

I was mobilised while still a student at the University of Latvia. Those who were called up first were given a choice of where to serve – in the German defence forces, to be part of the Latvian Legion or to do technical work or work in a factory. There was a rumour that if you volunteered to work you would be sent to Polish coal mines. Germans spread this gossip so people would be frightened and volunteer for military units.

We were called to a big hall on Lāčplēsa Street [in Riga]. On a podium at the top table was a senior German officer and a translator keeping a respectful distance from him. The General looked at my personal details on the enrolment sheet and the translator started to translate and I said: 'I don't need a translator. I know German'. The General looked pleased. 'Excellent,' he said. 'Well, you have three choices'. I volunteered to work. You should have heard the Germans swearing! Then they gave me a form to sign and said: 'Next'.

The guys standing outside asked me what happened – they'd heard the turmoil. I told them and they all said they'd volunteered to work too, not to fight!

That's the difference between the Germans and the Russians – at least the Germans kept their word. If they promised they'd do it, they did it. Maybe the General didn't like the fact that choices were given but he had to respect them. After a week all choices were cancelled.

I worked all through the German time as a railway technician, repairing equipment. It wasn't great but I could use any train at any time without tickets or needing a special permit. That was very useful when I was in the *Kurelieši* movement operating a radio transmitter.

Silins was one of the main organisers of going to Sweden from Latvia towards the end of the war. The Swedish were very interested in German plans in Latvia, particularly to know German plans towards Sweden, especially whether they intended to occupy Sweden. They were very sensitive about this. When Silins came from Sweden they gave him some radio transmitters. In exchange they said they would take care of refugees, a case of 'You do something for me, I'll do something for you'. I was told that – I don't know whether it's true.

But in the *Kurelieši* in Latvia there was no-one who could use a radio transmitter. When I served in the Third Jelgava Infantry I was a radio telegrapher and it was easy for me, so that's how I became the radio man. It was terribly impractical. The radio was in a massive box, so heavy we couldn't lift it. I rebuilt it into several parts in bags so we could transport it more easily. And that's how my very interesting life began.

I learned the codes and worked out how to use the transmitter and then the tasks began. Upelnieks [Kurelis's number two] was my boss. He gave me information which needed to be transmitted to Sweden. That happened three times a week. The first time I did it the electricity suddenly went off, then came on again. That was a warning. The Germans were trying to find our transmitters. They would turn off the electricity in Riga bit by bit so they knew which district the transmitter was in. As soon as it went off I stopped transmitting.

I did that for around one and a half years, [moving] around Latvia, always changing my place. I was transmitting military information but we also had a secret code for Latvians. The Swedish didn't know this code. There were two levels – the open code we were transmitting to the Swedish but also another hidden message. 'From where, what time, will the next boats come from Courland to Sweden'.

When things started to go badly for the Germans General Kurelis called me into his room and said: 'OK son, you've done enough. We can't do anything here any more. Take your family – it's your turn to go. Give the transmitter to someone else'.

So we left in September 1944 from the coast south of the Užava Forest.* Leaving was quite dramatic. Our boat didn't arrive when it was meant to. We were five nights and days without food living in a hut in the forest waiting for the boat. I had a wife and a one year-old girl. We were totally unprepared.

There was a group of important politicians who had to be taken to Sweden for security – we were just an unimportant group of people. Someone led us on foot through the forest to the dunes. I had a very small bag but I remember the Karlsons from Riga who were shop owners and they had rolls of carpet with them. They made us take those carpets through the forest. That was too much. We just got angry and threw them in the ditch.

At the coast it wasn't easy. We couldn't sit there and wait. It was terribly cold and windy and rainy and German patrols were going round all the time. The Germans had ordered the Lithuanian brigade to do the patrols. Once the Lithuanians saw one of the boats. They let it go and fired in the air, then told the Germans they had arrived too late. This was in January or February 1945. But the Germans put them all in a line and shot every third one as a warning to the others.

[Our] boat arrived exactly on the night Liepāja was bombed. We're on the beach at midnight in the dark. We can see the boat but it can't get closer because the water's too shallow. We cannot get in the boat because the water's too deep. It was so close but we couldn't get there!

It was good luck that we found a small fishing boat in the dunes with oars. It was half full of water so we baled it out with our hats, put the women and children into it and we men pushed it out to the boat. The best moment we heard was … 'puk puk puk'! The engine started!

---

*   South of Ventspils down the coast towards Jūrkalne.

Those boats weren't very good. Many sank. That's all they could get. Some broke down at sea, others wouldn't start. But ours did. 'Puk puk puk' … and we are heading off into the fog.[7]

I turn the page to the story of the best-known of the Gotland boatmen, Pēteris Jansons.

I could speak a little bit of German and a little bit of English so I was sent to Stockholm. I had a little bit of business in Stockholm. In the street I met a friend from the naval academy. He asked me if I'd be interested in going back [to Latvia].

'Oh, yes I would. Oh yes,' I said.

We pretended that we are fishing like Swedes. Fuel was brought to us by Swedes by car. We dropped Leonīds Siliņš along the coast. Then there was someone called Kalniņš, and Edward Andersons … I really don't remember any more … then we went back. When we got to Sweden the Swedes asked: 'Where have you been? Why have you been so long?'

We said we couldn't find the nets or the hooks. And the Swedes said: 'Your nets are caught in your propeller. That's why you can't find them and your boat is so slow'. We didn't know anything about fishing really, but we went back and picked up the men we'd left and they had four or five more men with them. We didn't know who they were but eventually we found out. So they were the first contacts. We had to go over every two weeks no matter what the weather or how bad the storms were.

One time I went with Jānis Fonzelis and another man who was later captured. We let that man off near the coast to make contacts. We had some weapons with us, some medicines, some money, food vouchers, vouchers for vodka … a lot of stuff. We were supposed to wait one night and one day and then come back the next night to pick him up. In that time he will make his contacts. We went back to get him: nothing. So we waited another day and went back again. Nothing. Then we discovered that we're running out of oil, and then we're running out of fuel. We have no reserve fuel so we can't go back. We decide to go to Riga Bay.

Jānis Fonzelis is from Mērsrags[*] and so are his parents so we'll go there, try to fix the boat and go back. So we get to the coast and it's so shallow there that we can't get the boat to the beach, and we see two German soldiers on horseback. I tell Jānis to go and talk to them, tell them we're fishermen from Ventspils or Liepāja and our motor is broken and we have to repair it. And if it's not going well, I tell him: 'Fall on the ground, fall to your knees and pray to God'. Because I had a weapon and could kill those Germans.

In those times nobody waited for long. Whoever was faster lived longer. If you were slow you got shot. But Jānis spoke Swedish very badly and didn't know German. He knew only Latvian. I already knew Swedish very well – it was in

---

*   A coastal town on the Gulf of Riga side of Courland.

my blood. So if I got out I might mix up my languages. Jānis was a very good talker. He could talk logs into planks. It worked, and they left. He came back and said: 'They believed me'.

We had to get the bits of the motor out so we could repair them and then we had to unload the radios and the weapons and the money and the medicines. We had to make three or four trips to get everything dug in on the coast, then we went to Mērsrags. I had a machine gun and Jānis had a gun and two hand grenades. I also had a number to call in Ventspils if something happened. We walked all night but Jānis got so sick he couldn't walk anymore. I started to kick him and hit him to get him to snap out of it but when he saw his parents' house he started walking so fast I couldn't keep up. I was tired too, terribly tired. His parents were very welcoming and gave us some food. His sister was there as well as his mum and dad.

I called that number and they promised to find us in the morning. We both went to sleep in the haybarn very late. In the morning I heard several cars come into the yard and lots of people talking in German... German SD officers and soldiers.* So I said to Jānis: 'We have to give ourselves away expensively'. We could have killed three or four of them before they killed us.

Then I heard someone say in Latvian ... 'But Mārtiņš...'

When I heard that I realised these must be our people so we went out to meet them. It turns out they were our guys dressed in German uniforms – I don't know whether there were Germans too – so I told them where the stuff was and because they were in uniform they could operate freely. I remember this moment very clearly because this was the moment I was ready to sell my life very dearly.

Then in October I found a big boat called *Zvejnieks* [*Fisherman*].† When we came with that boat there were many actors, writers, doctors – 10 or 12 doctors – and very good men. But we found this out only later. We never knew who we were taking. Suddenly I felt the boat was overloaded. I looked at how many people there were and said: 'I can't take any more'. When I went round the Kolkasrags‡ I started to feel the boat has only two centimetres of water under it. I was young and had a girlfriend in Gotland so I had to get back. I told every-one to take off their coats and clothes and throw them overboard – fur coats, everything. Sort the suitcases out and throw the clothes into the sea. It really helped. Because when the wind blows clothes get wet and heavier and we would all have sunk.

We made it to the coast of Gotland but I didn't tell anyone in the boat that we were close in case they all rushed to the side and the boat capsized. In the end we all went happily into the harbour – all 150 people on board. As we unloaded

---

*   SD:*Sicherheitsdienst* or Security Service – a special branch of the SS.
†   One of the most famous of the boats which ferried refugees between Latvia and Gotland.
‡   The northern tip of Courland where the Baltic meets the Gulf of Riga.

the boat some people couldn't walk because their legs were numb. The trip had taken roughly 42 hours.[8]

A wooden sculpture in the shape of a sail now stands on the main road into Jūrkalne to commemorate these voyages.[9]

By the end of the war the Courland coast was one of the few routes remaining for those wishing to avoid capture and questioning by the Soviets, especially for soldiers who had taken part in the darker episodes of the war.

Some Swedish newspapers accused the Latvians of smuggling out Nazi war criminals, which, although strongly denied, harmed the entire evacuation process.[*]

One lasting controversy from this period of exodus to Sweden still rankles today. In May 1945 Sweden interned 149 Latvian soldiers who had arrived from Danzig to avoid being captured by the Soviets. A month later the USSR demanded that Sweden extradite them. Despite protests from church leaders and unions and the refusal of the Swedish Army to co-operate, Sweden sent them back. The fate of the group is not entirely clear: two were executed, some freed and the majority sent to labour camps. Sweden's move prompted many Latvians to move on.[10]

By now the sun is setting properly so I get back on the road to make Ventspils before dark. The enormous freight terminal at the port city starts several kilometres outside the town centre. The cranes that unload ships can be seen from far away with signs indicating the various terminals; cargo, ferry, dry goods. The road bridge loops over the river Venta and into town past a big shopping centre and Rimi hypermarket.

My guesthouse is in the Old Town and as dusk falls I head out to explore.

Pils iela [Castle Street] leads me into the centre of the town past charming early 20th Century art nouveau style buildings which are a little neglected but very pretty. The streets are lit by what look like Jack the Ripper era, Sherlock Holmes-esque gas lamps spaced out at lengthy intervals, making the lighting shadowy and a little spooky.

In the centre of town there are lots of original wooden houses and shops but some are so neglected they appear on the verge of collapse. An ancient wooden grocery store occupies the corner block right in the very heart of the main square. It's for rent but it's all shuttered up, the paint peeling.

It's like a postcard from the past: low rise, old tech, unloved – and it's probably cheaper to let this fall to the ground over time then replace it rather than repair it. The rules in Latvia are that historic old buildings have to be restored properly. Across the road on Liela iela [Main Street] there's a red brick building that dates back to 1767.

These are the main streets in the centre of the Old Town of Ventspils, but at 7.30pm on a Friday night the place is deserted. Most of the houses are shuttered up, abandoned, uninhabited or decaying. There's only an occasional light in an entire street. All the shops are closed. There are a couple of people in the library reading. I thought

---

[*] See Stephen Dorril's book *MI6* for further details of British secret service recruitment of former *Waffen-SS* soldiers and SS men wanted by the Soviets for war crimes, particularly Chapter 16.

with it being a port city this place would be buzzing at night but no, it's dead. There is nothing going on.

The wind gets up as I turn into Market Square. I'm getting closer to the harbour and the wind is rattling the shutters of the market building. Now I can see water and big cranes unloading cargo across the canal. As the wind has picked up so the temperature has dropped: it's a proper port evening. A fisherman steps off his boat to smoke a cigarette and make a final phone call before he sets out night fishing. I decide to turn in.

The next morning I meet Artūrs Tukišs, curator of the Ventspils Outdoor Museum, an eclectic collection of boats, narrow gauge railways and coastal-related exhibits. At 26, Artūrs is part of the new wave of Latvian historians and very passionate about his history. He's an expert on Latvian railways, a mine of valuable information and the guardian of countless stories about the Courland battles.

With us is Artūrs' girlfriend Kristine Graudina, on hand with her phone to translate words that stump our combined language abilities. Between the three of us a fascinating but sobering story emerges of engineering triumphs, lonely deaths and a tortured nation.

We talk about the physical impact of the war around Ventspils and its strategic importance. Each of the services – Wehrmacht, Luftwaffe and Kriegsmarine – had a headquarters in the city and SS units were also based here but, Artūrs says, one of the frustrating things about modern Latvian history is that no-one knows the details. Everyone who did is dead.

The Nazis did a considerable amount of heavy engineering work to improve links between the main towns and cities in Courland aided by a ready supply of slave labour.

> All this area is a big wood, in reality. The roads weren't good. The railway was the best way to move people, military equipment and supplies. The narrow gauge railway connected all the small towns in Courland, from Ventspils to Dundaga, Talsi and Roja. All through the war the Germans brought wood out of the forests and took it to Germany. Passengers went by the narrow gauge lines too, plus troops, munitions, supplies. I've seen pictures of tanks on the narrow gauge railway wagons.
>
> In 1944 the Germans decided to finish the railway line from Ventspils to Liepāja. The Latvian government wanted to do that in the 1920s and 1930s but didn't have the money. They started building a bridge over the [river] Venta in the 1920s, and built the left and right side but not the middle. The Germans designed a section to fit into the middle and lifted it into place to finish the bridge. Then in three months German troops built a railway line from Ventspils to Liepāja. In three months!*

---

* They were of course helped in the construction by the forced labour of PoWs and civilians brought from Russia.

The Germans expected a big [Soviet] landing all along the coast. From Tukums to the sea there were trenches through the forest, fall-back lines through the woods. We know those troops were Kriegsmarine, not Wehrmacht. Near the coast diggers have found dogtags from Wehrmacht, SS and Kriegsmarine. We don't know where the SS were based on the coast, but the dogtags were found in Lielirbe. And not Latvian Legion: they were from a German SS unit. And then only half the dogtag, too.

Ventspils had an air base, built in 1938 in Latvian times. There were fighter units in Ventspils, German Messerschmitts. The second reserve was in a village called Tārgale* and Piltene [further south]. There was a reserve airfield near Ventspils and after the war Russian troops collected military equipment there. All the local boys and girls explored all the burned-out tanks and damaged equipment seeing what they could take.

People came to siphon off the fuel, and any equipment that was stuck in the woods was blown up and the scrap taken to the metal works in Liepāja. Some of the tanks and vehicles were used as targets for gunnery training. The tanks had First Aid boxes and medicine was in short supply after the war so all the boxes were taken out. My friend's grandmother has a medical box from a German Panzer. She still uses cream from one of the tubes for rheumatism… the tube was manufactured in 1934!

Every Latvian family has war stories and Artūrs is no exception.

One Legionnaire told a story about when he was a machine gunner. When they heard the shouts of the Soviet infantry – 'Urrah' – they would start firing. The 'Urrahs' would stop, and then the next wave would come. They would fire and fire until there was a pile of bodies in front of them so high they couldn't raise the angle of fire of the machine gun any more. The Soviet troops just kept coming.

My grandfather lived near to Degoles village [near Tukums] and a red brick school there was used as a hospital. Near the hospital there was land used as a graveyard. Soldiers who died were buried there and birch trees were used to make crosses – and they started to grow. An old lady who was living there from the wartime, a very old lady, said that when there's a fog you can see the ghost of a German soldier walking around the building. Only in fog. And he has only one leg.†

My grandfather said that after the war large packs of wolves roamed through the woods because there were so many bodies there. These wolves weren't afraid of humans either. Special teams of hunters were sent to shoot them.

Because the Germans sowed so many minefields around Pampāļi the Soviets forbade people to go in the woods. A few years ago an old grandmother was

*   Across the river from today's airport.
†   The author visited Degoles two years later. The red brick building is still there.

in the forest there collecting mushrooms when she spotted a big one near a tree. She knelt down to cut it with her knife and there was a German soldier lying near the tree – a skeleton, wearing a helmet, with a gun and a few hand grenades. Near the hand grenade was the mushroom. This soldier must have been wounded and lain down resting against a tree and died. And no-one had found him.[11]

We talk about my journey to Ventspils through the swamps and forests north of Liepāja. I mention a memorial sign to the massacre at Saka of civilians supporting Red partisans. Inquiries in Pāvilosta drew a blank, I tell Artūrs – does he know anything about it? He nods.

'Perhaps,' he says. 'I know of a story about partisans in that area that might be the same incident'.

There would have been a lot of movement up those coast roads and into the interior, he tells me. The region north and east of Liepāja was an important supply route from the docks at Liepāja to Kuldīga where the central command was, and to Aizpute, where German troops were held in reserve.

A partisan group was operating in the Grini swamps around Saka; men who had fled to avoid being mobilised into the Latvian Legion. Then a Red partisan group commanded by Macpāns arrived and this group joined forces with them. The Macpāns partisans operated in the woods west of Saka and Pāvilosta, around Apriķi, Cīrava and Alsunga. There were 30 to 40 people in this group, operating in the back of the German 18th Army units cutting communications, blowing up bridges and other things, supplied by Soviet air-drops of weapons, ammunition and food into the forests with small groups of commandos inserted three or four at a time to support and strengthen them.

The partisan attacks disrupted operations rather than devastating them but German commanders decided a crackdown was needed and sent police units to clean the forests of these partisans. After the brutal German massacre of civilians at Zlēkas SS *Obergruppenführer* Jeckeln ordered the 'cleaning' of the forest in Saka – a term which usually meant it was sealed off and anyone caught inside the security ring was killed.'[12]

Artūrs has offered to show me round the Old Town so the three of us climb into my car and drive the short distance into the centre. We walk through the town along the snowy streets to the end of the main road. He points to a larger building on the opposite side of the road. It looks like an old-fashioned school or a hospital. Artūrs tells me that in its lifetime it has been both.

---

*   This may tally with Herbert Knēts comment about the Macpāns partisans in the table on p121: 'Unit defeated 26.02.45'

> This was the first school for ladies in Ventspils. After that it was a school for all the best pupils in the area. This was a hospital for the Legionnaires and the German troops. And also a place for mobilising soldiers and training them, as well as a hospital. You would report here to join the Army: when you got shot, you'd come here to get better.

We walk from the Old Town along street after cobbled street of boarded-up, decaying wooden houses, lit dimly by those turn-of-the-century streetlamps. We turn into a square with an impressive building on one side which, with its balcony and stucco finish restored, looks like an important civic building.

Artūrs gestures towards the cobbled square and relates another story from the twisted and tragic history of Ventspils.

> In World War One the Germans occupied Ventspils. At the end of the war the Red Army came into Latvia and took the town. A German soldier wounded in the battles had been left in the hospital but the Bolsheviks didn't shoot him. When the Germans came back and cleared the Bolsheviks out they rounded up all the men from Ventspils and lined them up in this square. The German soldier was brought out to identify everyone who had collaborated with the Bolsheviks. All the men he pointed out were taken down to the river and shot. One book says 30 people, a second book says 300. We have an account from a priest who was alive at the time – he says 150. We think he is right.

A sudden silence falls among us. It seems unthinkable that no-one knows the exact figure. But there's worse.

> The Germans shot the men and then left the bodies there for three months as a warning to the people of the town. They wouldn't let the wives collect the bodies. Then after three months they said: 'OK, you can bury them'.

Latvian history has a way of slapping you in the face with its unexpected brutality. We walk back to my car past the library, past the shuttered grocery store and past a statue of a man in what appears to be a Red Army uniform. Artūrs sees me looking curiously at the figure and explains.

> That's Jānis Fabriciuss, a Ventspils boy who was in the Tsarist army, in the 1917 Revolution. He fought in the War of Independence. Many Latvians don't know his name or what he did.

I have to admit I've never heard of him. We look him up online on Kristina's phone and find his entry in the *Great Soviet Encyclopaedia of 1979*, a source which nowadays carries a warning that the information might be outdated or ideologically biased. We take the chance anyway.

Fabriciuss, Jānis: Born 14 June 1877 near what is now Zlēkas, Ventspils Region, Latvian SSR; died Aug. 24, 1929, near Sochi. Hero of the Civil War. Member of the Communist Party from 1903.

The son of a Latvian farm labourer Fabriciuss graduated from a *Gymnasium* in 1894. He joined the revolutionary movement in 1891; from 1904 to 1907 he served a sentence of hard labour and later lived in exile. He joined the army in 1916 and served in World War I as a senior non-commissioned officer in the 1st Latvian Rifle Regiment. In 1918 he distinguished himself fighting against the German interventionists and the detachments of S. N. Bulak-Balakhovich.

In late 1918 and early 1919, Fabriciuss served as commissar of the 2nd and 10th Rifle divisions during the liberation of Latvia. In August 1919, as commander of a detachment, he helped defend the Soviet rear against attack by the cavalry of K. K. Mamontov.* In October 1919, as commander of the 48th Brigade of the 16th Rifle Division, he helped rout the troops of General A. I. Denikin.† He also fought in the Polish-Soviet War of 1920 and took part in the suppression of the Kronstadt Anti-Soviet Rebellion of 1921.

After the war Fabriciuss commanded a division and a corps and in 1928 became assistant commander of the Caucasus Army. He died in an air crash in 1929. Fabriciuss was awarded four Orders of the Red Banner.[13]

It seems strangely ironic, or weird even, to have had 50 years of Soviet occupation and keep a statue to a soldier who, even though he was local, was in the Red Army. Or perhaps there's a simpler explanation: he's still embraced precisely because he's local, and did well. By this point in my journey I'm getting used to the shrug of the shoulders that comes with such seeming contradictions. That's Latvia, I guess.

I say goodbye to Artūrs and Kristine and return to my hotel, stamping off the snow outside and heading up to my room. I have a couple of stories from Ventspils that have been given to me by Māra Zirnīte at the National Oral History Archive in Riga.

One is that of Valentina Lasmane, a key member of the secret network smuggling refugees from Courland to Sweden. Her father was Latvian, a Red Rifleman and later a civil servant. Her mother was Ukrainian – she was born in Ukraine when her father was working there. She was introduced to the resistance leader Konstantīns Čakste and involved in the underground movement by her university friend Leonīds Siliņš. She was in this network during the first Soviet period and also during the German occupation.

While working as a teacher in the east, she ran errands for the Resistance, the LCC, the Latvian Central Council. The boys in her class stole ammunition and rifles from German trains coming through her local station at Pļaviņas and hid them in caves around the banks of the Daugava for *Kurelieši* partisans nearby to collect. The girls baked bread which was left alongside. In 1944 she was working as a cleaner in

---

* The crack Cossack cavalry fighting for the White Russians in the Civil War.
† The decisive defeat of the White Russian Army.

a Legionnaires' hospital. When the wounded were told they were to be evacuated to Germany many deserted. Lasmane got them civilian clothes.

Then the manager of the Central Council in Courland asked her to come to Ventspils and help others. Her interviews give a vivid insight into conditions in the final days of Nazi-occupied Latvia.

> Ventspils was full of refugees. There was not enough food or accommodation. If you didn't have an address in Ventspils and you got caught you were locked in a camp and sent off to Germany.
>
> We had our own photographer who made passport photos. We had Krastiņš, a graphic artist from the Academy of Arts, who could make anything. He could draw all the German birds [pictured in the passport].
>
> But nothing would have been possible if it hadn't been the end of the war when the German military was corrupt. You could get anything in exchange for butter and gold.
>
> My task was to clarify the situation for each refugee. For example it is fairly easy with a sick child. A Legionnaire: he has to get away. I had to group them before a boat came and you never knew how many places there would be in the boat – maybe 100, maybe 55. Usually it didn't work out as you planned.
>
> Everything happened in the dark. We gave tickets to those who were OK to go. But then along come so-called 'outsiders' who have to wait. Everybody has a password. Small boats approach the big boat with two people who ask for a password. What do you do if somebody doesn't know the password and climbs in anyway. Will you push him away in the dark?
>
> One day we received a message which I de-coded.* When it was decoded it seemed absurd. 'Bring to Sweden a *žīds*.†
>
> I decoded it a second time but it was the same. 'Bring a Jew'.
>
> [In his book Leonīds Siliņš also mentions the message: 'It is important that you bring some Yids too'.]
>
> Then I remembered that I knew of one Yiddish woman. She had escaped and lived in Dundaga near to Olita [a girl in their group].

Valentina decided to go and get her. She got a car and fuel and her artist made a fake travel permit for the trip.

> We had a good idea. I became a secretary for an SS unit and the driver would be Frišenfeld. He borrowed an SS uniform with a cap. The only problem was that his German was very poor and there were check-points where questions might be asked. But that is why I was there. They made me up like an SS girl with make-up and clothes according to the fashions German girls wore. All the

---

*   From the people in Sweden sending the boats.
†   Pronounced 'jeeds', an old Latvian term for a Jew, similar to the slang derogatory term in English 'yids'.

checkpoints were Waffen checkpoints and the SS were higher. Proper SS would not talk to some Waffen checkpoints.

So we go. Friŝs is driving and I am smiling at them. It was around 12 when we arrived in Dundaga. I asked Olita where the Yiddish woman was?

She didn't know. No more Yid. All the forest have been cleared by the Germans combing them not for Yids but for partisans. With dogs.

I say to Olita: 'Show me where you took the food for them'.

She agrees, so we go there and we are walking through the forest chatting and we've nearly reached the next hamlet when I see something moving in the forest. It's not an animal, but a human. So I run down the slope and as I get closer I see a Yid – yes indeed! It's a Yid!

I literarily jump on him and say in Russian: 'You're coming with me! You're coming to Sweden with me!'

He tried to get away but I held him like you'd hold a diamond. I stunned him by speaking Russian – he told me that later. He knew Russian but was completely stunned when suddenly in a forest a women in trousers shouts at him in Russian something about Sweden. We went together to the coast to wait for a boat.

Why a Yid? We suspected – and later found out it was true – that there was some money from America for the evacuation of refugees, specifically Jewish refugees. If they took a Jew over, the benefactors might send more money.[14]

She and the Jewish man went on a boat which was designed for 45 people but actually carried 167. She didn't want to go to Sweden but a message came saying that she might be arrested. That could put the entire organisation at risk. So she went to Sweden with her sister and later her brother joined them and some time after that their mother and father too.

The Jewish man stayed in Stockholm too and invited her many years later to his 80th birthday party where he announced her to everyone and said: 'Here sits my guardian angel'.*

The second story is shorter and relates the memories of the day of capitulation of Lydia Doronina from Pāvilosta.

The 9th of May [the capitulation] was a terrible day in my life. Because we were in Kurzeme, in that siege encirclement all the time. The Kurzeme Pocket – that's what we called it.

While our Legionnaires were defending the front and there was hope for Latvian independence, the rest could escape. But not everybody managed it. We were waiting for the last boat, and it did not come. We were all arrested.

Interviewer: Where were you waiting for that boat? In Liepāja?

---

*   Valentina Lasmane later edited a book of 130 eyewitness stories from Latvian refugees who went to Gotland and Sweden called 'Over the sea 1944/45' which was published in Sweden in 1990.

Lydia: We lived at the seaside. Pāvilosta and Jūrkalne – they're near the sea.

My father's house was only one kilometre from the sea. My father had connections with the men ferrying people across. The guard and border guards were all bribed with my father's pigs and something else, I don't know … (she laughs).

Then the Army men came, spread in a chain, combing all the forests, all the fields, everything. They were looking for men. All the men were taken to filtration, as it was called. My father was in filtration for several months. (She sighs). It is terrible to remember it. In our house we had a telephone, a radio, that we had buried in the cowshed under dung. Everything was hidden.

Some stuff – clothes, some other things – were hidden in the firewood shed, in firewood piles. My cousin's wife had hidden her baby's clothes and diapers and suitcase in the firewood. But they came and searched and destroyed everything.

They took everything, all the belongings they could find. From my handbag they took a watch, a nice little watch from the old times given to me by my grandmother that could be worn around your neck.

And that Latvian who lived with us as a refugee, that Red Army man's wife who knew them, she came forward and said: 'My husband is in the Red Army. Don't touch these people. They have been very good to us'.

There were Russian prisoners [that lived with us]. They took them away. They considered them to be criminals: they were arrested. Stalin did not permit anyone to surrender. Those who were captured by Germans? They all were criminals.

And they could torture their own men?

That is unspeakable. It's not possible to comprehend'.[15]

Notes

1   Lumans, pp.364-365.
2   Lumans, pp.365-366.
3   E. Andersons, L. Silins, *Latvija un Rietumi [Latvia and the West – The Latvian Central Council: Kurland after the Capitulation]* p.511.
4   Information boards Pāvilosta.
5   Meler, pp.261-264.
6   Lydia Doronina interview, Oral history archive, University of Riga, courtesy of Māra Zirnīte.
7   Boris Mangolds, National Oral History Museum interview; courtesy of Māra Zirnīte.
8   Pēteris Jansons, National Oral History Museum interview; courtesy of Māra Zirnīte.
9   Information boards Jūrkalne.
10 Occupation Museum website at http://www.occupation.lv/#!/en/eksponats/05VII.2/latvian-legionnaires-being-handed-back-to-the-ussr-by-sweden (accessed 2 Feb 2016) and Gilmour, J. *Sweden, the Swastika and Stalin.*
11 Interview with author, January 2015.
12 Rubiks, *Patiesiba ir dziva: dokumenti liecina* p.40 [translated by Daiga Kamerade].
13 N. D. Kondrat'ev, Jan Fabriciuss – *The Great Soviet Encyclopedia, 3rd Edition* (1970-1979).
14 Valentina Lasmane, National Oral History Museum interview, courtesy of Māra Zirnīte.
15 Lydia Doronina, National Oral History Museum interview, courtesy of Māra Zirnīte.

17

The SS State in Dundaga

The Nazi hold on Europe had given them access to millions of men who could fight for them, but they needed training. Courland offered space away from the front lines and the reach of Allied bombers to train replacements. Tank crews especially were needed to tackle the seemingly inexhaustible lines of Soviet armour.

Nazi leaders identified the flat fields of northern Courland as an ideal training ground once the forests around the village of Dundaga were cleared. Jewish prisoners from the Kaiserwald concentration camp in Riga could be sent there to do that. The tank training camp was just the first phase of a bigger plan to create a new World Order, an SS state to breed the next generation of the Aryan master race. Courland was just the place – and the Jews in the Riga ghetto could build it.

Through autumn 1943 and early 1944 Jews were sent from Kaiserwald to Dundaga and put to work building a large training centre at *Seelager Dondagen* [Sea Camp Dundaga] linked to Ventspils and Mazirbe by rail, and enlarging a camp at the Suzi estate [*Suschenhof*] on Kisezers Lake. The commandants at Dundaga – Max Kröschel and Gustav ['Iron Gustav'] Sorge – were merciless – outright sadists. The Jews in Riga soon referred to this camp as a killing centre.[1]

One of those Jews was Margers Vestermanis, born in Riga in 1925, aged 16 during the mass murders at Rumbula and Bikernieki. He was one of a few thousand Jewish survivors held in Kaiserwald in Riga's Mežaparks district and transferred to Dundaga as forced labourers.

> In *Seelager Dondagen* the visions of a new SS Order were realised to a considerable extent. The isolated, wooded area mostly surrounded by the ocean was an ideal terrain for military and ideological training of an SS offspring with a nameless supply of prisoners as slaves. *Seelager Dondagen* [Sea Camp Dundaga] was probably the only colonization experiment [of] Himmler in the temporarily occupied Soviet territories, and was halfway realized. It shows what the objective of the Nazis 'New Order in Europe' would [be] like in practice'.[2]

By 1944 there were SS units stationed all over northern Courland. Among the specialist units were construction battalions, geological teams, medical units, transport specialists, site management, tank repair shops and military police. There were bases in Mazirbe, Stende, Roja, Talsi, Dundaga Castle, Jaundundaga and Popervāle. The population was cleared from three villages – Dundaga, Ārlava and Lubezere – to create *Seelager Dondagen*.[3]

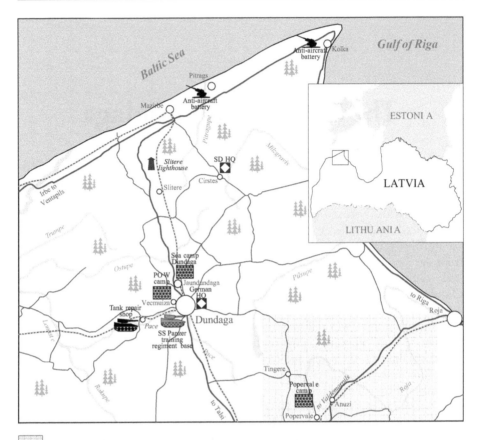

Area of operations of Vestermanis partisan group

Narrow gauge railway

Map 5 Northern Kurzeme During Wartime.

The work would be carried out by Jewish prisoners from Latvia, Lithuania, Czechoslovakia, Hungary and Poland and several thousand Hungarian Jewish women from Auschwitz. Sources vary as to whether it was 2,000 or 5,000. There were also Dutch volunteer workers and skilled workers from other countries including Czechoslovakia and France.[4]

Conditions were appalling. More than 1,000 civilians, including 500 women and 100 children, lived in cloth tents, sleeping on straw, 18 to 20 per tent. Wood could be burned in a small metal pipe to generate a little heat. Their heads were shaved and they were given striped clothes to wear, surviving on a piece of bread in the morning and watery soup in the evening.

They set about building a training camp for the Wehrmacht in the middle of a forest, paving roads, chopping down trees and constructing buildings and installations. The mortality rate at Dundaga was particularly high: in winter 1944 between

10 and 20 prisoners died every day. 'The Holy One blessed be for He takes us in *minyanim*' [a quorum of 10 for prayer] was a common saying among the Dundaga labourers.[5]

In May 1944 several thousand Hungarian Jewish women arrived at the camp from Riga, brought in on open cattle cars. Their work included uprooting and dragging tree stumps from the forest with horse-drawn equipment. When horses were not available, four women took their place. Not surprisingly, many died.[6]

More prisoners arrived each day to replace those who died. To dispose of the corpses camp commandant Kröschel had them dropped into the sea through the ice. But when the ice started to melt in the spring the corpses floated to the surface.

Kröschel feared the corpses might be carried across the Baltic Sea and end up in the hands of the Swedish Red Cross, leading to international protests and reports in the newspapers. So he ordered his prisoners to wade up to their necks in ice-cold water to fish the dead bodies out of the sea and then burn them on the beach. Many died of pneumonia as a result.[7]

The Popervāle camp was set up in an area of dense forest and fields. Prisoners arriving there found no shelter provided for them. They had to sleep in the open and many died as a result.

The Popervāle prisoners were used to clear forests for rifle and tank firing ranges, roads, bunkers and barracks. Margers Vestermanis was one of these prisoners. Others, like Avraham Shpungin and Matis Frost, worked in the troop supply warehouse in Dundaga, loading and unloading supplies. Tipped off that the camp was being moved they decided to escape and chose the method 'in plain sight': they hid in a cowshed right under the noses of their German guards for 10 months until the war ended, fed by locals. The area of Dundaga where this happened is almost exactly as it was 70 years ago and the original buildings are still there.'[8]

Shpungin's experiences at Dundaga are appalling to read. He describes Kröschel as an elderly, grey-haired, cruel veteran of several concentration camps including Sachsenhausen and Buchenwald: 'a true believer in the destiny of the German Reich [who] hated Jews even more than he hated the Russians'. This hatred manifested itself in cruel and sadistic punishments, one of which involved having a prisoner beaten senseless for begging some extra food from villagers, then tying him to a fence, pouring ice-cold water over him and leaving him to freeze to death.[9]

The rapid advance of the Soviets into Latvia in summer 1944 meant the defence of the Reich had to take priority over other plans, and the SS state was abandoned. When the Red Army reached Tukums towards the end of July the order was given for the camps at Dundaga and Popervāle to be cleared. The prisoners were to be marched to the coast. Some were shipped to Gdansk and then to the Stutthof concentration camp. Others ended up in Liepāja prison and were killed there 'as a result of military operations'.[10]

The prisoners from Popervāle were organised into a column and marched away as the Russians approached. Margers Vestermanis made a break for freedom when

* See Map 6: Dundaga in wartime and now (p.173).

he knew he couldn't continue and was one of the few prisoners to survive to see the end of the war. He fought as a Soviet partisan in the forests and later founded the Riga Jewish Museum, devoting the rest of his life to documenting the Holocaust in Latvia. He speaks Latvian, Russian, German, Yiddish and several other languages but not English, so he declined my request for an interview and sent me instead some responses that were already translated.

> Surviving the Holocaust was a mere accident. I was young, physically strong and the most important, I had the will to resist. After several unsuccessful attempts to escape an accident helped me. Due to the approach of the Red Army at the end of July in 1944 the concentration camp Dundaga was moved in a strong pace of 'death march' to ports in Liepāja and Ventspils.
>
> Many people died on the way but when our path ran through the forests near Ugāle, many people made a last effort to jump the ditches at the sides of the road and rushed to the forest. I was one of them.
>
> I managed to join the anti-fascist partisan troop of Latvians who did not want to join the SS Legion. In our troop, there were also Soviet prisoners who escaped from German camps and even one German deserter, Luftwaffe *Oberfeldwebel*[*] Egon Klinke, who became my friend.
>
> During this time the German Army put a lot of effort into going through forests searching for those who escaped, and on the 26th of December our troop was destroyed. My German friend Egon and I were among the few people that managed to escape but after five days – on New Year's Eve – I lost my friend too. I wandered around the forest until 9 May 1945 as an 'armed partisan loner'. Without help from Latvian people I could not have survived in the forest during that time.[11]

A contingent of 830 Dutch civilian workers were caught in the final days of the camps in Latvia, part of a labour contract signed between the SS and the Dutch Nazi Party. Sent to Latvia to work in the camps in Dundaga, Popervāle, Vaiņode, Jelgava and Riga, they were unhappy at being treated like slaves by the SS despite wearing *Organisation Todt* uniforms.[†] Around 300 Dutch managed to get a boat out of Liepāja in January 1945. The rest were left behind to become prisoners of the Soviets.[12]

Ārlava consists of its Lutheran Church, a few farms, a lot of forest – and not much else. I am parked in front of the church looking at, more or less, where the Popervāle camp was. The church is on a slight rise so I can see quite a long way: fields, forest, farm. Fields, farm, forest. I slip the car into gear and head back along the forest track that brought me here. Once onto the bigger roads I see how the Jewish prisoners

---

[*]   Air Force sergeant.

[†]   The Nazi civil and military engineering labour organisation which built, using forced labour and PoWs, the Atlantic Wall, the Autobahn network and the V1 and V2 launch sites in northern France, Belgium and the Netherlands.

might have escaped from their guards. By leaping a drainage ditch along the edge of the road a man might make the cover of the treeline and from there plunge deeper into the forest. In a concerted break left and right there might have been too many escapees for the guards. Or maybe, as they were in a rush to get away from the advancing Red Army, the German guards may not have lingered too long to search for them.

Dundaga is another ten minutes by car north of Popervāle. The village is dominated by, and built around, its castle. Dating back to the 13th century it's the largest and oldest castle in northern Courland. In the war it was a hospital and a headquarters for the SS. Around it stands a Lutheran Church dating from 1766, some former stables for the estate which were converted into a syrup factory, and a brewery dating from 1902 but now used as a dairy.

A group of elderly ladies is waiting for me outside the castle's thick oak door. After introductions we go inside and sit down around a table in the tourist information office. The office manager Ālanda, the daughter of one of the ladies, has come along to translate. The first to speak, Jautrite Freimane, was a schoolteacher here. She has put many years of research into the fate of Dundaga's Jews.

> When the Germans first came to Dundaga in July 1941 all the Jews were killed. Then in Spring 1943 the SS in Berlin started the plan for the camps at Dundaga and Popervāle to build roads and barracks for the tank training area. There were Jews from all of central Europe here: Czechoslovakia, Hungary, Austria, Lithuania; as well as from Latvia. There were 14,000 Jews in Jaundundaga, in three camps.[13]

She marks crosses on my map.

> Here, here and here to the east – here was one to the west. These are all camps – barracks style camps. The buildings were put up very quickly in small locations, made of thin wood; very simple buildings.
> This is the Jaundundaga camp to the north. Popervāle: 7kms from Dundaga to the southeast where the Jews were employed for building a camp, *Seelager Dondagen* ... and a PoW camp in the Vecmuiza district to the west. There was a tank repair depot close to the village, to the southwest, and a big security police depot about 10kms north.*[14]

I move across my tourist map of the Dundaga region circling the camps that she mentions. As we fill in the camps and depots the landscape gradually becomes crowded. We add searchlights, flak batteries and gun positions to the coastal area, plus railway depots, reserve areas, soldiers, equipment and vehicles to the picture, plus tens of thousands of refugees and armed partisans of all persuasions lurking in the forests. Suddenly northern Courland looks like a war zone.

---

*   Around Cirstes.

One of the ladies, Aina Pūliņa, starts to tell her story. In the summer of 1944 she was 14. Now she is 85.

> I remember the day when the Jews were taken to Ventspils. I lived in Laukmuiža at the time.* I saw a column of Jews that was 200 metres long. They were very tired and walked very slowly, wearing striped clothes with German guards with dogs. I ran and told my mother that the Jewish people were being taken away. My mother gave me bread to take to them. They took this bread and the soldiers didn't say anything. Later we heard that around Ugāle the soldiers allowed some people to escape, to run into the forest.
>
> In real life there had been good relations between Jewish people and the local inhabitants. Our neighbours were Jewish, with a young family – five children: Berta, Jossells, Jutka, Dora, Olga. They disappeared one day.
>
> In the very centre of Dundaga there were some Jewish shops – very different shops. Local inhabitants were shocked that they weren't here any more. 'What happened? Why aren't they here any more?' The first reaction was shock, then misunderstanding. Eventually, step-by-step, they pieced it together.[15]

I ask Aina if she knew what was happening to the Jewish population.

'People knew they were prisoners under German rule. Even the children knew that'.

'Did you know they were being killed?'

> No. Different stories went around. We heard that people were killed in the camp. As in life … people mentioned things, said things. In 1944 the Russian Army was coming back. Society here was in chaos. No-one knew what was going on or what will happen. Everyday life had to go on. There were farms, people had to live, had to work. There were things that needed doing.
>
> During the *Kurzeme Katls* [Courland Pocket period] there were very many Germans and lots of people from other places who came here – refugees from Vidzeme and Latgale. The Russian front was coming. There were very many soldiers and refugees. The density of people here was very high. There were a lot of soldiers, civilians, refugees. There was equipment everywhere.
>
> Near our house there were tanks dug in, assault guns, trucks, horses. In the trucks there was food, supplies, equipment – everything that was needed for the Army. I liked horses a lot and they were nice… big Dutch horses with short tails. Every square metre was full of people and equipment.

As we talk Aina says the overriding feeling among Latvians was to get away. No-one wanted a second Soviet occupation: the memories of the *Baigais Gads* were too vivid.

'That was a terrible experience,' she says. 'No-one wanted that again'.

---

*   A village to the south of Dundaga.

Aina and her family got a boat out of Ventspils in October 1944, the *MS Gotland*, later bombed and sunk with thousands of casualties. She was lucky. Russian bombers couldn't find the ship in the storm and the marker flares they dropped blew out. Her family moved from Dortmund to Dresden just as it was bombed, then to Prague and Ukraine. When the war ended they were on the wrong side of the partition of Europe and were returned to Soviet Latvia.

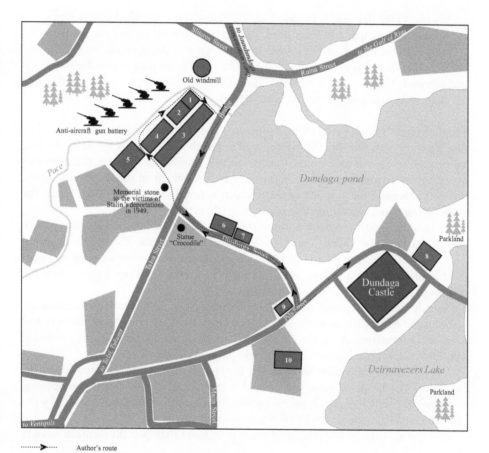

······>···· Author's route

Key:
1. Prisoners' quarters (Guards patrolled around warehouse area – buildings 1-4)
2. Wartime warehouse
3. Main troop supply depot and loading dock
4. Stables where Frost and Shpungin hid
5. Living quarters for German guards and the two families that used the stables opposite
6. Dundaga dairy
7. Living quarters for German officers
8. Bath house
9. Aptieka (chemist) in former dwelling house
10. Platform for anti-aircraft gun.

Map 6 Dundaga in Wartime and Now.

I show everyone a map of Dundaga that I have brought with me. It was drawn by Jewish survivor Avraham Shpungin and shows where he and Matis Frost hid for ten months. The area is on the other side of the lake to the castle, then a troop supply depot. Using the lake and river as landmarks we start to get a feel for how things were in 1944. Slowly – incredibly – it starts to make sense.

We walk around the lake and down a slope to the red brick house where the two men hid out for ten months. They were quite literally under the noses of the Germans. There were soldiers living next door to them, above them and opposite them. Jautrite points at the doors on the ground floor.

> In the 1930s that was a blacksmiths. Up there, above the blacksmiths was a haybarn. Shpungin and Frost lived there at the top window, and the German soldiers were next door. They lived there for ten months, until the end of the war. The Germans never realised. There were six or seven Jews in Dundaga who survived. They stayed until 1949. When the deportations happened they didn't want to be sent away so they went to Israel.[16]

Today there is a family living there. Around the back of the buildings we find the river that Shpungin ran across to lay a decoy trail to put the guard dogs off – as marked on his map. We follow it to the old ruined windmill, now home to an enormous stork's nest. In the wartime four anti-aircraft guns were positioned on the flat ground above the river alongside the junction of the roads to Ventspils and Vidale. Apart from the guns having gone, everything else is as it was 70 years ago.

We head back past the dairy and towards the 120 year-old *aptieka* [chemist] in an area called Doctors' Valley. There is a memorial stone for the 357 people deported from the Talsi region to Siberia in 1949. It's a sculpture of a person sleeping in a bed, their head resting on a pillow, inscribed with the message: 'When I go to sleep my dreams of my country will be my pillow'.

Directly across the road is a statue of a crocodile, a memorial for Dundaga Legionnaire Arvīds Blūmentāls. He escaped from Latvia at the end of the war and went to Queensland, Australia in 1951. There he hunted crocodiles, re-inventing himself as 'Harry the Hunter' and becoming a well-known character.

When hunting crocodiles was banned Blūmentāls started prospecting for opals. He set up a shop at his mine and turned it into a tourist attraction. The opening scenes of the film *Crocodile Dundee* are set in Dundaga: the statue was donated by the Latvian consulate in Chicago in 1995 to commemorate him.[17]

The crocodile statue is symbolic of something more than just Blūmentāls, Ālanda says.

> We know just a few stories from the war in Dundaga. One of those is the story of the Crocodile Hunter. There were three brothers. One died in the war, one went to Siberia and one went to the war in the Legion aged 17. After the war he travelled to Australia and became the Crocodile Hunter [Crocodile Dundee].
>
> All Kurzeme history is in this symbol of a crocodile. Our soldiers were fighting in the Kurzeme Cauldron [Courland Pocket]. The idea goes deeper than

just the crocodile hunter. He is the symbol but his fate in his life also represents the way thousands of other lives were destroyed in the wartime – and after the wartime – by the Soviet system.[18]

Standing in front of this stone crocodile, just a hundred metres from the hayloft where two men hid themselves from certain death, I feel a sense of the gulf between how Latvians may have wanted to live their lives and how they were forced to. From this green countryside which Blūmentāls and his brothers called home the three were scattered to the winds. How he must have reflected on his fate compared to that of his two brothers.

Back at the castle, we say goodbye to Jautrite but Aina and Ālanda offer to show me where the Jewish camp was at Jaundundaga. We drive for a few minutes north of the town then pull up alongside a large field. There is a memorial stone by the side of the road: low, dark and easily missed in the twilight.

When the war ended, this field was excavated to reveal a pit filled with the bodies of 1,200 Jews, brought from all over Europe to be used, abused and then dumped in this lonely place. It was Jautrite who went through the archives of the Soviet Commission on Fascist Activities to discover where the bodies were and arranged for the marker stone to be placed there.[*19]

Aina wants to show me something else before it gets too dark and cold. The winter fields have a dusting of snow and a certain stiffness from the frost.

I follow Ālanda's car along the sand roads, my winter tyres crunching the snow. Occasionally a house pokes out from the treeline of the forest. To left and right fields are trimmed with dark green pine forests. One or two trees line the road. Every now and then there is a stork's nest on a telegraph pole, empty for the winter. This is truly the Latvian countryside.

We jump down into the field and walk across frosted grass. As we reach the trees at the edge of the forest there is a simple white wooden cross amid the pines with a sign. It reads:

> The field is a burial ground for wounded soldiers from the castle's hospital from different countries. Many of them died and were brought here. All those who served in the German Army.

There is another small sign, made from thin steel welded to a metal pole.

---

*   Latvia has set up a Presidential Commission of historians to research what happened in its territory during the Holocaust. It notes: 'More than 70,000 Latvian Jews and more than 20,000 Jews brought to Latvia from 1941 to 1944 from other occupied countries of Europe (Austria, the annexed parts of Czechoslovakia, Hungary, Lithuania) and Germany proper were killed. The total annihilation of Jews in Nazi-occupied Latvia was the worst crime committed in Latvian territory in the twentieth century. It stands out because of the indescribable sadism with which it was committed and the huge number of victims'. (Latvian Presidential website, Commission of Historians report: www.president.lv)

Here lie German and Latvian soldiers who died in the years 1944-45.

I turn and look back on the field we have just walked across. The grey snow-filled clouds are tinged with pink and the sky streaked with yellows and whites as the sun sets, turning the tufts of grass reddish-brown in this field where mortally wounded German and Latvian men breathed their last. It's not an official graveyard – it's just a field outside Jaundundaga with a wooden cross marking it. The grass crunches under our feet as we walk back. I wonder why there's no memorial apart from the cross and the sign. Aina has a suggestion.

> Maybe in all the Soviet time this was a bad place – they are German soldiers – and no-one was taking care of it. Since independence there have been a lot of things to do and it seems no-one has found it their mission to do something to get a place like this in order, or to tell society more about it, to concentrate attention on it.

We walk back to the car and I say goodbye to Aina. She shakes my hand and thanks me for coming.

> Mine is a good story compared to others. I'm not sorry that I didn't manage to escape to the west. I was thinking about my grandfather [who lived here] and his woodworking business. First the First World War came, then the Second World War, then the Soviet time. All his dreams were destroyed.
>   Maybe they would have escaped to the west and spent all their lives having a successful business but dreaming of their homeland. Many Latvians in the west are still dreaming and hoping that their children and grandchildren will return to Latvia. And some are coming back – we read that in the newspapers. Very few … but still they are coming.[20]

I drive back to Talsi and stop at a café to eat. My head is full of thoughts about what I have just seen. The more time I spend in Latvia the more I understand that Latvian people don't always say what they mean. The crocodile is like a secret symbol that many wouldn't understand. The crocodile is a fate-line. It's about everything involved in the Courland Pocket, then and now: it's about destiny, living, dying, families being separated. It represents America, Australia, Siberia… the graveyards, the brothers' cemeteries, the vast cemetery at Lestene with Arte Dumpe's statue of a grieving mother – and it's about a Latvian boy who survived, escaped to Australia and hunted crocodiles.

Notes

1 Angrick, Klein, Brandon The 'Final Solution' in Riga, *Exploitation and Annihilation, 1941-1944*, p.388.
2 M. Vestermanis article in Lexikon der Wehrmacht, The SS Seelager Dondagen.
3 Lexikon Der Wehrmacht webpages at http://www.lexikon-der-wehrmacht.de.
4 Ibid.
5 D. Blatman, *The Death Marches: The Final Phase of Nazi Genocide*, p.61.
6 Ibid.
7 B. Press, *The Murder of the Jews in Latvia: 1941-1945*, pp.191-192.
8 G. Schneider, *The Unfinished Road: Jewish Survivors of Latvia Look Back* Chapter 12, 'The Terrors of Dundaga' pp.151-163.
9 Shpungin, *The Terrors of Dundaga* p.152 in Schneider.
10 Angrick, Klein, Brandon, p.412.
11 Vestermanis, Interview in English sent to author, 2014.
12 JewishGen.org: 'Report on an inspection trip', by B.J. Hoekstra.
13 Jautrite Freimane, interview with author.
14 Jautrite Freimane, interview with author.
15 Aina Pūliņa, interview with author.
16 Jautrite Freimane, location visit.
17 Dundaga, tourist information website.
18 Ālanda Pūliņa, interview with author.
19 Ālanda Pūliņa, interview.
20 Aina Pūliņa, interview with author.

18

A Beautiful Beach where the Tanks Reached the Sea

The Christmas Battles had drained the German and Latvian defenders. They had withstood unimaginable artillery shelling, almost constant air attacks, wave after wave of tank assaults and overwhelming numbers of Red Army soldiers throwing themselves at their positions. It was vicious and exhausting hand-to-hand combat in sub-zero temperatures, with front line troops spending many hours knee-deep in trenches full of icy water waiting for the next attack.

A headcount of German men and machines was taken: 400,000 men, broken down into 375,000 soldiers, 20,000 Luftwaffe, 12,000 *Waffen-SS* and police, 10,000 civilians and *Hiwis* [labourers]. There were also 10,000 PoWs.[1]

The fourth battle would be shorter, even more intense and take a staggering toll on the Red Army's reserves of men.

Almost the entire southwestern corner of Latvia erupted when Soviet artillery opened up on 23rd January. The attack was aimed at three places: southeast of Liepāja at Priekule – the plug in the bottleneck into the vital port city, still keeping supplies flowing in and evacuees out; south of the road and railway junctions at Saldus which kept supplies and reinforcements moving along the front, and northwest of Dobele, defending the southeastern flank of the Courland Pocket and protecting the head-quarters at Kuldīga, the reserves at Dundaga and the port at Ventspils. Three separate Soviet army groups attacked along a front line roughly corresponding to the area between the Lithuanian border and the A9 Liepāja to Riga highway, from Priekule as far east as Dobele.

The Red Army hurled huge numbers of men at the German and Latvian trenches, sustaining almost inconceivable casualties for the territory gained. One Wehrmacht report estimated that 45,000 Soviet soldiers were lost and 541 tanks destroyed in ten days of fighting. Finally on February 5th the fighting died down.[2]

When a consignment of snow camouflage coveralls, felt boots and fur hats was unloaded at Liepāja's docks in February 1945, the German and Latvian soldiers knew there was now no way out.[3]

Fresh supplies reached the Red Army front line troops too. At Vaiņode 200 American Sherman tanks were unloaded, sent as part of the Lend-Lease arrange-ments. Artillery regiments and mortar brigades moved up to train their guns on the defenders of Liepāja and Saldus, aiming to split the frozen swamps of the front line and strike for Ventspils.

178

Gottlieb Bidermann returned from leave following the fourth battle of Courland between 24 January and 3 February 1945 to find his unit, the 438th Grenadier Regiment, in positions south of Liepāja.

> Positioned in a marshy, low-lying area the soldiers had constructed a log palisade with a floor of sand that was somewhat higher than the surrounding terrain. Warm bunkers had been constructed up to the very front line, and those who had no iron stove had fabricated chimneys and fireplaces of stone and clay.
>
> There remained an abundance of firewood. The troops preferred to burn split birch as it created little smoke to betray their location. When one entered the bunkers from the cold and damp air outside it was as though one had stepped into an oven. The troops protested loudly when the bunker door or shelter-quarter hanging over the entrance was left open to the cold air outside. The loud, vociferous protests usually implied that the soldiers would 'rather stink than freeze'.[4]

One of the greatest German air aces of the Courland Pocket who died at this time was Otto Kittel, squadron commander of the JG-54 'Green Hearts' fighter wing. Initially a wingman covering other squadron 'aces' he built a fearsome reputation as JG-54 fought across the Eastern Front, especially at Kursk. He picked up decoration after decoration as his tally rose first above 100 kills, then 150, then in early September 1944 to 200. In epic engagements in October 1944, that tally rose to 250, earning him promotion to *Oberleutnant*.

On 14th February 1945, the day after recording his 267th victory, his Focke-Wulf 190 flew into a group of eight Ilyushin Il-2 ground attack planes and was shot down in flames.[5]

I park once again in Harmonijas Street in Tukums and walk across the cobbles to the museum. The road still looks like a scene from the 1920s. Perhaps it always will. I am shown into the office of the director Agrita Ozola. With her is an elderly couple, Livija and Leonhards Stanga. They will tell a remarkable story of love and resilience in wartime, of determination to fight the Soviets, an assassination attempt against the First Minister of Soviet Latvia, Vilis Lācis, and then years of hard labour as a result in copper mines in Kazakhstan.

Leonhards is a slim man in a dark jacket with a roll-neck cardigan underneath. On his jacket he has badges identifying him as a Legionnaire.

> My family lived in a small house, the third house from the railway station in Tukums. When the Russians came in 1944 I was up at the crossroads on the road between Riga-Jelgava-Tukums-Ventspils, on a farmstead there. We had friends on Riga Street, on the road up from the railway line. When the Russians first entered the town in tanks they met these people. The tanks stopped and the Russians shouted to them. 'How far is it to Berlin?'
>
> Our friends didn't understand so they answered 'Berlin is a long way away'.

Then the Russian tank commander said: 'We'll push the Germans into the sea' – so our friends told them how to get to the coast at Klapkalnciems ... 'Just follow Riga Street all the way to the sea. That's the way to Klapkalnciems'.

The Russian tank commander gunned his engines and set off for the sea, where he filled up bottles with water and sent them to the Kremlin as proof that the Russians had reached the coast, generating the famous story.[6]

Livija met Leonhards at school when he had to re-take a year. He was studying in Riga when war broke out and he was ordered to report to a mobilisation centre on Raina Bulvāris. Then the new recruits were sent to Danzig, training in special battle methods.

I was very good at shooting. I had special training on the [MG42] machine gun known as the 'Bonesaw'.[*]

In 1945 we were sent to Liepāja. From Liepāja we went by train to Ventspils and then to Tukums. Then we were marched off to Lestene, where there had been a battle raging since Christmas.

I set about getting myself the best, most modern weapon. The front line soldiers always had the best equipment. Then an officer spotted me and remembered that I'd been very good on the Bonesaw so I was added to another squad of men as a machine gunner.

It was a good gun. We could fix it into many different positions so that if men from my section were in front of me I could fire over their heads. It was lightweight, too. Many, many Russians attacked. Even though it was my first battle I wasn't afraid. I had a machine gun, and I'd seen what the Soviets did when the KGB cells in Riga were opened in 1942 after the Year of Terror.

The Russian soldiers attacked in one big group, then another. They just ran at me and kept coming. I can't really say what happened. I was just shooting. My unit was in a special pocket like a D around the front of the trench with the Bonesaw at the top of the D, so it had a wide field of fire. We were just shooting and shooting.

After that we moved to a farmstead near Lestene called *Paugibelas*. On the way from Pētertāle to Lestene we noticed that there wasn't a single tree that hadn't been damaged by shellfire. All the trees were smashed.

Around 15-16 February a big battle started, the 5th battle of Kurzeme. There was so much shooting and bombing and smoke it was so dark that it was like day was night. We needed to pull back – we couldn't stay there. Suddenly something exploded close to me and I couldn't feel anything any more. I just lay there.

---

[*]   The MG42 could fire 1,200 rounds per minute. Each belt fired carried 50 or 250 rounds. British troops knew them as 'Spandaus' as the name of the factory which made them was stamped on the base plate.

Because I was one of the machine gun specialists I had a Parabellum pistol.*
A Russian turned me over looking for weapons. The Russian guy found the
Parabellum and as he took it from me I came round: I'd been unconscious and
I'd been wounded in the leg. Some other guys were also found alive.

The Russians started to select those who had SS badges on the collar. They
were shot on the spot. The younger guys had a badge of the sun on their collars
– [identifying them as a Latvian rather than German unit] – and they weren't
shot.†

We were taken prisoner and moved to a bunker behind the lines. Everything
was taken off us, even handkerchiefs. It was very cold because it was winter. I
was interrogated many, many times and we were marched to Jelgava to a soldiers'
camp. After that we were sent to Karelia‡ to work on the Belomor Canal.

I ask Leonhards why he hated the Russians so much. He swallows. 'When the
Russians came [to Tukums] in summer 1944 local Communist sympathisers seized
power and had many local people shot'.

At this point the conversation becomes a little strained and Leonhards begins to
look uncomfortable.

When I got back from Karelia I was sure I needed to fight against the Soviets. In
1944 it was more like I was a young boy and all my friends were fighting – that
wasn't like a conscious decision. But it was in 1946 and 1947 that I decided to
join a group of partisans and take part in the struggle against the Soviets.

I still can't quite put my finger on what drove him on so much to carry on fighting
after surviving first the war and then a period of punishment. He could have just got
on with his life. Why become a partisan? I ask Agrita to ask him again why he hated
the Russians so much.

Leonhards sets his jaw.

I went with my father to Riga and I saw what they did. And I experienced
summer 1944 in Tukums. So I was quite sure that these Russians were really
something …. [he harrumphs].

The KGB cell I saw at the beginning of the war.§ I can't describe it. I didn't
see bodies because they were gone, but I saw the room where they shot people.
It was soundproofed. The insulation material which had been on the walls had
been taken off and you could see the bullet holes in the wall, and there were
special gulleys for the blood to drain away.

---

* A semi-automatic pistol also known as a Luger.
† Latvian Legion Chief of Staff Artūrs Silgailis notes that the Rising Sun badge was issued to
  15th Division soldiers from autumn 1944.
‡ Between Finland and St Petersburg.
§ The execution cell at the Stūra Māja KGB HQ in Riga.

I've been in those KGB cells several times, actually. In 1942 and then again this summer [2014] to see the KGB exhibition. And it wasn't like it used to be at all... it was a very small part of what it was like ... tiny, tiny. It was like a theatre. Nothing like it used to be.

Leonhards became involved in a local resistance group, was recruited by partisans and in October 1947 was involved in an attempt to assassinate Vilis Lācis, the Chairman of the Council of Ministers of Soviet Latvia, as he drove through Riga.

Riga-born Lācis began his working life as a manual labourer who wrote a hugely successful novel *Zvejnieka dēls* (*A Fisherman's Son*), published in 1933. He had links to the Communist underground, rose to prominence through the dockers' union and then worked as a librarian in Riga writing *A Fisherman's Son*, which was re-printed many times and made into a popular film. He became a favourite of Ulmanis during his period of autocratic presidential rule and when Latvia became part of the Soviet Union in 1940 he became extremely powerful.[7]

As Interior Minister and then Chairman of the Supreme Soviet in Communist-era Latvia until 1959, he signed orders for the arrest and deportation of 58,000 people; 14,000 in 1941 and 44,000 people in 1949.[8]

The gang were betrayed by the girlfriend of the ringleader – Krastiņš – and Leonhards was initially sentenced to death. Luckily for him death sentences were suspended at that time and instead he was given 25 years' hard labour in a gulag. He served nine years underground in a copper mine at Džezkazgan in Kazakhstan – and it's here that a leather wallet he produces so gently from his pocket enters the story.

Livija visited Leonhards in the camp – all the way by train from Tukums to Kazakhstan – and gave him a leather wallet as a present. She only had the money for a one-way ticket so Leonhards' friends in the camp clubbed together to buy her a ticket back. When Stalin died the hardline attitude to the Latvian soldiers eased a little and some considered guilty of lesser crimes were released. Among them was Leonhards, who arrived back in Tukums at the beginning of August 1956 after a train journey lasting five days. He married Livija six months later – and still uses the leather wallet she gave to him.

After Leonhards has told his story Agrita and I drive out to the nearby town of Pūre to meet another veteran of these troubled times. On our right we pass the woods at Vecmokas where the Jews of Tukums were shot in 1941 by local fascists.[9]

Agrita's mother lived in a house by the railway line a little further along. She used to tell Agrita how she'd hear the Soviet planes bombing Tukums and their engines roaring as they turned for home over her house.

An elderly man in a windcheater and baseball cap is waiting for us as we arrive outside an apartment block. This is Kārlis Vārna. He greets us both cheerily and jumps in. We drive back down the road for a short while then turn into the forest and along a track, pine trees on either side. This area was the reserve for troops defending the front line east of Saldus. From here it was a journey of 40kms to reach the front at Džūkste, Lestene, Jaunpils or Blīdene. Compared to there, Pūre would have been paradise. Mr Vārna becomes animated.

This was 'Jaunā Berline' [New Berlin], a centre for the defence of Courland. It was called New Berlin by locals because it was so big. There were about 100 bunkers here in the forest. It was like a town, a military camp. They even had a cinema. It wasn't a hospital – the hospitals were in schools and regular medical places. Look, there. There's a bunker. Pull over![10]

A short distance from the track there's a depression in the forest floor about a metre deep, perhaps more, filled with tree branches and moss. Mr Vārna makes digging motions and points out the edges of the bunker as being man-made.

All the forest was full of bunkers; half underground, half on the surface.

They were made from wood and turf was put on top of them for insulation and warmth but also protection. After the war people wanted wood to build things, so they came here and stripped all the wood linings out and made cupboards and chest of drawers. After the war there was a brewery here. When the potatoes were ready and it was time to make spirit we needed wood for heating, so we were sent to this camp to strip the wood out of the bunkers so it could be burned.

Mr Vārna outlines the history of Jaunā Berline as we drive further along the forest track. The camp was built in autumn 1944 after the evacuation from Riga, housing not only soldiers but also civilians from Riga and eastern Latvia, often sharing accommodation.

With a sweep of his arm he points to where the headquarters was situated at the centre of the camp, an area the size of a football field. He laughs at the memory.

There were pictures of this camp in snow in Soviet-time magazines. They were like cabins with doors, dug into this beautiful forest. Jaunā Berline ... like a holiday camp.

As we talk on the path through the forest a woman rides past us on her pushbike. Mr Vārna tells me his war story.

I'm from Smiltene originally, from Vidzeme region. I was born in 1924 so I was mobilised, but you were given three choices. The first was to join the Legion, the second was to join a work organisation, a labour battalion, or the third was to work as a helper with the Luftwaffe. I registered for labour service in the work battalions. In 1943 I was digging turf for heating. I started to work in Latvia but I was sent to Germany, digging turf there.

After a year of labour service all the lads were switched to the Army, trained in Poland and sent to Courland. I was in the Legion for six weeks before I was wounded, near Jaunpils, in my first battle, in between Blīdene and Biksti. I was shot by a Russian sniper in the leg and hand when I was working near the front.

You know how it is… bullets flying everywhere. One went though my leg and hand.

There's a book about us all, an illustrated book by Juris Barkāns. That's the story of what happened to our group in the war.*

When I was better I got five days off. I came to Pūre on the 4th of May 1945 to visit my relatives – so I spent the last few days of the war here. I was here for the capitulation.

There was no official announcement that the war was over. One day the Germans left, the next day the Russians arrived. That was it. Because I was working in the Labour Service I kept my civil passport, and they weren't confiscated, so the next day – 9th May – I went to the office of the experimental gardening centre where they grew seeds and so on and asked if they had any jobs. And the director said: 'What are you doing?'

And I said: 'Well, I've finished working for the Germans. I was in Germany and now I'm back'. And the director said 'OK, then you can start now'.

I was in my German uniform of course with a Corporal's stripe so I changed into my work fatigues and started there and then. I didn't get sent to any camps, I wasn't a prisoner, I wasn't deported to Siberia… nothing. I just carried on working here. I did get to visit filtration camps, but only to work there.

I had six very good friends from school who joined the Legion and fought in Courland. In six weeks two were shot and killed, and four were wounded. In one group of children in Smiltene there were 15 boys and 15 girls. At the end of the war there were three boys left.

The light has now almost gone and the temperature is dropping. I decide it's time to take Mr Vārna home. He continues talking as we drive back along the track out of the woods.

For Latvians Germans were Enemy Number One for years, way back in history. As you know Germans went into East Prussia because of Hitler.† They were paid for everything that was left here, property and houses. But when the Soviet Union occupied Latvia for one year, that changed everyone's view towards them and they became Enemy Number One.

No-one wanted the Soviets to come back. My uncle fought for the Russian Army for four years in the First World War. He was four years at the front, forced to do it. So in a way he was fighting for Latvia's freedom, in this time against the Germans. But in 1941 when the Germans came in he celebrated

---

* This book – *Atminas Par Maniem Dienesta Laikiem [Memories of my Period of Service]* is on sale in most bookshops in Latvia. It's a combination of personal wartime memories of Barkāns and his friends, including Kārlis, illustrated with sketches he made from his time in the front lines and later as a prisoner.

† The agreement in the Molotov-von Ribbentrop Pact for the Baltic Germans to leave Latvia.

– even though he'd fought against them in the First World War. This time the Germans were coming to save Latvians from the Russians.

He turns to me:

> I have a joke. I tell people: 'I wanted to build a new Europe [one of the Nazi aims] but nothing happened. Then I wanted to build a new world, a Soviet world, but … nothing happened!'

He throws his head back and laughs at the irony of what he's lived through: laughing too, no doubt counting his blessings every day, that Fate – in the form of two small pieces of metal passing through his hand and his leg at high speed – dealt him a lucky deck of cards and a long life.

My hotel in Tukums is in Pils iela [Castle Street], the street where the German commandant had his headquarters. At the end of the war, like military musical chairs, the Soviet Army commissariat moved in. Next to it is a small cemetery, the last resting place of 17 Soviet soldiers who died in the battles for the town in 1941, 1944 and 1945. There are also two people remembered here who were killed by national partisans in 1946.

When the Germans were marched out as prisoners, the Red Army moved in to occupy the town. Local people were either turned out of their flats or forced to share them with Soviet soldiers stationed there. This ensured a constant military presence which helped discourage anti-Soviet demonstrations.

Internal security units guarded roads and railways with orders authorising action 'to fight bandits'. Anti-partisan security was tight but even so partisan groups killed 17 security police between 1944 and 1950.

Huge security bases were set up, and several 'New Towns' built to house Soviet officers and their families.

The mass deportation of 1949, like that of 1941, was intended to break partisan and public resistance to Soviet rule and the collectivisation of Latvian agriculture. Today railway tracks at Tukums station, driven vertically into the ground, remember the names of the camps that people from this region were sent to.[11]

In the morning I say my farewells to Tukums. It's eight-thirty on a grey, foggy, drizzly morning. Visibility is down to 300 metres. The whole of the town is shrouded in wet, clinging fog.

I park at the top of a hill opposite the Old Town known as the *Malkalns* or Clay Hill. An old blue and white Gaz lorry is straining slowly up it laden with a cherry-picker ladder, a symbol of the years of Russian occupation and the technology that is so old here.

On this hill stands a dramatic sculpture visible from the town: three figures carved in the shape of an oak tree. The large central figure represents Mother Latvia. The two smaller figures on either side represent two sons separated by the war, fighting on opposite sides against each other and their friends. It's made by Arta Dumpe, the sculptor who carved the figure of Mother Latvia in the Lestene Cemetery. It towers over me, a giant representation of a mother's pain at her sons being torn from her. But what irks me here is that there's nothing to explain to the casual passing visitor what this monument represents – in English, Russian, German or even Latvian.

It's almost as though the process of remembrance in Latvia is a private reflection, one which the outside world either isn't invited to or enabled to share.

When I started on this journey I felt these events weren't remembered enough but I'm wrong about that. There are plenty of reminders – and still plenty of people for whom the memories are only too vivid.

What I'm also beginning to understand is that Latvian remembrance seems to operate on two levels. There's the remembrance of Latvians among their fellow countrymen and families, and their remembrance with outsiders – who might represent a threat to them at a later date. It seems that caution and perhaps also understatement are active elements in the process of remembrance.

For a while I look over the town imagining exactly what Tukums went through in 1944: waves of planes swooping over and bombing the town; explosions and fires breaking out, the shouts and screams, people trying to organise themselves against attack, soldiers running around. Perhaps the tanks parked in camouflage pits on the flat area down by the railway station below me would be a target, with a ring of anti-aircraft guns firing, protecting the vital supplies and reinforcements coming in at the railway station just next to Leonhards Stanga's house.

But I'm here for a reason. I walk to my car and drive back down the hill to Riga Street. This morning I intend to re-trace the route of the Soviet tank unit which reached the sea through Tukums seventy years ago.

The road winds past ponds and lakes. There are fishermen at the edges with their rods. Then a stretch of forest, the protected woodland of the Ķemeri National Park, a deep dark green beautiful mass of pine trees spaced at regular intervals. I pull the car over at one point just to listen to the silence and to look at the paths heading into the trees. I'm reminded of the massacres in the forests: such violence amid such beauty.

The road emerges from the forest through the small village of Klapkalnciems. I cross the coast road to a car park in the woods before the beach. There's a wooden boardwalk over the sandy dunes with picnic tables dotted amid the silver birch trees. These are the wooded dunes of Jūrmala [*Jūrmalas kapas*]. The trees run right down to the white sandy beach.

It's fantastic. The sand, the sea, the Gulf of Riga as flat as a millpond, lapping at the beach. It's so quiet, so beautiful, so peaceful. And there's no-one here. It's a scene of utter tranquillity. Perhaps on this very spot the Russian tanks stopped and the crews ran to fill up their water bottles with seawater to send back to the Kremlin, no doubt shouting: 'The sea. We've done it! We've reached the sea!'

They had closed the net on Riga and sealed the Courland Pocket, if only temporarily.

The war was into its final stages. When the Russians took Riga a few weeks later fate closed in on the Germans and the Latvians fighting alongside them. Now the only ways out were through Liepāja or Ventspils, or by fishing boat to Gotland and then Sweden – and the Baltic was now under threat from the Soviet air force and navy. Alone on this deserted beach, at nine-thirty on a foggy Monday morning, I'm standing at a fleeting moment of history.

Notes

1   Kurowski, p.168.
2   Ibid, p.182.
3   Ibid, p.183.
4   Bidermann, p.276.
5   Kurowski, pp.279-284.
6   Interview with author, August 2014, Tukums, translated by Agrita Ozola.
7   Latvians.com website, quoting "Latvia—Our Dream is Coming True" published by Soviet Booklets, London, England, in December, 1959. http://www.latvians.com/index.php?en/ CFBH/LatviaLācis/LācisA-05-author.ssi.
8   Latvian Ministry of Foreign Affairs website: http://www.mfa.gov.lv/en/policy/informa-tion-on-the-history-of-latvia/briefing-papers-of-the-museum-of-the-occupation-of-latvia/ soviet-mass-deportations-from-latvia.
9   Local story told by Agrita Ozola. More details in *Jewish Latvia*: site to remember p386.
10 Interview with author, August 2014, Tukums, translated by Agrita Ozola.
11 Author visit to Tukums, August 2014.

19

If These Trees Could Tell Stories

At 0700 on 20 February 1945 2,000 artillery guns, mortars and Katyusha rockets opened up all along the Courland front between Džūkste and Priekule. Massive infantry attacks supported by tanks were launched northwest of Dobele and southeast of Liepāja.[1]

Despite an overwhelming superiority of numbers the Soviets made no significant progress against the German and Latvian defences in eight days of continual attacks. For another week Red Army generals ordered their men forward in repeated attacks on the front lines around Saldus. Eventually, in early March, after astronomical casualties and huge losses of armoured vehicles and aircraft, they called off the offensive. The fifth battle of Courland had cost the lives of 70,000 Soviet troops; 19,000 alone in attacks on Liepāja.[2]

Six hundred armoured vehicles and 178 aircraft were destroyed. The only objective they achieved was capturing Džūkste.[3]

Wehrmacht estimates of the Russian losses over the five battles of Courland to that point were 320,000 dead, wounded or captured; 2,388 tanks lost, 695 aircraft, 906 guns and 1,140 machine guns.[4]

The reality of such enormous Red Army losses is apparent as I arrive at Priekule cemetery. It's a vast graveyard on the outskirts of town with nine walls of grey concrete blocks standing three metres high. Each block is inscribed with thousands of names. There are 23,000 dead Soviet soldiers remembered on these walls, casualties of the six Courland battles from October 1944 to May 1945.

At the head of this row of sombre walls is an enormous dark grey statue of a woman holding a baby above her head. The message is clear, of a future delivered from evil. There are some flowers in a small bouquet at its base.

A section of the main boundary wall has a roll of honour for men awarded the title 'Hero of the Soviet Union'. On brown-flecked marble plaques are the names of six men, four of whom died within three days of each other in the fifth battle, attempting to capture the town where they now rest. The stories of their valour are extraordinary.

Vassily Alexandrovic Igonin was drafted into the Red Army in January 1943 aged 18, serving as a machine gunner with the Second Baltic Front. On 21 February 1945 he was fighting near Liepāja when a German Tiger tank broke through on the left flank. Igonin took a hand grenade, threw himself under it and blew the tank up, dying in the process. He was awarded the Hero of the USSR posthumously.

Vladimir Sergeevich Samsonov was 19 when he joined the Red Army artillery in 1941. By February 1945 he was a senior lieutenant in the Second Baltic Front, commanding a battery. On 23 February his squad was taking part in the offensive near Priekule. Samsonov destroyed five German tanks and killed many soldiers and officers but was badly wounded and died soon afterwards. He was awarded the Hero of the USSR posthumously.

Some men commemorated here were already Heroes of the Soviet Union before they were killed in action in Courland.

In September 1943 Mikhail Ivanovich Chebodaev crossed the River Dnepr in a boat and destroyed a machine gun position that was pinning down Red Army forces. He then held off strong German counter-attacks despite being outnumbered. He was killed in action at Liepāja on 25 February 1945.

Feodor Sergeyevich Berestov, a Kazakh, joined the Red Army aged 20 and fought with distinction in Belarus and the Baltic, notably in the battle of West Dvina in June 1944 when he destroyed a machine gun position with grenades then killed eight Germans in hand-to-hand combat. He was promoted to Junior Lieutenant but was killed at Priekule on 27 October 1944. He is buried in the cemetery's Bed of Honour.

Ivan Petrovich Goorov died on 28 November 1944 in one of the battles for Liepāja. Four months earlier at Yamno he had assumed command of an artillery squad when his commanding officer was killed and fought off a German attack.

One man fought with distinction in Latvia but was killed somewhere else. I'm not sure why he is here but his bravery is beyond question. Ivan Yakovlievich Grigoriev was a tractorist from the village of Lopukhovka who joined the Red Army tank forces in June 1941. Three years later he was fighting in Latvia. On 26 August 1944 his tank ambushed 30 German tanks, destroying six and killing many infantry soldiers. Six months later he was killed in action in modern day Slovakia when his tank was hit and caught fire. Grigoriev fought on, destroying more German tanks before he died.[5]

This is undoubted bravery and astonishing sacrifice, though the stories engraved on these plaques are in Russian only. Alongside the sombreness of death on such a vast, de-humanising scale there's a strange air in Priekule, and I can't work out what it is. The location of the cemetery on the edge of the town is almost as though the scale of this loss of life would overshadow it if it were nearer. At the same time, although I have no evidence to support this thought, I get the distinct feeling that this is a place the town wishes was somewhere else.

Two months later I am sitting in the Mayor's office with a local historian and a Latvian man who speaks English but is wary of my intentions.

I have asked museum curators and tourism people to help me find out more about what happened in Priekule during the war. Calls have been made and now I'm back.

A timber specialist called Mārtiņš Cerins has agreed to talk to me, initially at least, to find out my 'angle'. He is a local man who has returned to Priekule after four years in America studying the art of housebuilding using forest timber. Now he builds new wooden homes and restores those that have been neglected for decades. There is plenty of work for him in Latvia, that's for sure.

I have had to overcome a certain amount of suspicion to reach this point as apparently some previous interviews between local people and journalists have ended badly. I'm told of one journalist applying what's been called a 'pro-Soviet spin', after which the people of Priekule vowed never to speak publicly again. So the meeting begins cautiously. After I have explained that I have no angle other than gathering some true stories of what happened here Mārtiņš and historian Lidija Treide agree to tell some stories. I ask Lidija why Priekule was at the epicentre of such gargantuan clashes.

The Russian 51st Army came this way with a plan to go through Priekule and on to Liepāja. Why Priekule? There's a railroad which was a major supply line and a strategic road going through here that all the heavy machines used to get to Saldus from Liepāja. They planned the offensive operation for the evening of February 14th with the support of the 6th Army on the right flank at Vaiņode. The offensive line came from the south and was 4-5kms wide with Priekule at the centre. The reserve was in Purmsāti.* The plan was to attack very quickly and gather reconnaissance on German defences then to react to developments. They got to within 800 metres of Priekule – rifle range – but the problem was they attacked across swamps, so digging in was a problem. The Germans evacuated all the civilians from Priekule and sent them to Aizpute and Kuldīga. Then they fortified the town and built complex defensive lines in depth, to the front and on the flanks.

At this point she picks up a pen and marks out the boundaries of the town to illustrate what she is saying, drawing in the direction of attack and defence.

The approaches to Priekule were swamps, with woods further back to the left and right. The Russians pulled huge numbers of Katyushas into the woods to fire on the town and the German defences. In the town Vaiņode Street was the main defensive line, ready to take the full frontal onslaught.

On February 20th the artillery starts firing and the attack begins. One division lands a left hook on Priekule, avoiding the main front line. Another division goes right in a pincer movement but is repulsed and fails. The centre of the town was so heavily fortified the Soviets decided against a frontal attack and in the evening of the 20th a third division was sent round in a wider right hook to attack round the back and encircle the Germans, but this failed too.

The following night at 9pm the Russians finally managed to surround the Germans and after hours of heavy fighting and shelling the Germans surrendered. A whole division, the 127th, surrendered. They had over-estimated the strength of their own defences and hadn't expected an attack in such numbers. Even though they had taken massive casualties the Soviets were too strong. The fighting was so bloody there is no actual figure for the losses. On the 22nd to the west side of the town the Germans attacked and re-took Priekule. The Russians reached the outskirts of Bunka and got to within 10kms of Liepāja. Priekule changed hands five times.

One German soldier told me that he was sent to the east of the town with 20 tanks, ten soldiers on each tank. Nearly all of them – 200 soldiers – were killed.

---

*   To the southwest.

He survived and was captured by the Russians and interrogated. The Russian officer was very intelligent and talked to him in German. He survived the war, went to Estonia as a PoW, then went back to Germany where he lived for the rest of his life. He came back to Priekule in 2006 and went around the town [with me] remembering what he did here.[6]

Mārtiņš pinpoints the swampy, heavily wooded terrain around Priekule with its good visibility and fortifiable defensive positions as distinct advantages to the Germans and Latvians.

Why did the front line form where it did? Because of the landscape. From a military point of view there was a better defensive landscape in Courland. Liepāja was well fortified from the First World War and the Germans put a lot of resources into there to defend the supply routes; the port and the railway. The fighting was so intense in Priekule because of the railway.

The Germans and the Latvians knew the landscape and could bring shells down precisely on roads, columns of tanks or infantry. The Soviet tanks were caught in bottlenecks because the roads were very narrow. For artillery you need spotters but if you're attacking it's difficult to get spotters in, so they were shooting blind.

The German and Latvian Legion tactics with the infantry and machine guns were inventive too. The Russians tried to get positions at the top of the hills but the Germans set up defences in the low spots. When the Russians came running down the hill the Germans opened up with machine guns and they didn't have anywhere to hide. The only cover was behind the bodies of their fallen comrades. The Soviets lost so many men because of the landscape. Courland is the perfect place to defend.

In my family three brothers of my Grandma went into the Legion. Her father was a Latvian Rifleman serving Lenin. His sympathies were to that side but his three sons chose to join the other side: not for the politics, but for adventure. That's why they joined. Their father was against it. He said: 'If you join the Legion, you're out of my family'. But they went. They survived – and then all three were sent to Siberia. The last one died two years ago.

The biggest problem is that we had to live side-by-side with the guys who were shooting at us. Both sides, Russians and Germans, said to the Latvians: 'You're fighting for your freedom. Now is your hour'. And they believed it. At Džūkste the 19th Division faced the 130th Latvian Riflemen – Latvian against Latvian. That's the price we pay for living on the cusp of Eastern and Western Europe. That's our tragedy. That's our destiny.

Maybe the key to our survival is that we didn't side with one side alone. If we'd all sided with the Germans we'd all be dead. My great grandfather was a Rifleman for Lenin. When the Russians came back in 1940 the family said 'Let's run'. And he said: 'No way. I fought for Lenin. They're not going to touch me'. And they didn't.

As a man who works with timber and wood Mārtiņš has an interesting perspective on the war in Priekule. The shelling was so intense in this area that the trees are still full of shrapnel. We drive to the east where the Germans repeatedly repulsed infantry attacks so he can show me.

We walk through a wood of oak and birch trees growing in a river valley, with steep banks up to the fields. The Germans prepared detailed strongpoints and overlapping defensive positions here to inflict maximum possible casualties. The Soviets attacked across an open field straight into the fire of Bonesaws spitting out 1,200 rounds a minute supported by mortars and artillery. That's before they reached the frontline trenches at the top of the slope where we are. We have an absolutely clear field of fire across this flat ground all the way back to the trees.

If any men reached this side of the field alive the Germans could fall back to positions down the slope if they needed to. Then the Soviets would be attacking downhill with the guns at the bottom of the valley cutting them down and more on the opposite bank ready to open up if they made it to the river. It would have been slaughter. Wholesale, bloody slaughter.

We head into the woods, our boots crunching in the snow. It's beautiful among the trees, despite the reason we are here.

'The wood is full of shrapnel. I'll show you,' says Mārtiņš, pointing from left to right.

'You see up there? There was a building up there. You can see the stones. All flattened. Here – this was a bunker'.

We stop. He points to the edges of the wood.

'We're on the east of Priekule where the Russians tried to flank the Germans. It's a flat area but it's full of trees to the east and there are trench lines crossing it and going down into the valley. There's one line here with a second line further back and individual positions on the slope. It is just madness to attack across here. You wouldn't stand a chance'.

No wonder there are stories of the bodies being piled so high the machine guns couldn't tilt high enough to keep killing the oncoming soldiers. Mārtiņš points across the field.

> The Soviets wore white snow camouflage smocks. When a bullet went through a soldier a white cotton ball would spray up. The man would keep running because of the adrenalin and blood pumping, but the gunners knew if they saw a white cotton ball they had hit him and they'd just start firing at the next wave. After the battles the treelines and bushes were full of – if you like – snow, because of all the bullets covered in white cotton from the camouflage smocks.

That's why there are 23,000 dead Soviet soldiers in Priekule cemetery then.

We walk a little way over to a group of trees Mārtiņš is planning to clear for a motocross track he is building. The area in front of the trees is flat: deliberately, Mārtiņš says. This was the firing position for three mortars. I look more closely. Three definite cleared and level areas can still be made out.

All these oak trees are no good for planks because they are full of shrapnel. They can't be cut. The metal goes blue when it reacts with the wood. All the trees from here to the Liepāja road will be full of shrapnel. This puddle is a shellhole …

He reaches down and from a frozen puddle picks up what is clearly recognisable as the base of a shell.

This is what's left of a shell. Lying on the surface. All these trees are full of shrapnel. The war is everywhere, still.

He twists the shell round to show me. I take a photograph of him with it and he throws the shell base back into the frozen puddle.
'If these trees could tell stories …'[7]
With that we walk back to the car and drive back to town. I get the feeling that I have only begun to scratch the surface of the stories that abound in Priekule.

Notes

1   Kurowski, p.186.
2   Kurowski, p.310.
3   Silgailis, p.149.
4   Kurowski, p.203.
5   Gravestones from Priekule Cemetery, translated by Sasha Skvortsov, with biographicals details from 'Heroes of the Soviet Union'.
6   Lidija Treide, interview with author, Priekule, January 2015.
7   Mārtiņš Cerins, interview with author, Priekule, January 2015.

20

The Last Resting Place of a Soldier

March 1945 came. With a winter thaw setting in Soviet infantry massed along the front waiting for the air attacks and artillery barrages to end so they could launch one last assault on the German defences. This would be the sixth and final battle of Courland.

It began on 7 March with a two-pronged attack, northwesterly on Pilsblīdene and northerly towards Pampāļi. The Latvian 43rd Grenadiers were moved west of Zebrus Lake to counter this thrust. Arriving there on 17 March the regiment was ordered to counter-attack against Soviet forces which had broken through west of Blīdene railway station. Some of the scenes described by Latvian Legion commander Artūrs Silgailis are like a 19th century army fighting a modern one.

> The spring weather had started and the melting snow had converted roads into an impassable quagmire. The Russians were equipped with American Caterpillar vehicles while the Germans had to rely on horse-pulled vehicles. The burden of transport was actually carried by horse-pulled wagons of Latvian farmers. Due to the terrible road conditions the regimental units arrived piecemeal at their destination.[1]

The men went straight into combat. They suffered heavy losses but managed to stop the Russian advance 1.5kms from Blīdene railway station.

German Army gun captain Gottlieb Bidermann was in positions to the west between Saldus and Skrunda when the final Soviet offensive began on 18th March.

> Streets and roads [were] little more than bottomless quagmires over which nothing could travel without great exertion. The earthworks and machine gun positions seemed to be devoured by the grey-black mud and even the activity on the Soviet side came almost to a halt, the impassable roads spoiling any immediate plans for a further attack.[2]

Despite almost constant shelling, fierce combat and attacks from the air for days on end, the German defences held. Their system of fortified farmsteads took a heavy toll on the Red Army's men and machines. But the constant pressure forced them to give ground and fall back to new defensive positions.

Through March German lines were stretched. Armoured units operated more like quick reaction teams heading from one crisis to another. But by early April Soviet attacks were falling off in intensity, their generals almost sensing the futility of further loss of life.

On April 4th the sixth battle of Courland ended. The new German commander of forces *Generaloberst* Carl Hilpert strengthened the defences around Priekule once more to keep Liepāja's harbour open as long as possible.

April saw only local skirmishes across the whole front east to west. On the night of the 3rd of May the guns opened up again. Russian loudspeakers bellowed towards the German positions: 'Berlin has fallen. Germany is at an end'.[3]

With Hitler's suicide on 30th April, his successor Dönitz stepped up Operation Hannibal, attempting to evacuate as many troops from Courland as possible before the inevitable capitulation.

On the 7th of May Hilpert was informed of Germany's impending surrender. He was given orders to ship out as many men as possible before it came into effect, especially the sick and wounded. All reserves plus one officer and 125 men from each division would be first on the boats.[4]

Hilpert's final order as commander of *Heeresgruppe Kurland* [Army Group Courland] was issued that evening:

> Marshal Govorov* has stipulated that the ceasefire is to start at 1400 hours on 8 May. Units are to display white flags in their positions immediately. The commander-in-chief expects loyal compliance since the further fate of all the Kurland fighters decisively depends on it.[5]

On the 9th of May the German unit commanders surrendered to the Soviets. One highly decorated *Oberst,†* Joachim von Amsberg, described his feelings.

> At 1400, accompanied by a trumpeter, an interpreter and an *Unteroffizer*, I moved forward with a white flag on the front fender of the staff car to the first Russian strongpoint. From there I was escorted to a Russian division headquarters where I signed the surrender agreement. I then went back to the regiment and spent the last twelve hours of the night in freedom. They were the last hours that I spent as a free man for the next ten and a half years.[6]

In the final week of the war Admiral Dönitz was negotiating surrenders to the Allies in both the east and west. The British agreed that ships at sea could continue their voyages. The Russians and Americans insisted that embarkations at Liepāja, Ventspils and at Hela‡ must stop at 0100 on 9 May 1945 and that these ports be handed over at that time.

---

*   Leonid Aleksandrovich, the Soviet commander in the Baltics, who had masterminded Soviet forces during the 900-day defence of Leningrad then led the drive to push the Nazis back west.
†   Colonel.
‡   Hel in Poland.

Dönitz ordered a frenzy of activity to get as many ships in the Baltic as possible ferrying people back to Germany. On 7 May 20,000 people left Hela in a fleet of torpedo boats and destroyers.[7]

A desperate shuttle of humanity began. German torpedo boats were much larger than a British or American vessel; more like a small warship. Soldiers crammed onto the decks, squeezed into cabins, found anywhere there was space. On one torpedo boat 2,000 men crowded aboard.[8]

All the available boats, fishing vessels, ferries and tankers that could float mustered off Latvia's two Baltic ports. Troops were still arriving in the ports at 8pm on the 8th of May with the last boats due to sail at 11pm.

Four convoys left Liepāja with approximately 14,400 troops on 65 boats. Two convoys sailed from Ventspils carrying 11,300 men on 61 ships. As the last ships left Liepāja advance Soviet forces arrived and started firing at them. Two tugs loaded with soldiers were captured.[9]

As the convoys sailed away so too did any last hopes of escape. Discipline had been maintained until this point but now there was widespread panic. Soldiers seized practically anything that would float and attempted to escape by sea. Some reached the convoys and were taken onboard. Others made it to Sweden only to be turned over to the Soviets later, but many drowned. For the rest, on the 8th of May 1945 more than 200,000 men of Army Group Courland laid down their arms and became Soviet prisoners.[10]

The Courland Pocket was over. Forty-two generals, 8,000 officers and 180,000 men surrendered, along with 14,000 Latvians. On May 9, on the orders of Admiral Dönitz, the German armed forces sent out one final message.

> ...Our armies in Courland tied down superior forces of Soviet infantry and tanks for months and won immortal fame in six great battles. They rejected all possibility of an early surrender. Only seriously wounded soldiers and fathers with many children were flown out to the West. The staff and officers remained with their troops. In accordance with the conditions signed for, at midnight the German side ceased all movement and fighting...
>
> Since midnight the guns have fallen silent on all fronts. By order of the *Gros Admiral*, the Wehrmacht has halted what has become futile fighting. With that, almost six years of heroic struggle has come to an end. It has brought us great victories but also difficult defeats. The Wehrmacht has maintained its honour: it has submitted to massively superior forces.
>
> The Wehrmacht remembers in this most difficult hour its comrades who have fallen in the face of the enemy. The dead compel us to unconditional loyalty, obedience and discipline to the Fatherland, which is bleeding from innumerable wounds.[11]

Almost seventy years later I'm sitting in a second floor flat in Skrunda with Jānis Blums, an elderly man who fought in that last battle. With me to translate once again is Courland tourism chairman Artis Gustovskis. Mr Blums gathers a collection of diaries and family albums around him and refers to them as he tells his story.

I was in Kurzeme in the 15th Division. I started my war service in Russia and in February 1944 I had my first real battles. I took part in the Legionnaire's Day battles on the Velikaya River. After that I had special training as a forward patrol scout – we went out first to check out the situation, to look for the enemy. New guys came in at the end of 1944 who didn't know anything so we did a lot of training between September and November 1944 in Pomerania.

On 22 January 1945 there was an alarm because the Russians came through the front line [in the Danzig area] and we were moved up. The front line moved around a lot [in two days of hard fighting]. It was chaos really. The Germans would advance and then the Russians would attack from the side. An officer next to me was wounded as we were standing in a yard. A bullet came in through the roof and he was wounded. The officer said to me 'Take the men and get them out of here'. There were 35-40 men. We were cut off and I led them out of there but I was wounded in the back of my leg.

This is the happiness of the soldier. I had a long military coat with a cigar box in the pocket. The bullet hit the cigar box instead of going into my leg. If I hadn't been wounded I would be dead, because all the others were killed. There was shooting everywhere. It was like a killing machine.

They took me to hospital. I could walk again after a week and was discharged to Neubrandenburg where the division was being collected. There was a ration of flour, bread and very simple porridge and we were told the wounded would go to Denmark. The doctor checked me and said I was almost fit for combat. But I wanted to get back to my friends at the front. I was sent to Stettin* as there was a Latvian battalion there. There were four of us, friends staying together. But it was chaos. If you didn't have the right documents the Germans could kill you.

There were lots of deserters and people everywhere. The Germans were very strict and controlled everyone. There was an office where they were gathering soldiers for the Kurzeme Front and we went there. There were about 80 soldiers who had volunteered to go back. We were given new uniforms, boots and two loaves of bread and sent to Swinemünde† to wait for a ship to Liepāja. That's more or less all we had to eat.

We waited for about a week. Swinemünde was the only way out of there, by sea. This was about the 8th, 9th or 10th of March. Swinemünde was like a resort and it was empty.

---

* The German name for the city of Szczecin in Pomerania, then part of Germany. At the end of the war it became part of Poland and its German population was expelled. On a visit to America in March 1946, Winston Churchill used Stettin in a speech warning of the future of post-war Europe: 'From Stettin in the Baltic to Trieste in the Adriatic, an Iron Curtain has descended on the continent'. The speech, titled 'The Sinews of Peace', is considered by some as the start of the Cold War.

† The port of Świnoujście in modern Poland.

Mr Blums picks up a book of his war memories that he wrote in 1979. The Occupation Museum in Riga has a copy.

> 11.3.45. We got onto the ship. It was a day like today: very rainy, cloudy, misty. There were a lot of soldiers collected together but the four Latvian friends stayed together, like the four musketeers.

He looks at me. 'I can't remember their names now, unfortunately'.
  He reads again.

> The ship is standing in the river like a gate to the sea. On the bank of the river there was a train full of refugees. Suddenly the air raid siren sounded. Everyone must leave the ship. But the people on the ship said: 'No, we won't leave'.
> And those four Latvian friends go to the side of the ship with a view over the river and the warehouses on the other side. They see bombs falling and exploding everywhere and the aircraft are directly overhead. They're English. About a hundred planes, bombing for an hour. In the middle of the river was a big ship. It was hit, and exploded. But the friends jumped into the cabin of the ship and the planes flew over very low. The sound was so powerful we were almost blown over by the noise alone.
> A lot of ships were hit and blown up but our ship escaped. By this stage in the war the bombing was happening all day and all night.
> When the bombing was over we left the ship. But in that one hour 2,000 people were killed, mainly civilians, because the town was full of refugees. That's what one officer told me. That night all four of us slept in the forest. The next morning the ship was gone.

He looks up at me as Artis translates and takes up the story from memory.

> We got the next ship to Liepāja and then on 14 March caught a train to Ventspils. The tracks had been bombed so we had to get off one train, cross the place where the rails were smashed and then get on another train. In Ventspils we got another train to Tukums, and from there we walked to Remte where we joined up with the 43rd Grenadiers. There the Colonel checked out what training we'd had and then gave me a Bonesaw.
> We were told to support a unit coming out of Blīdene station. On the Soviet side was an Estonian division known to be very strong. I was positioned ready to support our men but only four out of twenty five came back.
> At Easter we were sent to the front line trenches. There was still snow on the ground. I was moving forward across a field when I came across some of our men who'd been killed by a Katyusha [rocket] explosion. They'd been crossing the field when they were killed. They were all lying dead in a row. It brought me up short. It was very emotional. It's hard to say what killed most men. I was lucky. I have an Iron Cross, but it's in Germany. I was issued with one but the war finished before I received it.

We break for tea and biscuits. Artis takes photographs of Mr Blums and I take photographs of his wartime pictures. One is of a thin boy in a uniform that is too big for him. His arms are too long for his tunic. Mr Blums laughs. 'I was only a skinny little lad'.

He was born in Majori in the Jūrmala district of Riga in August 1925. His father had been a soldier before him, fighting in the Tsar's army. He volunteered for the Legion with a friend on 18 March 1943 and went into the German Army a week later. Now, a year short of 90, his hands shake as he opens his father's diary at an entry written in fountain pen marking the birth of his new son, Jānis.

He saw his parents for the last time on 5 January 1945 before he returned to Courland. They made it to Germany and after the war emigrated to America. Life would take him in the opposite direction – to Siberia.

On the night of 6 May the men came back from the Remte front during the night. We started to walk to Gaiķi and stopped for lunch there. The officer with us said: 'So, gentlemen. The war is over. You are free now. You can go where you wish to go'.

Some of the men were local. Twenty minutes later they were at home. But of course there were people who went into the forest to be partisans. Someone asked for my Parabellum revolver so I gave it to them. At 1200 the next day, 8 May, we knew the war would be over.

We reached a country house just past Varieba Mill and went inside. The place was full of Legionnaires, all gathered around a long table eating bread and meat and drinking the home-made spirit *dzimtenīte*. After we'd eaten we played cards. I lay down on the floor to sleep because I was so tired.

When I woke up I heard another Legionnaire asking if we had a driver in our team. There were two German trucks, a Renault and an Opel *Blitz** that was used by communications battalions to lay telephone cables. Our driver turned the ignition and the truck started. There were ten cans of fuel, so we filled it up and said: 'Where shall we drive to?'

We decided to go to Stende because the big German storehouses were there and there would be lots of food, cigarettes and schnapps.

More Legionnaires turned up and got on the truck. Now everyone was standing. Lots of people had guns and we were asking: 'What shall we do with these guns, because the war is over?'

A lady who lived nearby gave us a white shirt to put on the truck to show that we were not fighting, and we set off along the back roads. Along the way we threw the guns out of the truck. The ditches along the sides of the roads were full of guns that had been thrown away.

The truck was so overloaded that the axle broke and we were stuck. Lots of Legionnaires got out and walked off, leaving just our original group of seven.

---

*   A three-ton truck that was the backbone of the German military.

The driver cut down a telephone pole, attached it to the chassis and tied it up with telephone wire to fix it.

Heading for Kabile we suddenly ran into some Russians. The captain asked us: 'Where are you going?'

A few of us spoke good Russian. 'We're going home,' they said.

'OK,' said the officer. 'We'll let you go. But first I must get permission for you from the Commandant. Do you have something valuable to give me, like a watch?'

I had my father's pocketwatch which he'd given me the last time we'd met, in Germany in January. It was a very good watch, very valuable, made in the Tsar's time in St Petersburg by a famous watchman who had also made watches for the Tsar – Pavel Buhre, a very old brand name. It also had a chain.*

The officer started to search me and he found the watch.

'Oh, it's a Russian watch,' he said. 'Wait here, I'll get permission'.

The officer disappeared, leaving the Russian soldiers with us smoking and joking and firing bursts of automatic gunfire into the air. We were a bit worried that at any moment they might turn the guns on us. Who knows? The war is over. Anything could happen.

Then two Russian women soldiers appeared, one lieutenant and one sergeant. And they said: 'Give us your rings'. One man was so big they couldn't get the rings off his fingers for ages, but after that we drove away [in the opposite direction] to Sabile.

There we ran into more Russians who told us to get out of the truck and gather in one place. I'm still wearing a German uniform at this time but not with the SS insignia – one Latvian division had a fire cross, the other had a sun. Everyone had torn their badges off.

There were 500 men in that place, Gala Muiža. Then they marched us to Varme where there were a few thousand men, and from there to Sabile and on to Kandava. There we met a column of Russian tanks.

As we passed the last tank one soldier [riding on it] opened fire on us with an automatic weapon. Lots of prisoners were killed.

Even after all the stories of brutality I have listened to I'm still quite shocked by this one.

In Kandava the German prisoners were separated from Latvians. The next day we went by road to Tukums. Lots of people in the countryside came out and gave us milk and bread. We met another column of Russian tanks and this time we were stripped of anything valuable we had left. Mostly by this time all we had left were boots.

---

*   Pavel Buhre watches were originally made exclusively for the Russian Tsar. They were given for outstanding service to officials and cultural figures, to foreign diplomats as presents and as bonuses to officers and NCOs in the Tsarist Russian Army.

As we approached Tukums some Russian soldiers ran out and escorted us into the town. Those of us who had medals and insignia of rank were separated out. We were allowed to wash and then taken on to Schlockenbeck Manor.* We slept in a stable that night.

In the morning a Russian came along and told us he was now in charge. They made a list of names and told us we'd be going to Jelgava. There we washed, our uniforms were cleaned, any remaining watches and knives were taken off us and we were given the same uniforms back. On the 9th June 1945 I was sent by train to a labour camp at Komsomolsk† and then on to the Sea of Japan where I was until December 1946.

Then I was sent to Estonia where the Russians formed a special working battalion from the people who worked for the Germans or the German Army before. There were only three nationalities there – Estonians, Latvians and Lithuanians. They did different jobs there, mostly building. The officers had been filtered out and killed. We were just the ordinary soldiers who were left.[12]

The next morning I drive to Pilsblīdene to look at the last battlefield of the war. I cross the railway line heading north and turn left on the road to Remte. Two men clearing the hedgerows stop to look at me. A sign catches my eye but in the drizzle I can't quite make it out so I turn my car around and drive back. The sign reads: *'Brāļu Kapi Tuski'* which means 'Tuski cemetery of fallen brothers'. It's a soldiers' graveyard.

The cemetery is some way down a narrow single-track mud road. Laid out in a clearing among trees, with woods some distance to either side, are neat rows of black headstones engraved with four columns of around 25 names per column – making 100 names for each headstone. There are more than ten of these headstones, each at the end of a row of individual graves, some of which are Russian, some Latvian.

I notice the dates of death. All these men died within a very short period of time: between 18 March and 23 March 1945, in fact.

Here's a man from Varakļāni in eastern Latvia. V.D. Cakuls, born 1924, died 23rd March 1945. On the same day, Jānis Rimsans, four years his senior.

Russian graves often have pictures of the dead, and here's a very young-looking boy, 20 when he died. His stone is engraved with his name, years of life and underneath: 'Mama'.

Augusts Kiselevs, Jānis Brencans, Kārlis Brēkis: 23rd March. Aadam Koit, Richard Loodla, 18th March. Andrejs Klindžāns, Pēteris Samsons, 5th March. Alexandrs Paberzs, Viktors Sarkans, March 1945. Another Cakuls, Jānis Jura, born 1926, same year of death. They may have been brothers – this man is two years younger – but there's no sign where Jānis Jura was from, or even the day he died.

---

*   A fortified manor house for German barons dating back to the 15th Century, it is now a museum, hotel and cultural centre. It's located five miles east of Tukums on Rigas iela, the road from Tukums to the coast at Klapkalnciems.

†   To the northeast of Moscow.

More Latvian names. More Russian names. I walk to the far end of the cemetery. There is a large memorial stone with a Red Army star. It reads, in Latvian:

Eternal glory to them. Fallen in battle for our future.*

And then in a corner there is a tall grey slate stone with an inscription:

Under this stone lies a letter from veterans of the Great Patriotic War and Communist Youth from the Mangali shipyard [in Riga]. This letter was written on the 100th birthday of Vladimir Ilyich Lenin [in 1970] and is addressed to our descendants who will be alive in the year 2070.[13]

The Mangali shipyard was founded on the Daugava river in Riga in 1946 as the main repair base of fishing vessels in the western USSR. On Latvia's independence it was made a public corporation then privatised on 27 March 2001. In 2002 it was re-named Termināls Vecmīlgrāvis. The shipyard still operates today under private ownership but no-one there knows why there is a message from 1970 from the yard's Communist Youth under this tall stone in this remote burial place, or what it might say.[14]

I wonder whether anyone alive now realises there is a message from the past buried in this country graveyard, to be read half a century from now. It's a capsule from another time, another world, planted in the last resting place of these soldiers down a dirt road in the country in a land where once a burst of gunfire – perhaps fired by one of the men I have met and talked to – snuffed out the lives of these boys who had barely lived.

Notes

1   Silgailis, p.149.
2   Bidermann, p.281.
3   Kurowski, p.261.
4   Grier, p.105.
5   Kurowski, p.263.
6   Ibid, p.265.
7   Ibid, p.269.
8   Buttar, p.317.
9   Grier, p.105.
10   Grier, p.105.
11   Ludde-Neurath, *Unconditional Surrender: The Memoir of the Last Days of the Third Reich*, p.152.
12   Jānis Blums, interview with author, November 2014.
13   Author's visit to graveyard. Inscriptions translated by Daiga Kamerade.
14   Author's correspondence with shipyard, *Termināls Vecmīlgrāvis*.

---

*   *Mūžīga slava varoņiem. Kas krituši kaujās par mūsu tēviju 1941–1945.*

21

Even the Dead Were Bombed

Later that day I am standing in front of a ruined church in a clearing in a snow-covered forest in the middle of Latvia. The church has no roof, no windows and no doors. The walls are only really an outline of what was here before. This is Zvārde – a ghost town – shelled to the point of obliteration during the war. All the people who lived here were deported to Siberia and it was then pounded further into non-existence.

The walls of the church are surrounded by heaps of rubble even now. We clamber over them into the interior. Rows of pews are laid out inside the church boundaries for a congregation, as though people still come here to worship. My guide, museum curator Roberts Sipenieks, nods, anticipating my question.

> Yes, the church is still used. There's no roof; the place is destroyed. But it's their church. Wait until you see the graveyard.

There has been a church in Zvārde since 1567. It was made of wood until a stone church was built in 1785. That survived two and a half centuries until November 1944. Then the forest stood between the Soviet attackers and the German front lines, and the church was shelled into oblivion. It was completely demolished in 1954 when the area was used as a military zone.[1]

We are deep inside the Kursīši forest south of Saldus, miles from anywhere. There are no main roads, only tracks, and few signposts. It's beautiful. The forest air is fresh and clear. A rabbit lopes across the clearing.

This is a vast band of dense woodland between Saldus and the border with Lithuania. The forest runs west as far as Priekule and east to Dobele. There's just one road running south from Saldus to a small town on the border called Ezere. Amid these trees and lakes and swamps the Soviet tanks and infantry were pushed back time and time again, leaving devastating numbers dead.

Around here are names I recognise from the accounts I've read of battles and desperate encounters between Russian, Latvian and German. This is where the forti-fied farmsteads were: areas of resistance, places that changed hands time and again – outposts in this long-forgotten war of attrition. *Zvejnieki, Lācis, Stedini, Ozoliņi...* many names impossible to find on modern maps. But with a guide like Roberts Sipenieks, curator at the museum in Saldus to the liberation war hero Oscars Kalpaks, the wartime landscape comes to life. He knows the secrets of the forest. We turn away from the ruins of the church and Roberts points into the trees.

The forest is amazingly thick. When we were kids [in the 1990s] we would come in and find machine guns, bullets, bombs, grenades. At that age we weren't thinking with our heads. We'd find bullets from machine guns [MG42s] and take them home. If we found something we didn't know we would call someone older so he could tell us whether it was dangerous or not. We'd never call the bomb squad – never.

The local Jews from Pampāļi and Kursīši were shot in the sand dunes – thirty or forty of them. They were brought here in trucks, killed and buried. They [the Germans] let them reach the age of twelve, then shot them. All of them.

The Germans searched for places to bury their comrades: graveyards, quiet places, in woods. They marked them with crosses made from birch trees but of course after the war all the burial places were bulldozed by the Soviets. It's really only after the end of the Soviet times that the German authorities could come here and start searching for them.[2]

We bounce along the frozen country tracks in Roberts' Chrysler PT Cruiser, a modern American car, metallic red with 1940s retro mobster styling, which seems weirdly out of place for discussing such grim topics. Every now and then Roberts gently touches the brakes to stop them icing. His younger brother Rūdolfs is in the back. After a while we pull in at the edge of what looks like a field that's been ploughed up, but in a very strange way – it looks ruptured rather than ploughed by hand.

'This is the graveyard,' says Roberts. 'The Soviets used it for bombing practice'.

I look across what used to be a graveyard. There are stone tombs shattered to an outline of what they once would have been, simple wooden crosses marking where loved ones were laid to rest. It's a featureless landscape of brown vegetation, snow and pulverised graves. Soviet planes used the graveyard for target practice for decades after the war, from 1954 to 1993. A freshly engraved headstone carries the details of this final insult from the victors.

Sorry that we did not protect you.
For those buried in Rītelu cemetery whose places of rest were ravaged between 1954 and 1993 when this place was a target zone for Soviet bomber pilots and the holes made by bombs were repeatedly levelled by tractors.[3]

The control tower which guided the bombers in stands about a quarter of a mile away from this desolate place. Concrete posts jut out at strange angles amid the saplings that have sprung up in recent times. A solitary cross stands alone marking a grave, clearly having borne the brunt of some considerable force. Even the dead were bombed.

Roberts, Rūdolfs and I are heading for a remote farmstead to interview a former Legionnaire. His name is Roberts Miķelsons, who fought first on the Eastern Front and then in the Courland Pocket. We turn off the road and down several long tracks until we reach a group of farm buildings surrounded by fields. Roberts has been ringing ahead but Mr Miķelsons hasn't answered. The door is open, so we go inside.

Mr Miķelsons is a little surprised to see us. He's still in bed. We apologise and wait in the kitchen until he's ready. Roberts has suggested we bring a bottle of vodka for Mr Miķelsons and he pours us each a shot. The elderly man – pushing 90 – gathers some cold meat and bread that's on the table and accepts the vodka glass. Together we raise our glasses. 'Prieka'* we say, and down the orange liquid in one gulp. Roberts and Rūdolfs translate as Mr Miķelsons begins to talk.

I was born in January 1924 and was 17 years old when the war started. I lived in this same house. No-one was deported from my family and no-one was taken for the Soviet Army [in 1940].

The order was given in February 1943 to create the Latvian Legion. In March 1943 there was a mobilisation. One month we were in Saldus at school, the next we were at the front. I was in aircraft support, serving at Staraya Russa until 1944.†

In August 1943 they asked soldiers to relocate to the Latvian Legion and we moved to Volkhova. They took any Latvians – even deserters from the Red Army. The guys who were mobilised didn't really want to fight but the guys who were in the Legion already were really crazy. They always wanted to fight and win the Iron Cross so they were always attacking – and taking the mobilised guys with them. It wasn't an Iron Cross they were getting, but a wooden cross.

The volunteers had Bonesaws so they could kill more people but I had an old Czech carbine. It was so heavy I had to rest it on the edge of the trench when I fired.

When we got to Staraya Russa it was quiet, not much fighting at the time. But the snow was black from all the smoke and explosions. It was a game of chance who lived or died. Either you fight or you die. My cousin was killed at Volkhova – shot. I wasn't injured.

I was sent to Tukums in Spring 1945, near Valguma Lake.‡ There were three fronts. I was lucky – mine was the peaceful one. There were two other crazy fronts. All the time I was lucky. We had three units. The first and the third were in the fights and were mostly destroyed while the second one, where I was, was surrounded.

It was the last days of the war so everyone wanted to stay alive. The Russians weren't so keen to attack in the last days. I was in the 19th Division 10kms east of the main fighting and in the rear sections of the line – away from Blīdene, Džūkste.

On the 9th of May we signed the capitulation but fighting carried on for one or two days after the ceasefire. We didn't know about the capitulation for

---

*   Cheers.
†   Staraya Russa was occupied by the Germans between August 1941 and 1944 and was totally destroyed during the war.
‡   To the east of the town in what is now Ķemeri National Park.

a while. Fighting was pointless. They shot one of ours: we shot one of theirs. No-one attacked.

After we surrendered we were taken to the sugar factory in Jelgava. From there we went by truck to the railway: 45 people in a cattle truck. Some were on the floor, others were on the bench. There were holes in the floor and it was very cold. Anyone who died was dropped out of the truck onto the rails. A lot of people died.

We ended up on the other side of the Urals and got a boat down the Volga. We were working on the railway. We used gravel to create a level base for the rails to be laid. I was there 18 months [until the end of 1947], flattening out the hills to make the land level.

We pause. Roberts pours another vodka and we clink our glasses again and drain them. There are a few questions I'd like to ask, I say. What was he fighting for?

I was a landowner's son. My father owned 80 hectares. He was an 'old' owner – and that was a lot.*

In my opinion the Russians wouldn't give us any mercy so we had to fight. We were hoping that the Allies would come and save us. The Americans, the English. That was the main idea of the partisans. We were fighting for a free Latvia. We knew we wouldn't get any mercy from the Russians.

Having survived fighting in the war, 18 months in Siberia, fifty years of Soviet occupation and now 25 years of freedom, how does he feel now Latvia is free?

Luck was on my side. I was lucky not to experience the things some of my friends did. One stepped on a mine and had his legs blown off. Another was shot in the stomach.

The Soviet times were OK. We worked, and the work was OK. When I was sent back from Siberia I went to Tallinn, rebuilding the city in a work battalion. After that I came back here [near Ezere] where I've lived ever since. I have six children, 13 grandchildren and seven great-grandchildren with an eighth on the way. I've got no complaints.[4]

After we leave Mr Miķelsons' house we stop along the road between Saldus and Pampāļi. Roberts points to a wood on the horizon.

That wood is where Panfilov's division[†] was destroyed in the spring of 1945. The dead Soviet soldiers were buried in that ditch running across the field there

---

*   He had owned the land since before the re-distribution at the end of the First World War. Many people were deported for half that acreage.

†   The Soviet 8th Guards, named after the commander in their heroic defence of Moscow in 1941.

– about 200 men. They were all killed in a matter of hours. There were huge fights in all these forests in the war, especially in the final days. It was common for Russians to drop the dead in the ditches, cover them with soil and move on. The Germans buried their fallen comrades properly and marked them with a cross but the Russians bulldozed the graveyards and took the crosses away so no-one knows where they are.

In the 1960s my grandfather was digging ditches to lay pipes and they hit a trench with a German corpse in it. He said the stench was really bad.

We are on the way to Ezere to meet Roberts' grandmother, Biruta Sipeniece, who runs the museum where the German capitulation was signed. It's a large white house off the main road running parallel to Latvia's southern border with Lithuania. The road past the house is the old road to Lithuania but leads now only to the river – the bridge was demolished in the 1950s. The Soviet generals came from that direction to meet their Nazi enemies.

We walk to the river and look across it. Biruta explains the circumstances of the signing of the capitulation.

World War II ended here in Ezere. On the 8th of May 1945 at 6pm in the evening the German General Rauzer came here from Pelči Castle near Kuldīga and Soviet General Popov came from Lithuania. They sat down at the round table in the house and signed a capitulation paper for the Kurzeme Katls [Courland Pocket]. The next day the Soviet flag was raised above the Reichstag.

Ezere was halfway between the two bases. The German HQ was in Pampāļi and the Russian HQ was in Mažeikiai, 13 kms from here. The house was the first one across the border between Lithuania and Latvia. Both generals brought their staff and adjutants. There were guards all round the house and barbed wire everywhere. They signed the capitulation and that ended the war.

The Germans left and after that there was a lot of drinking. On the other side of the river here there was an Army barracks. One Russian major got so drunk that night he was sick in his boots.

We laugh. What a detail from history to be remembered for. Biruta leads us inside for coffee and cakes and starts to tell her story.

She was born in 1942. Her father worked in a German wood factory and was afraid he'd be sent to Siberia so he sent his family to the country and fled to Germany on one of the convoys leaving Liepāja. They didn't know whether he survived the war and didn't hear from him again until 1968. Biruta was one of the first to get a visa to visit Germany to see him and in 1975 he was able to return to Latvia before his death. She puts down her coffee cup.

That's what happened to Latvians. Many had to leave the country. My cousin was travelling to Germany with his mother shortly before the capitulation. The father had been wounded. They were in Warsaw in the station square where a huge crowd of people were waiting to escape to Germany and to the Allies.

Suddenly Russian tanks drove through the crowd, splitting it in half. My cousin was 14 and was caught on the Allied side of the tanks. His mother was on the other side of the tanks, on the Russian side. So she was sent back to Latvia by the Russians. My cousin was taken to England and given a job at a military base. After that he got a job at a café in Mansfield. He lived in Bancroft Lane.

Our roots are pure Latvian going back generations. Just pure Latvian. But because of the war my family is spread out around the world. I have relatives in Australia; cousins. My grandmother's cousins are in the US, the UK, in Germany.

We take a break to look around the house, full of period mementos including an impressive collection of medals, military caps and helmets, gas masks and metal water bottles as well as photographs of the many notable political leaders who have visited the house.

Over fresh mugs of coffee and more cakes we discuss modern times, including the struggle for the second independence in the 1990s. Biruta grew up near Cēsis, studied at a technical school near Bauska then came to Ezere to work. She met her husband here and in 1961 they married. I ask her how she feels having lived to see a free Latvia again.

When we were in school in Soviet times we were taught that everything was perfect. I worked in a *kolhoz** for years. I knew everything about grains, about the soil.

Until the 1970s we were occupied and we thought only about work and sport. From the end of the 1970s and 1980s we could get visas and visit Soviet countries like Bulgaria and Romania and see how other people were living. Then we started to think how things could be different.

When I visited my father for the first time [in Germany] I met a man who was a minister during the first freedom times in the 1930s. He said: 'It cannot stay like that. It will change, and when it does you have to be ready for it'.

When the barricades happened in 1991[†] my grandfather was the head of the *kolhoz*. He gathered everyone together who had mechanised vehicles and said: 'Who will go to Riga?' And everyone stepped forward.

They ran shuttles for two weeks with a minibus to Riga to get people there and back and to send food and supplies. Six people were shot on 20 January 1991.[‡5]

---

*   Collective farm.

†   Part of the Latvian 'Awakening'.

‡   An incident during the period known as The Barricades in 1991 when Soviet Special Forces troops stormed the Interior Ministry in Riga killing five people, following the previous killing of a lorry driver. In 2007 on Jekaba iela in Riga then-President Vaira Vīķe-Freiberga unveiled a monument to those who lost their lives during the confrontations.

Everyone knew that if the tanks came no barricades would stop them. If today we had to go to war my generation would be the first generation to go to war for Latvia.'[6]

We tour the house one final time as I try to absorb the spectrum of emotions that Biruta must feel as she looks out of the windows here and meets people perhaps visiting the land their fathers or grandfathers fought for and never saw again.

I'm reminded of those statues in Dundaga; not only of the crocodile but also of the figure asleep, using their dreams of Latvia as a pillow. In the visitor book at Ezere one person has written:

It's wonderful to know historical things are preserved for everyone to see. Leaving Latvia aged two in 1944 and arriving in America in 1951 and now coming back to see everything first-hand I am comforted and feel at home finally to be in my homeland. The Latvian family I did not know existed found ME in 2012 and now I have visited my homeland twice.[7]

Notes

1   Information board, Zvārde church [translated by Daiga Kamerade].
2   Roberts Sipenieks, interview with author, January 2015.
3   Memorial inscription, Rītelu cemetery, Zvarde. Translated by Daiga Kamerade.
4   Roberts Miķelsons, interview with author, January 2015, translated by Roberts Sipenieks.
5   *The Guardian* newspaper, 21 January 1991: https://www.theguardian.com/world/1991/jan/21/eu.politics and Latvian History website https://latvianhistory.com/2013/01/20/omon-against-latvian-independence-1990-1991/ and Waymarking memorial website: http://www.waymarking.com/waymarks/WMPNCQ_Barikades_Memorial_Riga_Latvia.
6   Biruta Sipeniece, interview with author, translated by Roberts Sipenieks.
7   Visitor book, Ezere Manor.

*   In total, eight people died as a result of The Barricades. Roberts Murnieks, a Transport Ministry driver, was shot by OMON forces on Vecmilgravis Bridge on January 16th. Five died on the 20th when OMON troops tried to storm the Internal Affairs ministry: two police officers, Sergeys Konanenko and Vladimirs Gomanovics; a young student, Edijs Riekstins and acclaimed ethnological film-maker Andris Slapins and his cameraman colleague Gvido Zvaigzne. Ilgvars Griezins died the following day in an accident constructing a barricade. Raimonds Salmins, a driver for the Latvian Writers' Association was killed by Soviet forces near the railway station on the morning of August 19th in attempts to suppress opposition to Soviet rule during the coup against Gorbachev.

22

Capitulation and Defeat

With the capitulation came the sounds of celebration along the front line: on one side at least. There was gunfire, singing, cheering, dancing and drinking. The vanquished on the other hand were preparing for the next day. Some would flee, some would fight on from the forests, some would head for the coast and try to get a boat out. Others would turn their weapons on themselves. The war was over and the Soviets had won. Now came the peace.

On the morning of the capitulation veteran German gun captain Gottlob Bidermann was dug in along the Vartaya river with the Fourth Heavy Machine Gun Company facing Russian positions. German fire was met with artillery shelling. Several Soviet planes flew over and dropped fragmentation bombs behind the battle-front, cutting communications between units. The Germans braced themselves for an attack but at 1200 they received this order from HQ:

> At 1400 the Courland army will capitulate. White flags are to be displayed along the front lines. All personnel will remain in position under arms. Weapons are to be unloaded, magazines removed and barrels cleared. Officers are to continue to command their units.[1]

For Bidermann, as well as for every man alongside him, the prospect now of surviving the war brought uncertainty rather than relief.

> I made the rounds of our position, speaking to the men of the unknown fate that lay before us and attempting to calm their nerves. We no longer feared the prospect of death for we had lived and dealt intimately with it for years, to the extent that death on a battlefield in the east was an eventuality that was to be expected; that our inevitable fate was to find a final resting place in an unmarked grave in Russia.
>
> The fear that possessed us was the fear of the unknown, of not knowing what was to become of us, and more importantly, of our families in Germany. We had long been aware of what happened at Katyn in Poland, where the Russians had liquidated thousands of Polish officers, and we had no reason not to expect a similar fate should we fall into the hands of the enemy. The philosophy of fighting to the death had become so ingrained within us during the past years that surrender, as we were now being ordered to do, was inconceivable.[2]

The Russians made contact with their German opposite numbers and approached Bidermann's positions cautiously. As the morning advanced one German officer shot himself, leaving a note saying 'Without an army there is no honour'. Several other officers who reacted wildly against the idea of submitting had to be overpowered.[3]

> At 1400 our position was marked with ragged shirts, socks and bandages stuck on the end of rifle barrels. With this sign of surrender a khaki-brown wave surged forth from the forest's edge opposite us. The Russians swarmed into our positions, their new uniforms and well-fed bodies a striking contrast to our ragged appearance, our bodies thin from malnourishment and bleached pale from months of living beneath the earth in bunkers. The Soviets ignored the weapons and equipment and ran among the soldiers still standing in their positions, ripping decorations and insignia from uniforms and tearing watches and rings from the upraised arms. I was still wearing my camouflage battle smock over my tunic and was thus spared this plundering.[4]

I turn down a sand road taking me to the village of Bunka where the fighting had been so intense. One German, a *Hauptmann** Daube was in the front line near Bunka at the capitulation.

> The Russians came towards our positions like a horde of ants, waving their weapons above their heads and gesticulating. Some of them wrapped their arms around our soldiers' necks and offered them vodka. One could almost have said 'the universal brotherhood of common man'. The condition however only lasted half an hour.
>
> A high-ranking Russian officer ordered that we lay down our weapons within thirty minutes at the church in Bunka or the fighting would resume.
>
> The regiments of the 126 Infanterie Division marched toward Liepāja from their individual command posts. Arriving at the road to Liepāja we saw a gigantic march column – soldiers of all branches of the service, some on foot, some on vehicles – proceeding like a great folk migration toward Liepāja.[5]

Having surrendered, Bidermann and his men were marched in a column to a prisoner collection point in a cemetery where, as night fell, they watched the Red Army soldiers celebrate their victory.

> Wildly firing over our heads with sub-machine guns, rifles and pistols, they danced in the light of flares fired into the sky while we were forced to lie flat on the ground to avoid being struck as tracer bullets bounced and ricocheted among the tombstones. The Soviets gathered around us rejoicing in their victory with a macabre dance, chanting 'Gitler kaput! Voyna kaput!' in an unending chorus, leaping and springing in ecstasy while firing into the air.[6]

*   Captain.

Legionnaire Pēteris Stabulnieks had just returned to front line duty after a five-day leave period which he'd spent drinking moonshine with farmers and soldiers near Ugāle.

In the afternoon of 8 May, like lightning in the clear skies we were surprised by the news that peace was made between the two battling sides. Even though we had awaited this news for quite some time now, the fact that it actually came was unbelievable. We didn't even believe the messenger who brought it.

Only when we saw the white flags in the front lines and groups of soldiers returning home did we really believe the news was true. Our orders were: if the Russian soldiers were to come unarmed we were not to harm them, but if they were to attack we should defend ourselves. In the afternoon silence had fallen over the front lines and only the Russian planes were breaking the rules of the peace by shooting at the rear lines of our soldiers.

In the dark we were leaving our front line positions and returning to the rear lines. We had covered around 10 kms while carrying all of our belongings, including guns and ammunition.

The Commander of our group who had come from the headquarters had caught up to us. Immediately he called all of the other Commanders to him to inform them of the current situation.

Afterwards, the Commanders gathered all the soldiers and made an announcement.

'Last night at midnight a peace agreement was signed. All war efforts have to stop. You are free from duty and no longer have to follow orders. You can now choose your own path.

Those who have homes right here in Kurzeme – try to get home as quickly as possible. And as for the rest, either surrender to the Russians or hide in the forest. We know there will be no pleasant times with the Russians so whoever wants to can come with us. We are not going to surrender. We will try to get to Dundaga. Make sure you take your weapons and ammunition with you'.

Such chaos broke out it was impossible to hear anything. Those who followed the Commander dropped their guns and ammunition and so did we. All the ditches were full of things people had dropped. Then everyone disappeared in their own direction.

Along the roadside as well as wherever you looked there were exploded cars and tanks and the ditches were full of every calibre of guns and cannons. Even though it was a time of peace we were not allowed to ruin the things given to us during wartime – but no-one wanted to give such precious things as tanks and military vehicles to the Russians.

The last ammunition of flak was still being fired in the air and the skies were filled with bright bullets and explosions. Everybody was worried as no-one knew exactly what tomorrow would bring. Seven of us who were going home gathered in a group and walked the five kilometres home to spend the night.

We got rid of all the medals and insignia and burned the documents we had with us. I pulled off my corporal's insignia and threw away my medals: I had the

most [among] the seven of us. First and Second Class Gold Cross, Silver infantry assault badge, Silver medal for close combat – there were only three of these
in the whole of my Battalion, 'Kurland' cuff badge and a Silver Medal for injury.

It was hard to let go of the medals as we had risked our lives to earn them and
now they were worthless. I also threw away the machine pistol but I held on to
a handgun which I had picked up from a dead German soldier.

We slept until the sun came up and then we ate breakfast. Our plans were
to walk to Kandava which was about seven kilometres away and after that we
would see what happened.

As soon as we left the house a Russian jeep drove into the front yard and a
Russian lieutenant stepped out. He greeted us and told us to go to the headquarters three kilometres from here. There we would get documents and be allowed
to go home… so we headed toward the headquarters.[7]

Legion commander Artūrs Silgailis estimates there were 14,000 Legionnaires in
Courland when the Germans capitulated. About 5,200 men were soldiers in the 19th
Latvian Division and another 2,500 men were with the Battle Group *Rusmanis* in the
Dundaga area. There were seven construction battalions of about 400 men each, so
in total about 2,800 men. Another 1,100 were in three Police battalions, 560 men
worked as Air Force helpers and around 1,000 men were spread across other units.
Many Legionnaires did not surrender but went into the woods to resist the Soviets
as partisans.[8]

At the capitulation the surviving Luftwaffe pilots flew to Flensburg and surrendered to the British. The commander-in-chief, the highly decorated First World War
pilot *Generaloberst* Kurt Pflugbeil, a veteran of the Battles of Britain, Stalingrad,
Kursk and the invasions of France, Yugoslavia and the USSR, stayed in Courland
and went into captivity.[9]

Some Nazis, including the commander of the 6th Latvian SS, *Obergruppenführer*
Walter Krüger, tried to make their way back to Germany. Krüger was a First World
War veteran who'd fought on the Somme then in the Baltic in the German Freikorps.
When Hitler came to power he trained first Wehrmacht then SS recruits. He was
decorated in the Siege of Leningrad and led the SS Panzer Regiment 'Das Reich' at
Kursk, before assuming command of the Latvians in summer 1944.[10]

He was a formidable tactician. Over three days during the Christmas Battles his
men destroyed 190 Soviet armoured vehicles from the waves of tanks and assault guns
sent against them in the hellish fighting around the fortified farmhouse of *Gibelas*.
Then in a New Year offensive ordered by Krüger they regained all their previous
frontline positions, including those at *Gibelas*.

In late March 1945 – the sixth Battle – the Red Army once again sent vast forces of
infantry and masses of armour against their positions. Every available man was sent
to the front to prevent a breakthrough, often involving bloody hand-to-hand combat.

When the capitulation came Krüger released his Latvian soldiers from their oath to
the German Army and Hitler. He organised them into groups of ten to help them get
through the Russian lines, marching by night, hiding in the woods by day. Krüger
would not get out of Latvia. He and a group of fellow German officers attempted to

reach East Prussia but were flushed out of a hiding place in some woods right on the border a fortnight after the capitulation. Taken prisoner he managed to fire several shots at his captors but then pointed his weapon at his own head and pulled the trigger.[11]

The commander of the 19th Latvian Division, *SS-Gruppenführer* Bruno Streckenbach was taken prisoner, despite switching uniforms to appear to be an enlisted soldier.[12]

A Nazi Party member from 1930, Gestapo chief in Hamburg and then a key figure in the creation of the *Einsatzgruppen* death squads, he was sentenced in 1952 to 25 years' imprisonment but was released in October 1955 and returned to Germany, where he died in 1977.[13]

Pēteris Stabulnieks was marched from Kandava to a holding camp in Lithuania, then onto Jelgava and eventually to Siberia.

> Lithuanians were very polite and helpful people. For the whole way from Zagare to Jelgava people stood on the side of the road and despite the shots fired by the guards, they gave us bread, meat and other types of food. Sometimes when mothers saw their sons or when wives saw their husbands they ignored the screaming and shooting from the guards and ran to hug their loved ones. Only with force can they be separated.
>
> When we reached Jelgava only a quarter of us remained. I was one of the men who made it to the end. After the last resting time [before] the city, when we still had to walk four kilometres, even I struggled to stand up. At first I crawled on my hands and knees for a bit until I could move my legs again. Even the hunger was forgotten during the walk despite the fact that we hadn't eaten all day. All we got in the morning was a cup of coffee.
>
> The guards had said that bread would be distributed on the way but they didn't want to waste time so in the end we had to starve. We were located in a field next to a sugar factory on the banks of the river Lielupe.
>
> The weather was bad and it started raining to add to the cold conditions we had already had to endure. There was nowhere to escape. The field was wet and we were soaked from above as well as below.
>
> We gathered pieces of wood and tin to put on the ground and sleep on. For three days we slept in the field and in the evening of the third day we were taken to the train station. There a group of wagons with closed windows waited for us.
>
> The smaller wagons were filled with 40-45 people. The larger wagons were filled with up to 90 people each. We were crammed like fish in a barrel. There was no space to turn around.[14]
>
> On the night of 5 July the wagons left Jelgava. We were being taken to the 'vast homeland'. As we passed other stations we dropped notes telling others of our departure. It got very hot outside and we started to run out of oxygen. We were tormented by thirst as it was very hard to get water. At night the journey was a bit more bearable as at least it wasn't as hot.

During the day we were given 300g of sugar and a few spoonfuls of plain porridge. It was a total nightmare for those who smoked. Their pipes were broken and the contents smoked by the guards. Half the echelon – 1,500 men – were left outside Moscow. The rest of us were taken further. No-one knew our destination.[15]

Bunka is not much of a place. I drive along a road bordered by fields of sticky brown mud, ploughed and waiting for next year's seeding. There's an occasional thin sprinkling of trees separating one field from the next. The odd farm here and there stands alone with tractors, hay wagons and irrigation bowsers parked outside.

I slow down and put the car into neutral, rolling towards a ruined church on a junction with the main road. There's a country lane off to the left. A small lake full of reeds sits behind it. A thin copse of trees grows through the ruins and what's left of its tower. There's a cross marking where the other end of the church was.

This must be the church where the German soldiers laid down their weapons to end the war. There is a large stone with a slate plaque fastened to it. It reads, in Latvian:

In this place in May 1945 the victorious Soviet Army accepted the capitulation of the defeated Fascist troops.

There's a quote from Latvian poet Eizhen Veveris, which reads, again in Latvian:

Only the memory of victory remains. Too much blood was shed for it.[16]

I am an Englishman standing on a low sloping knoll in the middle of the Latvian countryside at the place where the Courland Pocket capitulated and the Second World War ended. There is no information board in English, Russian and German like at other places in Latvia that a curious tourist might go.

There are no solemn markers, no explanation why this church has been left like this, no pictures of what it used to be like before or why it was chosen to be the point of capitulation. There's just a ruined church with a stone plaque in Latvian. Maybe that's all it needs. Perhaps I'm beginning to appreciate the Latvian mentality. There really is no need for a song and dance about the end of the war. Too much blood was shed for this victory. Now, in reality, seventy years later, it's only the memory of victory that does remain.

Half a million men were dead, wounded or prisoners. Millions of lives were shattered. Courland was a graveyard; a scrap yard, a weapons yard. There were dead and damaged, displaced, raped and mutilated people everywhere. Some knowing that their lives depended on making an escape, most knowing that escape was now impossible. Just staying alive would be the next challenge, and many – like the German commander in Courland who signed the surrender, Carl Hilpert – would die in captivity.

Maybe whoever put up this slice of stone never expected a curious Englishman to come along seventy years later wanting to know what these words actually meant.

Dobele is a small town on the outskirts of Jelgava, a place you pass through on the way to somewhere else. I'm heading from Ezere to Riga, so I pass through it. A tall statue of two figures in what appears to be a very large graveyard catches my eye. I park up and walk back.

It is a Soviet war graveyard on a colossal scale. It's the size of a football pitch with a surrounding wall waist high covered in plaques engraved with the names of dead men. In the centre is a raised platform, a plinth for the statue of two men that caught my eye from the road. The one on the left is clearly a soldier with a rifle slung over his right shoulder; bare-headed, wearing a snow camouflage greatcoat. The man along-side him is older, with a moustache and full beard and a furrowed brow, which gives him a learned but deeply sad air. He's wearing what looks like a military greatcoat, with his hands folded solemnly in front of him. He has the appearance of a man bearing deep grief and sorrow.

The statue is a masterpiece of expression. The young man shoulders his arms and goes out to do what has to be done: the older man – perhaps his father, certainly old enough to be – grieves for him when he sacrifices his life for the good of others, but understands that it had to be sacrificed.

Whatever one's perspective on this war, this statue – the monument to the Soviet Warriors – demands reflection. Lining this cemetery's walls are the names of thousands of men whose lives were cut short prematurely in the struggle to extinguish the evil of Nazism. The scale of sacrifice of the soldiers of the Red Army, whether voluntary or coerced, cannot be denied. Thirty names to a plaque – each a father, son, brother. Thirty plaques to a wall. Eight walls, maybe more. I lose count at 8,000 names.

Some individual graves are engraved with medals declaring fallen Heroes of the Soviet Union. Their stories of remarkable heroism have lifted them above the anonymity of death.

Major Maxim Mikhailovich Khaliavitski commanded a rifle regiment resisting a German attack on Jelgava, destroying ten tanks, two assault guns and causing heavy casualties until being outflanked and surrounded.

Khaliavitski's men fought on for three days, killing 500 Germans and destroying another 22 tanks and seven assault guns before the wounded commander led a breakout the next day. This time he was wounded again –fatally – but the breakout was a success and his men were saved. A street in his hometown of Lubnyi is named after him.[17]

Kazakh tank commander Senior Sergeant Valeri Feodorovich Velichenko fought to the death when surrounded by eight German tanks. He knocked out two with consecutive shots and destroyed a third before his tank was hit, his loader killed and his machine gunner badly wounded. Velichenko continued fighting and destroyed another tank before he too was killed.[18]

Pavel Ivanovich Khrustaleov was an expert reconnaissance photographer flying over the front lines around Dobele in October 1944. His plane was hit by gunfire which killed the radioman and machine gunner and punctured the fuel tanks. The plane burst into flames and span out of control, preventing him from baling out. Pilot Captain Anvar Gataulin steered the stricken plane towards German positions, crashing it into the ground. All three were presumed dead and decorated for their bravery but Gataulin was found alive later in a military hospital. The plane had blown up in the air before it hit the ground and the shockwave catapulted the pilot into some trees, saving his life.[19]

Another pilot, Vladimir Ivanovich Dogaev, a 24 year-old from a mining family from Donetsk in Ukraine was not so lucky. He earned himself a reputation as a ground attack pilot at Stalingrad destroying Nazi tanks, transport and infantry columns. On 25 February 1945 on a bombing run over Biksti near Jaunpils* his bombs triggered such a powerful explosion on the ground the shockwave knocked his plane out of the air killing the whole crew, including him.[20]

The graveyard is full of Soviet 'Heroes' who left their collective farms in Azerbaijan, Tajikistan, Kazakhstan, Novosibirsk and all corners of the USSR and gave their lives in the fight against fascism. Their bravery is extraordinary, destroying tanks single-handedly, knocking out machine gun posts or going down fighting against over-whelming odds in this titanic struggle.

In the fight against Nazism, women had an equal part to play. Some chose to become snipers, graduating from training at sniper school to spend entire days motionless in snow or camouflaged in cover waiting for their next target. Often they would engage in lengthy duels with enemy snipers – a demanding mental test. Some were formidable, and racked up several hundred kills each. Altogether they took a terrible toll on their enemy. One woman sniper is commemorated in Dobele.

Aleksandra Nikolaevna Shlyakova, known as Sasha, was 21 when she died. Originally from Ukraine she was drafted to sniper school in December 1942, gradu-ating the following August. She spent the next year picking off careless Germans as the Red Army pushed the Nazis back west.[21]

Sasha Shlyakova always wore a red headscarf given to her by her mother. She said it was her lucky charm. But her luck ran out on 7 October 1944 near Dobele when, struggling with a virus, she got into one fight too many and took a bullet.

When the Germans heard she was dead, the news was received with a mixture of relief and admiration. One of her female colleagues remembered:

> Our scouts captured a German officer. He was greatly surprised that so many soldiers had been put out of action in his lines, all of them exclusively with head wounds. 'A simple marksman', he said, 'would be incapable of such accurate shooting. Show me the marksman who has killed so many of my soldiers. I was losing up to ten a day'.
>
> The regiment commander replied. 'Regrettably, I cannot meet your request. It was a young girl sniper and she was killed'.
>
> It was Sasha Shlyakhova. She was killed in a sniper duel, betrayed by her red scarf. She was very fond of it. But a red scarf on the white snow is a very reveal-ing thing. When the German officer heard that it had been a girl he hung his head, not knowing what to say...[22]

---

* Not far from the graveyard.

The rifle Sasha Shlyakova used and the 69 deadly cartridges that each killed a man are on display at the Russian Armed Forces Museum in Moscow.[23]

Dobele's history is full of twists and turns. It's known as the City of the Sun as it is officially the sunniest place in Latvia. It's famous for its lilacs and for being the birthplace of Karlis Ulmanis, Prime Minister four times and later autocratic President. It's not actually in Courland but in the neighbouring county of Zemgale.

In 1275 an attack on the town by Livonian crusaders was beaten off. The market place dates back to 1495. On 9 June 1940 a monument to the soldiers killed in the First World War and the independence battles of 1918-20 was unveiled in Brivibas Street – Freedom Street – where I am now standing.[24]

Remembering the dead isn't straightforward or simple in Dobele. This is a town that has had the memory of its own fallen crushed.

The Soviet casualties in the fighting around Dobele during the Courland Pocket were incredibly high. The dead were buried in mass graves in the cemetery in Brivibas Street in 1944 and 1948. Then in 1950 – incredibly – the Soviets ordered the monument to the Latvian dead of the First World War and the independence battles to be blown up and replaced with the monument to the Soviet Warriors. More Soviet soldiers were buried there in 1970.

It would take until the end of the Soviet times – another quarter of a century – before the people of Dobele were able to commemorate the sons who died fighting for their nation's independence. By which time, of course, other struggles had taken precedence.

The tension of this complex and difficult situation is encapsulated in Dobele. The solemn, dignified brothers' cemetery for the Soviet fallen is a vast, sobering and very moving place but the destruction of the Latvian memorial which stood there before suggests an unpleasant undercurrent of contempt for the vanquished.

However, there is more. Across the road, opposite the train station, is another uncomfortable, disquieting commemoration marking another desperate period of Latvian history.

At the junction of the main road through Dobele there is what appears to be an open and uneven grave, painted pink and full of jagged blocks like it has taken a hit from a shell, rupturing it. It's eye-catchingly distressing and unpleasant, in complete contrast to the sombre cemetery opposite. There is a large boulder at the headstone and an inscription reading: 'Memorial to the victims of the Communist genocide 1940 – 1956' with a poem by Arvids Cebergs.

> God bless the land of my birth
> Bless its houses, fields and forests
> So that at some point in the future
> At the end of a long and difficult road
> Brothers can come home.[25]

More than 160 people from Dobele and the surrounding area were deported to Siberia in 1941 during the Year of Terror. Another 600 were deported in 1949. There are fresh flowers and new Lāčplēsis Day candles placed by the boulder so there are clearly people in the town who still honour their memory. Unfortunately there's no-one alive today to explain why that poem was chosen, or even who Arvids Cebergs was.[26]

Many notable citizens of Dobele fled Latvia during the Courland Pocket times to avoid the Soviet occupation. Among them was the writer Veronika Strēlerte, considered one of the country's most outstanding poets and whose poem 'The Shores of Kurland' opens this book. She left for Sweden in 1945 and worked as a writer, translator and editor until her death in Stockholm in 1995, aged 83. She's buried in Dobele Cemetery.[27]

With the return of independence a new monument to those who died fighting for liberation in 1918–20 was put up, near the ancient castle. It has become the symbolic centre of all remembrance events and state anniversaries. A dwindling band of war veterans and Legionnaires gathers here each year.

Notes

1   Bidermann, p.287.
2   Ibid, pp.287-288.
3   Ibid, p.288.
4   Ibid, p.289.
5   Kurowski, p.266.
6   Bidermann, p.292.
7   Gribuska, pp.64-67.
8   Silgailis, p.152.
9   Kurowski, pp.287-288.
10 Mattson, *SS Das Reich: The History of the Second SS Division, 1939–45.*
11 Kurowski, p.300.
12 Lumans, p.381.
13 G. Fleming, *Hitler and the Final Solution* p.52; Kurowski, p.300 and Matthäus, Böhler, Mallmann: *War, Pacification, and Mass Murder, 1939: The Einsatzgruppen in Poland,* p.9.
14 Gribuska, pp.68-69.
15 Gribuska. p.69.
16 E.Veveris, Memorial plaque, Bunka Church. Translated by Daiga Kamerade.
17 Headstone, Dobele cemetery. Translated by Sasha Skvortsov. Biographical details from 'Heroes of the Soviet Union'.
18 Headstone, Dobele cemetery. Translated by Sasha Skvortsov. Biographical details from 'Heroes of the Soviet Union'.
19 Headstone, Dobele cemetery. Translated by Sasha Skvortsov. Biographical details from 'Heroes of the Soviet Union'.
20 Headstone, Dobele cemetery. Translated by Sasha Skvortsov. Biographical details from 'Heroes of the Soviet Union'.
21 Headstone, Dobele cemetery. Translated by Sasha Skvortsov. Biographical details from 'Heroes of the Soviet Union'.
22 S. Alexievich, *War's Unwomanly Face.*
23 Article, Shotgunnews.com (Sept 28, 2011).

24 Dobele tourist information leaflet.
25 A. Cebergs, Monument, Dobele.
26 Author's correspondence with Anita Banzina, Dobele tourist information office.
27 Veronika Strelerte biography, www.laikraksts.com, Australian Latvian online newspaper. Issue 223, 10 October 2012.

23

Peace, of a Sort

When the Red Army advanced into Latvia in summer 1944 the Latvian Communist Party leaders Jānis Kalnbērziņš and Vilis Lācis followed, setting up a provisional government in Ludza, in the eastern border region.

Entire NKVD divisions crossed into Latvia to start weeding out collaborators. By October 1944 the Latvian Communist leaders had re-located via Daugavpils to Riga and on the 22nd – to an audience of 100,000 people gathered at a mass meeting in the capital – announced the return of Soviet rule. On 14 November Moscow authorised the return of 20,000 Latvians who fled east in 1941.[1]

But the Soviet government did not control Courland, and would not until the war with Germany ended on 8th May 1945. The capitulation would trigger a new episode of misery for Latvians, encompassing an occupation, the forced collectivisation of agriculture, the imposition of an alien and often hostile culture, mass deportations and a guerrilla war – as well as the settling of old scores.

> Along with the Red Army and the restored Soviet Latvian government, the dreaded Soviet terror returned, a replay of the *Baigais Gads** but with a fierce vengeance and a far broader commission to eradicate enemies than in 1940-41.
>
> Arriving on a cyclone of apparently wanton looting, plunder, rape and murder the terror soon assumed a more purposeful and systematic character. As the NKVD descended on the Baltic states its agents carried with them lengthy lists of old and new enemies to arrest and liquidate.
>
> Added to the names of those who had escaped arrest and abduction in June 1941 were the names of new enemies, headed up by those who had collaborated with the German occupiers. The NKVD sought out Legionnaires, *Aizsargi*,† police, civilian administrators working for the occupation, teachers, clergy and countless others for removal and liquidation. Those who had collaborated with the Germans were deigned 'war criminals'; those who had not collaborated and even in some cases opposed the Germans but were too nationalistically inclined were designated 'enemies of the people' ... Security squads reminiscent of the *Einsatzgruppen*‡ travelled throughout the Soviet countryside rounding up suspects either for immediate shooting or incarceration.[2]

---

*   The Year of Terror of 1940–41.
†   Home Guard.
‡   Nazi death squads.

The sixth and final onslaught on the unfortunate city of Liepāja had come on March 19 when another massive wave of tanks and infantry was sent against its fortifications. The German and Latvian defenders were short on food by then and ammunition, supplies and guns were being hauled by horses. But the defences held and inflicted another 70,000 casualties on the Red Army, to add to the 320,000 already suffered. The final battle in Courland ended in April 1945 as the Soviets took up siege positions and waited for Germany's defeat.[3]

While the world celebrated the end of World War II on May 8, the Soviets began their occupation of Liepāja. The following day an eye-witness reported that Soviet soldiers entered the city hospital, dragged out the wounded and the nurses and shot them all.[4]

Filtration camps were set up across Courland to process those who had survived the war. Village backgrounds were checked out. Legionnaires were sent to Siberia for lengthy stretches to work on construction projects. Many died there. Before the official end of hostilities as many as 70,000 were already in filtration camps, of whom 50,000 were deported.[5]

Work began to repair the shattered towns and cities and to rebuild railways and bridges, especially into and out of Riga. Prisoners and civilians alike were conscripted into construction squads to clear rubble and begin repairs. One immediate priority was to get the land back to agricultural use in time for the planting season and harvest of 1945. The return of Soviet rule meant the forced collectivisation of Latvian farms, and this in turn would lead to the 1949 mass deportation of those opposed to this measure.

Many demobilised Soviet soldiers stayed in Latvia after the end of the war. By the second half of 1945 26,000 demobilised soldiers needed jobs. In 1946 that figure had risen to 53,000. By October 1947 it was still 27,000.[6]

The German prisoners were kept strictly separated from the general population and used for construction work and rebuilding, preparing lumber and fuel and for cutting peat from the forests and swamps. Orders were issued for them to be moved through cities in daylight hours only when absolutely necessary.[7]

A report of 7 July 1945 detailed where 60,982 PoWs were assigned.

Preparing of heating materials: 17,060
Construction and renovation: 27,882
Producing materials for construction: 7,260
Work in production: 8,780

Prisoners of war worked on clearance and construction projects in Jelgava, Liepāja, Valmiera, Daugavpils and Rēzekne. They built a new tramline in Riga and worked in quarries, timber and lumber farms, sawmills and furniture factories. They cut peat and worked in factories producing cement, paper, flax, textiles, pottery, bricks, metal springs, ceramics, glass and abrasives as well as tobacco and beer brewing products.[8]

Living conditions were tough. Prisoners working at Riga's hydroelectric station slept in unheated dormitories on bare bunks without sheets or blankets and did not get the opportunity to wash, so were infected with lice. Many prisoners became ill, productivity dropped to 52% and the mortality rate was close to one death a day.[9]

The collectivisation of agriculture began with decrees as early as September 1944 and the first *kolhozes** were formed in 1946. Many farmers sold up and moved on rather than join them. It was only after the mass deportations of 1949 that this collectivisation process was accomplished – but even by the 1960s agricultural production had not reached pre-war levels.[10]

The end of the war did not mean the end of armed struggle though. In the immediate post-war years as many as 10,000 people joined the resistance, of about which 3,000 were killed. Roughly the same number died among supporters of Soviet power. These casualties were generally Communist Party members, members of the *Komsomol*, NKVD agents and informers and other unarmed Soviet activists. Latvian resistance groups tried to develop cross-border links with Lithuanian and Estonian anti-Soviet partisans but these remained weak, and although described as 'national partisans' these groups were unable to unite nationally, and so remained regional groupings.[11]

In a coffee shop on Raina Bulvāris, an impressive boulevard in Riga lined with diplomatic offices, university buildings and government ministries, I meet Zigmārs Turčinskis. He is part-farmer, part-historian and author of a book detailing partisan operations in Latvia in the immediate post-war period.

The book was born out of research he began when he became suspicious he wasn't being told the truth about his family's history. He was right.

> In the last years of Soviet times my grandmother told me only vague stories about my ancestors. She said they were killed in 1949 but I didn't know anything about them. I was studying in Riga at the start of the second independence times so I went to the archives and said: 'Can you tell me anything about Helmuts Zeklars?'
>
> They got the card out and it read: 'Helmuts Zeklars. The leader of the bandits. Killed 11 people. Shot in 1949'.
>
> And I thought: 'Ah. Interesting. My grandmother's cousin was the leader of the partisan group in Jelgava'. So I started to do some more research.

Zigmārs has a collection of photographs of partisans fighting the Soviets in the immediate post-war period. They are a motley collection of men of all ages, from teenagers to grandfathers, dressed in semi-military, semi-civilian attire, with the occasional woman brandishing a pistol. The partisans have Soviet PPSh machine guns, German machine pistols, Lugers, radios, typewriters, ammunition clips, compasses, binoculars. Their bunkers were sometimes two metres deep, with secret tunnels leading away and guards posted on the approach routes. Sometimes there were 21 people sharing a bunker.

---

*   Collective farms and work groups.

One photo shows partisans posing in the forests near Kuldīga, including a woman quite famous at the time, Friča Kārkliņa. She was killed in autumn 1946. Another famous partisan was Pēteris Čevers from Latgale. He had been an anti-Soviet partisan in the east before joining a German commando battalion that operated behind enemy lines at Stalingrad, often gathering information while dressed as a Russian. Zigmārs tells me he was considered so valuable that he was airlifted out of Stalingrad before the capitulation of General Paulus. He then joined the Latvian Legion 19th Division and became commander of an anti-tank company in the 43rd Grenadiers.

At the capitulation he led a group of men from his company into the forests where they fought on until February 1950 when his group was betrayed, surrounded and wiped out by State Security Ministry troops, known as Cheka [later the KGB]. Čevers escaped, only to be betrayed again in November and captured. He was executed at Riga Central Jail in August 1951.[12]

The partisans faced overwhelming force when the end came. One group of five men held out as long as they could against 600 Cheka. In another incident in 1950 12 partisans fought to the death after being surrounded by 550 Cheka. The corpses of partisans were often dumped in the centre of a town and laid out for a photographer, their lifeless hands manipulated to show them holding weapons. Some of those gruesome pictures are here.

I am increasingly feeling that the partisan war against Soviet occupation is actually more like another Latvian war of independence, except conducted like a guerrilla campaign – from the forests with whatever weaponry can be found and organised by local commanders. Zigmārs agrees.

In May 1945 most of the Latvian Legionnaires surrendered to the Soviet Army. But about 4,000 Latvian fighters went into the woods and started to fight against the Russians. They lived in woods across Courland but particularly the central woods and the northern woods around Dundaga, Kuldīga and Talsi, organised into groups. The northern group was in Dundaga; there was another around Kuldīga and Ugāle called 'the National Partisans' Organisation'.

In northern Courland the leader was a former German captain called Miervaldis Ziedainis and in the central part there was Ēvalds Pakulis, another German captain and Legionnaire.

The fighters were Legionnaires, civilians who escaped from the *Arājs* police battalions in 1941, people who escaped from the Cheka. Some people spent many years in the woods without medical supplies or anything. One man who was shot and wounded in a fight had a bullet lodged between his eyes. He spent eight years in the woods without any medical help.

In Courland most of the weapons were German; in Vidzeme to the east the weapons were mostly Russian. It was not a big problem to find weapons. They were supplied by the villagers, from the farms. That was not easy. Four thousand men in the woods after the war – everything destroyed, people were poor – it wasn't an easy situation. And dangerous as well. Risky.

Many of the deportations in 1949 were to break the partisan resistance movement and organisation. The war against the Soviets was mostly defensive, with partisans protecting their bunkers: trench positions around the bunkers, the approaches covered with machine guns. They never lived in one place for longer than a week. It was too dangerous. They were always mobile.

The hope of the Allies coming was like a religious belief. The partisans believed for years that the Americans and British would come. Until his capture in 1953 one of the leaders of the Northern partisan groups was learning English because he thought it would be important to be able to communicate with the Allies when they arrived.[13]

Some partisan groups fought on until 1952 despite not having enough weapons to go round. About 2,500 partisans were killed. Around 900 were captured, sentenced to death and executed. From 1944 until 1956 there were 12,000 active partisans in the woods. In the Soviet crackdown of 1949 45,000 Latvians were deported to Siberia. Being located on an ever-shifting crossroads of history comes with a high price.

Later that afternoon I walk through one of my favourite places in Riga, Kronvalda Park and the district around the National Museum of Art in Krišjāņa Valdemāra Street, known as the Park and Boulevard Circle area. The Museum of Art is one of a collection of impressive public buildings designed by the German architect and art historian Wilhelm Neumann (1849-1919).

It has a small but significant contribution to make to the story of the operation to recover art treasures looted by the Nazis, featured in the George Clooney film *The Monuments Men*.

Neumann began his career as an apprentice engineer in Daugavpils and became city architect at the age of 29. He went on to design the Riga Bourse in Dom Square and the Riga Synagogue in Peitavas Street which, because of its city centre location, was the only synagogue in the city to survive the Holocaust.[14]

In 1903, two years before Neumann built the National Museum of Art, he finished Pelči Castle near Kuldīga, a large manor house in spacious grounds with a balcony above a four-columned entrance. With a landscaped park full of mature trees where a Baltic German baron might stroll or go riding at his leisure it's the kind of bourgeois pile that would set a Soviet general's moustache bristling. Pelči Castle has a small corner in Latvian history as the headquarters of the Nazi General Staff during the Courland Pocket time, and it was from here that the staff car set out carrying the generals who would sign the capitulation.[15]

The Art Museum has its place too, as the scene of a tussle over the direction of post-First World War Latvian art. Neumann, a great advocate and historian of Baltic German art, became director of the museum before the First World War but when the Soviets took control of Riga in 1919 following the proclamation of Latvian independence the November before they replaced him with Wilhelm Purvītis (1872–1945).

Purvītis was the son of a farmer from Jaunpils whose talent was recognised by an art teacher when his family moved to Belarus. The teacher urged him to train at the Art Academy in St Petersburg, which he did, and went on to become an internationally famous artist, exhibiting across Europe and inspiring a new school of Latvian nature painting.[16]

Purvītis is best known for his beautiful snow landscapes, developed during painting trips to Iceland, Spitsbergen and across Norway. His stunning paintings of the Latvian winter have shaped how Latvians view their own country, and he is generally considered the most important Latvian artist of the late 19th and early 20th century.[17]

Through the 1920s and 1930s Purvītis used his international reputation to promote Latvian art abroad and to bring artists from across Europe to the Riga Art Museum, staging exhibitions there until 1939.

He was replaced when the Soviets returned to Latvia in 1940 but re-appointed the following year under the German occupation. As Soviet victory became inevitable he fled the country via Danzig with his wife and adopted daughter Marion but died a few months later on 14th January 1945 in Bad Nauheim near Frankfurt.

His legacy as an artist is considerable but much of his work was destroyed or lost during the war. Many of his paintings were in Jelgava: these were destroyed in the fires that raged in the battle for the city. Ten crates of his paintings were sent from Latvia by sea to Königsberg having been selected for Hitler's art museum – *The Monuments Men* connection – but the shipment never reached its destination. Several hundred paintings disappeared without trace – an enormous loss that remains a mystery to this day.[18]

Art historian Margriet Lestraden, an expert on Purvītis and curator of the collection based at his family home in Jaunpils, gave this explanation of the difficulties in piecing together facts about him.

> Until 1991 it was absolutely forbidden to do any research on the Nazi period. It was a one-way ticket to Siberia if they found documents in your house on this period or the free period (1918-1933). And to make it worse, a lot was destroyed.
>
> There is some confusion whether Purvītis fled the country or was more or less forced by Alfred Rosenberg* to accompany his paintings that were selected for Hitler's museum.† Then there is no certainty about the destroyed paintings. Nobody knows. There are stories that they were burned or bombed but there are also stories that they were found by the Allies (the 'Monuments Men') and handed over to the Soviets.‡[19]

---

* An anti-Semitic, anti-Bolshevik Baltic German from Tallinn considered one of the key influences on National Socialist ideology including the persecution of the Jews, *Lebensraum* and opposition to 'degenerate' art. He rose to high office in the Nazi Party and led a task force that looted art treasures and books across Europe. In 1946 he was hanged for war crimes and crimes against humanity after being tried at Nuremberg.

† Hitler intended to build an art museum with these looted treasures in his home town of Linz, Austria.

‡ For further reading, see www.monumentsmenfoundation.org.

Purvītis' remains were re-interred in Riga in 1994 by his daughter after Latvia regained its independence.

A short walk about six city blocks up from the Art Gallery and the Esplanade gardens on the edge of the Old Town and I'm standing outside an imposing six-storey Neo-Classical building on the corner of Brivibas and Stabu iela.

This is the Stūra Māja, or Corner House, where the Soviet secret police, the Cheka, operated from, and it has its own grim contribution to make to the chapters of Latvia's painful past. It is yellowing, grubby and neglected.

The mother of one of my Latvian friends used to cross the road with her children to avoid going too close to it. The building has a strange grip on the present society. Some feel it should be preserved; others break down when they remember the dark secrets released from behind its heavy doors. Others feel that those times are best forgotten. What Leonhards Stanga saw inside here motivated him so powerfully that he put his life on the life to stop it being repeated.

When the Soviet Union broke up in 1991 the Cheka moved out and the Latvian police moved in until 2007. Not much has changed since then.

Designed in 1910 by promising young architect Aleksandrs Vanags, the Stūra Māja was a very desirable address. It had sumptuous apartments, shops at ground level and even electric lifts. Three times over the next thirty years the Soviets occupied Riga and their secret police made their home at the Corner House, converting the apartments into offices from which they ran a network of terror.

Thousands of Latvians passed through the doors of the Stūra Māja, including the architect himself, executed in 1919 aged 46 for 'counter-revolutionary activities'.

I will get a guided tour courtesy of Aija Abens, a Latvian who grew up abroad as the child of emigres and returned post-independence to reconnect with her native country. She became involved in the campaign to save the Stūra Māja from demolition and to preserve its past. Aija, a tall and very positive woman with an American accent, meets me in the dreaded doorway.

This is the famous corner entrance where people were brought in for interrogation. It has an important – notorious – place in Latvian history. The initiative in saving it came from a grassroots campaign called *Mana Balss.* *That's unusual for Latvia, which has a terrible post-Soviet hangover. Most post-Soviet societies do. Latvians don't believe in grassroots because they don't believe it can happen.

Everything has to come from the top. [In Soviet times] you had no say: your opinion had to match the party line. There was no option for dissent. Dissenters were put in psychiatric hospitals, prisons, sent to Siberia or shot.

We haven't really come to terms with our history and this is a dark part of it. The Soviet version of history is different from the Latvian version of history. Because the Soviet version was taught for sixty years while Latvia was part of the USSR a lot of people have a falsified sense of history. We want to collect the

* *My Voice.*

memories of the people who were held here, especially those held in the 1940s and 1950s, because they are now getting thin on the ground.

My parents were refugees who fled from Latvia in 1944 when the Russians were coming. My father was born in Riga, my mother in Malpils. He fled with his father, who had been a general in the Latvian Army and who had fought in the Freedom Battles, so his fate would have been sealed. And my mother's father was a forest ranger. Because people in positions of some power were forced to collaborate with the Nazi regime his fate would have been sealed too. So I'm from Latvia but born in America.

My mother used to tell the story of how her father led them through the forest to Liepāja to get a boat out, avoiding the roads which were full of refugees. A lot were cut off and didn't manage to escape. My father made the same journey at the same time with his family but the two of them didn't meet until the 1950s, as teenagers in Philadelphia.

There were nine in my mother's group. She was one of six kids, plus my grandfather, grandmother and great-grandfather. My youngest uncle was born in the Displaced Persons' camps. They were there from 1944 to 1949 when they went to America. They all made it to New Jersey, although my great-grandfather died soon after they arrived.

I have a brother and two sisters. My brother lives in Riga. One sister lives in New Jersey, the other in New York. I came back to live ten years ago but I'd been back to visit before that. Then we called it the Wild Wild East: you'd hear gunshots at night as you walked through Jūrmala. It was quite scary and no place to bring young kids.

Aija walks over to a tall wooden chest of drawers and pats it.

This exhibit is a little poignant. It's a cupboard where the valuables of those being interrogated were kept. Some never got out to reclaim them: others were so relieved to be released they didn't ask for their watch back. Nobody ever got their stuff. It wasn't offered.

We move on through padded doors, past bleak cells, down lonely corridors. Each cell has a bucket in the corner. With 20 to 35 people in a cell at a time, sleeping head-to-toe on the floor in a room barely big enough for four, conditions must have been oppressive.

Lights were kept on 24 hours a day, the heating was on full blast all the time and there were constant interruptions as prisoners were taken out for interrogation, beaten unconscious then shoved back in the cell. Exercise breaks were taken cell by cell so no-one knew who else was being held at the same time. Prisoners were ordered to keep their heads down and not to talk as they made circles around the tiny yard outside, watched over by an armed guard.

We pass through a tiled hallway and reach a small narrow room around the back. This is the execution room. I've told Aija about Leonhards Stanga and how what he saw here spurred him to take up arms against the Soviets and then attempt to assassinate Vilis Lācis. Standing on this spot changed his life forever.

Aija pauses to allow the enormity of what she's about to say to sink in.

> This is the actual shooting gallery. People were only shot here in 1941 from January to June but then the Nazis came in and the Soviets fled and they found bullet casings and so on. There was rubberised padding around the room and a tiled floor with a drain. Now that's covered over with cement and linoleum. The Gestapo opened this place up and used it as propaganda.
>
> After the Nazis left and the Soviets re-entered Latvia, they didn't shoot people here any more. They shot them at the Central Prison. And in 1953 after Stalin died they didn't shoot them in Riga any more, they took them to Moscow. This wasn't the only place in Riga where people were shot. There were other places, but this was the most famous. This room was so blood-stained and pockmarked by bullets that it was re-decorated once it was no longer used for executions. Later this was the Cheka shop and the KGB came here to buy stuff from the West ... French cognac, American cigarettes, things like that.

Even with the room in its sanitised state I feel quite sick. I understand how Leonhards Stanga would have been so revolted by what he saw here 70 years ago. A step across a small corridor takes us to a garage with big double doors. Trucks could back right up to the execution room and deliver their cargo to the barrel of the gun.

> This garage was built to make it easier for the trucks to back in: they would leave the engine running while they shot people. The building doesn't have thick walls so this garage was supposed to make it easier to drag bodies out, dump them in the truck and then drive away. People were not buried here. They were buried in the forests nearby.
>
> We play visitors the last three minutes of the Polish movie *Katyn* to illustrate what happened here. The prisoners were taken to a small room, a pistol was put to the head, they were shot, dragged out, dumped in the truck and then driven away.

I feel revolted. In a strange way I feel numb at the sadism required to fire a bullet into someone's head at close range. There is always a darkness, a feeling of despair and an enduring depression that humans are capable of this. Aija continues.

> The Nazis used this place as propaganda – anti-Jewish propaganda. They said Jews were Bolsheviks and blamed them for all the activities of the Bolsheviks and all the killings here. They repeated this information over and over again: on the radio, in the newspapers. Of course the Bolsheviks were responsible for what happened here but Chekhists were also Latvians, Russians, Poles. It's not like they were all Jews. It wasn't one specific ethnic group that did all the terrible things in this country. But I'm sure that man [Leonhards] heard the Nazi propaganda so many times he came to believe it. In fact, if you ask older people nowadays who was responsible for what happened here, they will say 'the Jews'. Because that was the propaganda they were fed.

The Soviets continued to use this propaganda to say that the Latvians were Nazi collaborators and Jew-killers, so the Latvians feel very guilty about the fact that they were so terrible – which is actually not true.

Every nation had its share of people that committed atrocities but not every Chekhist was a Jew, and not all Latvians were Jew-killers. When you tell a story over and over again people start to believe it.[20]

Here too the German generals responsible for events in Latvia during the war were held before their execution. Among them was Courland SS police chief Jeckeln, responsible for the Zlēkas massacre in 1944 and the killing of 25,000 Jews at Rumbula in 1941, along with many other unspeakable crimes. Jeckeln's fate was to be publicly hanged from a wooden beam gallows in front of a crowd of 4,000 in Riga's Victory Square on the other side of the Daugava a year after the war's end.

It's called Victory Park because it was originally meant to celebrate Latvian victory in the War of Independence. Plans were drawn up during the years of the Ulmanis dictatorship of the mid-1930s for an enormous stadium to be built for magnificent national occasions – which of course came to nothing. The Soviets kept the name and celebrated victory over the Nazis there for many years. The park remained undeveloped for forty years after Soviet victory until 1985, when a vast monument was constructed.[21]

It's an enormous grey concrete column made up of several fluted fingers, each topped with a Soviet star. Heroic Soviet soldiers celebrate and wave their PPSh submachine guns on an enormous base. Alongside is a colossal Mother figure. Whether that is Mother Russia, Mother Latvia or just a mother isn't clear while the purpose of such an enormous statement seems to have drifted a little since Latvia's second – and longest – period of independence arrived just a few years after it was unveiled.

The city's Mayor is a Russian-speaking Latvian and former journalist, Nils Ušakovs. Born in Riga Ušakovs speaks Russian, Latvian and English and is married to an ethnic Latvian. His grandparents were Army officers who fought in the Second World War. Ušakovs' popularity with the public has grown steadily but his political opponents are uneasy, suspicious of his strong links to Vladimir Putin's United Russia party.

His Harmony Centre coalition won enough votes in 2009 to take control of Riga city council and draws its strength nationally from Latvia's Russian-speaking minority, around 30 per cent of the country's 2.2 million population.[22]

Harmony is now the largest single political force in the country but with 23% of the vote in the 2014 elections is still too weak to form a majority government. A coalition of ethnic Latvian parties has so far kept Harmony out of power.[23]

In an interview with the British newspaper *The Guardian* in 2015 headlined *'I'm a Russian-speaking Latvian patriot'*, he fielded questions about whether he recognised the Soviet times as an 'occupation'.

He smiled wearily and said: 'We believe there are no debates on the fact that Latvian independence was violated in a violent form by the strident usage of military force'.

So, is that an occupation?

'Precise wording has become politics itself,' he said. 'Whether it was an annexation, an occupation or an incorporation, better to leave that to historians. But nobody doubts that Latvia did not want to become part of the Soviet Union and was forced to'. [4]

As for the legacy of the war, he uses the example of his ethnic Latvian wife. Much of her family fought for the Germans he says, while both his grandparents were on the Soviet side.

And somehow we can live with this fact. It's time to move on. This country has huge challenges to face in the future and we can only do it if we're ethnically united … Ten years ago Russian mayors and vice-mayors sounded like science fiction. Right now it's just a part of our life. It will take a lot of time and effort but having a Russian prime minister is definitely possible'.*[25]

The modern controversy over remembrance in Latvia also revolves around the Soviet monument, where the May 9 celebrations of Soviet victory are held each year.

According to the organisers, the 70th anniversary of the end of the Second World War attracted 220,000 people to a parade here, although this figure – translating into one in ten of the population of the country – seems rather unlikely, given that this figure was an increase of 70,000 on the organisers' estimate of numbers the year before.[26]

One mayoral candidate said the memorial should have been brought down back in 1991 with the rest of the Soviet-era monuments and replaced with amusement rides and sports facilities, with metal plates in several languages describing 'the true meaning of Soviet liberation for the Latvian people'.[27]

The issue has been raised in the country before when Latvia's Defence Minister Artis Pabriks called it 'outmoded'. Neo-Nazis tried to blow it up in 1997 by planting a bomb around its base. The blast was prevented. Ultra-nationalist Igors Šiškins, who also tried reviving the wartime pro-fascist group *Pērkonkrusts* [*Swastika,* or *Thunder Cross*], was sentenced to two years and eight months in prison for the bomb attempt.[28]

The 16 March Legionnaires' procession at the Freedom Monument is also controversial and sensitive. In 2012 neo-Nazi Šiškins, now released from his jail term, invited representatives of ultra-right movements from Ukraine, Russia, Germany and Poland to the commemoration of Latvian *Waffen-SS* legionnaires in Riga. Representatives of anti-fascist organisations vowed to turn out to oppose them. The march passed off peacefully.[29]

---

*   Nils Ušakovs served three terms as Mayor of Riga until 2019 when he was suspended amidst political turmoil surrounding an investigation into corruption in municipal companies, although he was not charged with any crimes. He stood for and was elected to the European Parliament in the same year.

In 2014 Prime Minister Laimdota Straujuma banned government ministers from taking part in the march.

> All the ministers have consent on and understanding of the fact that the nation-wide Day of Memory of Fallen Soldiers is November 11 and that's why they'll abstain from the potentially provocative public actions.

Her order was ignored by Environment and Regional Development Minister Einārs Cilinskis, a nationalist, who said: 'A nation that does not respect its heroes has no future'. Straujuma sacked him.[30]

The procession of veterans has been condemned for glorifying Nazism by the Russian government and the Nazi-hunting Simon Wiesenthal Centre. One reason for this is that some of those who served in the Latvian Legion had actively participated in the mass murder of Jews prior to its formation.

In 2014 Dr Efraim Zuroff, the chief Nazi hunter at the Simon Wiesenthal Centre explained his opposition to the marches as glorifying the most genocidal regime in human history.

> Contrary to the claims of the marchers, who present the SS veterans as fighters for Latvian freedom, the Nazis had absolutely no intention of granting the Baltic countries independence. Although these units played no role in Holocaust crimes, many of those who served in them actively participated in the mass murder of Latvian Jewry and of foreign Jews deported to Latvia prior to their joining the *Waffen-SS*.
>
> Glorifying such persons is an insult to the memory of the victims of the Holocaust and a total distortion of the accurate narrative of World War II.[31]

The following year he made an equally strong condemnation of the march.

> This march is the tip of the iceberg of Baltic efforts to re-write the history of World War II and the Holocaust, to hide the crimes of local Nazi collaborators and try to falsely equate Communist and Nazi crimes.[32]

Although the controversy remains, in recent years the protests have passed peacefully.

Notes

1   Lumans, p.374.
2   Ibid, pp.375-376.
3   Ibid, pp.361-362.
4   Ibid, p.381.
5   Ibid, p.376.
6   Plakans, *Experiencing Totalitarianism* p.380.
7   Ibid, p.159.

8   Ibid, pp.159–169.
9   Ibid, p.141.
10   Ibid, p.141.
11   Ibid, p.142.
12   R. Landwehr, *Siegrunen* 81, p.15.
13   Zigmārs Turčinskis, interview with author, Riga, January 2015.
14   Latvian Art History website www.makslasvesture.lv.
15   Author's visit to Pelči Castle.
16   Author's correspondence with National Art Museum historian Edvarda Smite.
17   Purvītis House website: http://www.purvitishouse.com/purvitis01%20ENG.html.
18   Author correspondence with Dr. Jānis Kalnačs, Professor of Vidzeme University of Applied Sciences.
19   Author correspondence with Margriet Lestraden.
20   Aija Abens interview with author, January 2015.
21   Latvianhistory.com 27.10.2013 The Soviet Victory Monument in Riga.
22   The Baltic Course, 02.06.13.
23   *The Guardian*, 05.10.2014.
24   *The Guardian*, 15.06.2015.
25   Ibid.
26   *Baltic Times*, 11.05.15: May 9 commemoration in Riga attended by 220,000: organisers.
27   Russia Today Online: Latvian party calls for demolition of Soviet Liberator Memorials (3 May, 2013).
28   Ibid.
29   Latvian Centre for Human Rights article: Radical nationalist Igors Siskins invited representatives of the ultra-right movements from Ukraine, Russia, Germany and Poland to Riga on 16 March.
30   *The Guardian*, 14.03.2014: Latvia minister faces sack in Nazi memorial row.
31   Wiesenthal Center, 'Operation Last Chance' statement 16 March 2014.
32   Wiesenthal Center statement 16 March 2015: 'Wiesenthal Center Protests March of Latvia SS Veterans'.

24

Escape from a Death Camp

I'm passing the Riga Jewish Museum set up by Popervāle survivor turned partisan Margers Vestermanis. I wrote to him and asked if he'd be interviewed for this book but he declined: he was ill and didn't speak English so he sent me the answers included earlier. The next time I was in Riga I got some further details about his experience from his deputy at the museum, Ilya Lensky. Now I'm in Riga again, this time with my Latvian wife Daiga, so we drop in to check another query I have. Mr Lensky is out but is expected back. We're invited to look around the museum while we wait.

We browse through exhibits telling a tragically familiar story of thousands of innocent people being massacred, illustrated with what remains of their mortal presence: shoes, spectacles, suitcases. It's terrible to see those pictures again of the half-naked women on the dunes at Šķēde.

After a few minutes the office manager comes back into the museum with an elderly man alongside her. 'This is Mr Vestermanis,' she says. I introduce myself in Latvian and he nods, mutters something and walks away into the next room, striking up a conversation with museum staff at the ticket desk.

One of the museum exhibits is the bayonet Mr Vestermanis used in the forest. We drift into the next room and continue looking around. I get the feeling Mr Vestermanis doesn't want to talk, so I'm not planning on asking him to.

A little later the office manager comes over and asks if we have any questions. I nod. I have many questions. It's worth asking one or two if I get the opportunity.

She leads us over to Mr Vestermanis and introduces us again.

'You have some questions?' Mr Vestermanis asks.

'Yes, about Dundaga,' I say, with Daiga translating. 'I'm interested in how you survived in the forest for so long. What did you eat? Were you in concentration camp clothes? How did you change them?'

Mr Vestermanis looks at me, then at Daiga, raises his eyebrows and begins to speak. 'You are the first one interested in Dundaga,' he says.

At first I take notes on a spare piece of paper. Then as he gets into his stride I ask if we can record the interview on Daiga's phone.

What follows is an extraordinary impromptu interview which continues for four hours, long after the museum has closed. It was light when we went in and dark when we came out.

> I was in the first group at Popervāle in November 1943. There was nothing. We slept on the ground. After a while we were allowed to have a fire and we had one potato each. We were building barracks for the Panzer Grenadiers. First we

234

built a good house for the chief with wood, and heating, then for the guards, and then we built these cardboard tents for ourselves. Lots of people died so they had to be replaced.

The Germans planned to take out all the farmers [around Dundaga], clear the farms and forests and build manor houses for SS officers. The plan was that Soviet war prisoners would work there and then Jewish prisoners from Kaiserwald. Teachers at the school in Ārlava have collected documents from local farmers who were told: 'Do your harvest and then report to this point where you will be taken away with everything you have got'.

They had lots of work done there, big building work. They took prisoners in groups from Riga to Stende and then by narrow gauge railway to Lube. I know Lubas Mill very well because I was a Soviet partisan. I wasn't the only Jewish partisan, and not the last Jewish partisan but now I am the last surviving Jewish partisan.

'Iron Gustav' Sorge was the commandant at Dundaga. He was the son of a blacksmith from Eastern Prussia which was in Poland in those days. He wasn't very good-looking, he wasn't educated. The only thing he was good at was beating people up. He was very proud of that. Everyone said: 'You are stupid, but you are very strong'.

He and 'Pistol' Schubert were guards at the notorious concentration camp Sachsenhausen, and tortured and killed numerous prisoners. Whatever happened, Schubert got his pistol out and shot. At his trial in Bonn in 1956 Schubert insisted he'd done nothing wrong. Sorge said: 'I don't remember exactly what I have done but if this eye-witness says I have done it, I will accept that'.

When Soviet tanks started to come into Latvia [in summer 1944] Sorge received an order from Jeckeln to do something about the camp at Dundaga.

At first Jeckeln ordered him to shoot the prisoners but Sorge said there were too many – about 5,000 people. So the plan instead was to move them to Liepāja.

In the afternoon Sorge got up on a carriage [to address the prisoners]: 'My children. I have a task to deliver you to the Allies untouched so we have to get you out of this war zone. I will take you safely to the Allies. Everybody who can't walk, don't worry. We have carriages' – they'd got them from farmers. 'Everybody will get 400 grams of bread,' he said. Usually it was 200 grams. And he said: 'If you haven't got it, then tell me'. He was behaving like a father to them.

You could hear the sounds of fighting from Tukums. There weren't many guards around because most soldiers had been taken to the battle. Most guards were Latvian police auxiliaries. Sorge had a motorbike with a machine gun on it so he was going round and round the column. My right leg was very swollen. I couldn't take my wooden shoes off.

The second day the column stretched longer and longer. At a certain point they let the farmers with the horses go. In the horse-drawn carriages were the Hungarian women, and they were told they'd have to carry the ones who couldn't walk. We already knew that if you couldn't walk you'd be shot, but they [the women] didn't. Even though my leg was very swollen I said 'No, I can walk. I'm fine'.

We walked along further and we heard shots. There was a girl – Daisy Brown – whose mother was in the carriage. She wanted to go to see her but they wouldn't let her. In her memoirs she writes about how she heard the shots. Everyone who couldn't walk was shot.

There was a deep ditch on either side of the road for draining the fields, then very thick forest, firs and pines, right up to the road. When we got to Ugāle I decided that I couldn't walk any more. If you can't walk, they shoot you. I tried to persuade my friends to come with me but I was the only one to go. I knew that after Ugāle there was no more thick forest, so I jumped over the ditch. I was 18. The Germans were shouting: 'Stop! Halt!' I thought: 'I've escaped. I'm not going to stop and let them shoot me!' They didn't chase me – they just shot at me a few times. I was wearing concentration camp clothes when I ran away. Stripes, but without stars. A number on the left breast. I don't remember it.

For two days I lay in the forest, in moss. That's one of the happiest moments of my life. No-one was shouting at me, no-one was making me go anywhere. I took my numbers off and buried them in the moss. I took my jacket off and hid that in the moss too, but I didn't want to go without trousers. We had concentration camp underwear too – full of lice, but underwear nonetheless – and without stripes. If I had had proper trousers I would have been fine. I was walking round the forest thinking: 'I'm not going into any rich houses'. Every rich Latvian farmer had a telephone.

I found a house that didn't have a phone, so I hid in some bushes and watched the house for half a day to see who was living there. There was a farmer about 45 years old and his wife and someone who turned out to be their daughter.

When the evening came and the sun went down there's smoke coming out and they're making dinner – it's the end of July – so I went to the house and said: 'Hello. Could I have some dinner as well?'

They had a massive frying pan and I could smell bacon frying. Oh my… I can still remember that. The man looked at me. I had my head shaved – that's what they did in the camps – and lice everywhere. The man said: 'Alright. Come here'.

But the woman said: 'No, go away. Don't eat. Go and sit by the oven'. And she went out. They didn't have a phone and the closest house was several kilometres away. I was thinking: 'Where has she gone?' But I decided to wait.

She went to the farm and milked the goat then made some special dumpling soup for me. She told me: 'Sit here and wait'. But I was afraid everything would be eaten!

She brought a big bowl of soup and said: 'Don't eat too fast'. It was very hot so I couldn't. She saved my life. If I had eaten the dark bread with bacon I would probably have died. Very many people died because they ate too much the first time. You get diarrhoea immediately and then terrible cramps if you haven't eaten for a while.

'How long was it since you'd had a proper meal?' I asked.

I hadn't had a proper meal since 1941 [three years before]. I hadn't eaten properly since the entire concentration time began. Even in the ghetto we were starv-
ing. We went to the concentration camp in October 1943 and we had starvation
rations there.

When I had eaten I said to her: 'Well, I might need some trousers'. So the
man took me to the barn and there was a pair of Latvian Army military trousers
on a pile, but they were covered in patches – bright blue, black – and the man
said: 'They are still good. You can have them'.

So I put them on over my concentration camp trousers, because it was getting
cold. Of course they wanted to get rid of me as soon as possible. The woman
gave me a loaf of bread but cut it into a brick by cutting the sides off. It was
possible to tell where each individual loaf of bread was made and so to identify
the house. She scooped out the inside of the bread and filled it with cottage
cheese [*bizpiens*] then put the top of the bread back on. The farmer asked me
'How did you get to our house?'

I told him how I lay in the bushes and watched the house for half a day. He
took me by the hand over the meadow and said: 'Follow the Venta. That's where
the bandits are'.

For three or four days I walked through the forest. It was very dark and quiet
at night and the Germans wouldn't go through the forest. Then one night I
heard some men coming. They were armed; I could hear their guns brushing
against the bushes. They were *Kurelieši* [national partisans] but I couldn't be
sure – they might have been Soviets or provocateurs – so I was careful what I
said.

One night I was sleeping under some trees and I heard a woman and man
speaking in Yiddish. She was crying and he was comforting her. And it turned
out be my cousin and his wife Riva from Liepāja! They had run into the forest
shortly after me. She was crying because she was pregnant. In a concentration
camp pregnant women were sent to the gas chamber.

For seven to ten days we walked through the forest to Lube* where we knew
what was going on. Baptists live around Ārlava and we knew they would help
us. In Popervāle camp we didn't have water because it was on a bog. So we went
to farmers, the Baptists, to ask for water. We had big buckets to fill. We made
acquaintances with some and we could speak with them because the Germans
didn't understand – we could speak in Latvian and we got to know each other.
When we were walking through the forest I was thinking – 'Well, we know
Farmer Bērziņš, and Riva is pregnant and underfed and autumn is coming –
and you can go safely to Baptists. We are children of Israel, they are children of
Israel … so you are safe to meet them. Perhaps we should go there'.

---

* A village just north of Popervāle on the road to the coast at Roja.

It was the end of August already and the nights were getting colder. One of the Baptist women gave Riva a coat and made a little hut out of branches of fir trees so she could sleep there.

We arranged a meeting with Alfreds [the local partisan leader]. They didn't take just anybody, in case of provocateurs. I met Alfreds and said: 'I'm not alone. I have a cousin and a woman in the forest. My cousin, you know, he's properly Jewish'. And Alfreds said: 'Well, that's all I need'. Because in that group there were Russian prisoners and a German deserter, Egon Klinke.

But Alfreds said: 'I can't take a pregnant woman'.

We had lots of deserters from Riga, especially a recent intake from the 15th Division Latvian Legion who didn't even have uniforms. They ran away [to avoid] being boarded onto the boat [to Germany] and went to Kurzeme and joined Alfreds' group. They looked at me and said: 'He looks like a Riga boy, just about the right age'.

But in Courland they speak in a special way – the Ventini dialect – and I thought they were laughing at me because I was speaking very good, proper Latvian – so I became Margers Cekuls, and I was from Riga.

The rule was that you didn't ask personal questions: where are you from, where is your house? If you asked those questions you didn't live long. There was one Russian guy who asked lots of questions. He wasn't a very pleasant guy. One day Alfreds asked me what size boots I wore. I said: '42, 43'. And Alfreds said: 'Try these'. He gave me a pair of German boots marked 'Technical Support Force' that had been worn by the Russian guy. We never saw him again. I didn't ask what happened to him.

They dug a bunker [for Riva and his cousin] in the forest and we delivered food to them in a big pot with bread. Usually it was me who took the food but one day the German [Egon] said: 'We haven't taken food to your Jews'. I was supposed to be a Latvian boy so that was a hint he understood, but he didn't do anything about it.

Everyone [in our partisan group] was excited that Riga had been freed but then lots more Germans started to come into Courland at the beginning of the Kurzeme Katls.* We started having more problems as there were too many people so we stopped shooting and sat quietly.

Then after a while the Germans started to comb the forest to clean it. We were near Roja and they cleaned the forest between the road and the river. They cut an empty zone 10 kms wide so they could push the partisans and everyone else out into the clear zone and then shoot them down with machine guns. We were lucky. It was light on the road but still dark in the forest. The commander spotted what was happening and shouted 'Scatter'. He was the first to run. I stayed with the German guy Egon as he had experience in the army and had been in battles. Later the KGB asked me: 'How did you survive? It was impossible'.

---

*   Courland Pocket period.

We decided to stay in the forest because it was too light. There was snow so we crawled to avoid leaving footprints. We saw an empty barn on an abandoned farm and went in. We heard people walking around and shooting. If they'd have opened the door they would have seen us. One and a half days we lay there in that barn. If they'd seen footprints they would have looked, that's for sure. We were absolutely frozen – so frozen we couldn't speak. We were waiting for a snowstorm, then went towards the road because we knew a forester there, Lumanis. We could see Germans driving on the road and movement on the narrow gauge railway all the time. We saw a hut there. I told Egon: 'Don't say a word. I will speak'.

We went into the hut and there was an old man there, close to death, reading a Bible, and an old woman. They were very poor but the hut was warm. We said: 'Can we warm up a little bit? Could you give us some hot water?'

She said 'No. But you look so bad you can take my bed and I will cover you up.' I was very dirty. Then the German said – in German: 'What did she say?'

The woman looked at us and said: 'What's going on?' So we told her.

After that she went to milk a goat and gave us each a cup of milk, and told us to stay here and get better. There were Germans driving on the road, searching. Anybody could have come in at any moment.

I had a rifle and Egon had a Walther pistol. We said: 'You know if someone comes in we can't just give up. There'll be shooting'.

And she said: 'It doesn't matter. You're human beings. You're staying here'.

A couple of days later it was New Year and Egons had got himself a girlfriend. We'd gone to sleep in a barn nearby. It was warm there and nobody locked barns in those days. We just had to make friends with the dogs and take something to give them to stop them barking. There were lots of refugees around and Egons had a girlfriend in that house. Lots of people were going – locals, *Schutzmanns*[*] – and they were making moonshine. I decided I wasn't going to go.

He [Egons] got totally drunk, so drunk, and started to sing German soldiers' songs. Everybody went: 'What's going on?' And the *Schutzmanns* came and took him away. Two soldiers took him by the hand and said: 'Come on friend, let's go and drink some more'.

As he got up they took his Walther pistol from his belt and took him outside. But he had a stick grenade in his jacket.

He was pushed by the guard and fell and as he fell the grenade exploded. He still wore his aluminium dogtags. I'd said to him to take them off and throw them away: 'We are going to get captured someday and your family will have trouble'.

'No,' he said. 'I am a German soldier and I will be tried by a German court but you – you will hang from the first tree like a bandit'. So I said: 'Does it matter?'

---

[*]   Local auxiliary police commanded by Germans, managed by the SS.

I found in the archives a few years ago that Egon fell on the 1st of January 1945. They might not have understood that he was a deserter. Egon was a driver in the German Army. He drove an anti-aircraft truck. When the Russians attacked he drove into the forest and scattered. When I met him he was wearing a very good quality Latvian forester's outfit. I never asked him where he got it, nor where his machine gun was, nor why he was wearing a Walther pistol.

After that I stayed in the forest until the 9th of May. I knew a couple of people in some houses but you could never tell if you could stay there, or if some of them were provocateurs. Riva and my cousin were found and taken to Talsi, and after two days they were shot.

When I came out of the forest, the KGB Smersh security unit said to me: 'So who are you and who knows you?'

And I said: 'Everyone knows me, but nobody knows who I am. They think I'm Cekuls but I'm not Cekuls'. They hadn't heard about Dundaga or Popervāle concentration camp!

One of them said: 'Well, I came from Latgale all across Latvia to the western border and I haven't met any Jewish. Suddenly here you are saying you're Jewish'.

Well, they expected me to speak Russian, but I don't speak Russian very well. They took me away, told me I'd be safe and locked me in a camp. I knocked on the door and shouted: 'I have something to tell you! I can prove that I'm Jewish. I will show you my only document on the table if you want!'

Previously I had hidden my Jewish credentials away.

They said: 'You say you've been in a Jewish camp but you're the only one. And you say you were a partisan – but again, you're the only one'.

We were allowed to go to the town but only for two hours and one day I saw Alfreds [the partisan leader]. He had hidden under the floorboards of a dress-maker's house with his wife for five months until the war ended. Here was my commander! But maybe he was worried I'd tell people he was the first to run? I said: 'We must stick together'. He became a police commander in Talsi and said: 'This is my partisan'.

When it came to the first Midsummer Solstice celebration I was going on patrol with two Soviet soldiers. In every house we got a little drink of beer and all Kurzeme was totally drunk. I don't remember anything. Everybody was glad to have survived the war. But in the morning we couldn't find Alfreds. And then ... Alfreds is dead. Officially, he killed himself. Shot in the head. But he was a great friend of many women. He was very good-looking. His wife knew all about it. He went to every woman. Even in the forest he managed to get gonorrhoea. He needed an injection in his private parts. In the bunker it was quite funny when the commander was injecting himself. Everybody was having a good laugh.

A young girl lived with him and his wife, a girl from the countryside, and perhaps things happened. Maybe she was pregnant. The position the body was found in was a bit suspicious. But nobody knew – and suddenly my main witness was not there.

I couldn't get out of Courland after the war ended until one of my friends who worked as the director of a bank made me some papers saying I was a tax inspector and needed to go on a training course in Riga. If I'd have stayed in Courland I would have had to join the Red Army in September, and because I had a High School education I would have been sent to surgeons' school – which is at least three or four years' service.

I met one of my concentration camp friends in Riga and he was in a seaman's uniform. He told me there was a naval school on Kronvalda Bulvāris so I went there too. He said: 'They won't take you with your glasses'.

But I didn't want to go in the Army. There was a military school for the river patrol squads so I learned all the letters on the eye test and passed with perfect sight – without glasses. When winter came I started to complain about my eyesight. 'I had such good eyesight but now it's getting worse and worse'. Then I went to Law School and after that to study history at University in a military department. I ended up a USSR Senior Lieutenant military specialist and translator ... but I got into trouble because I tried to publish documents about what happened to Jews'.[1]

It's now 9.30pm and dark. We've been talking for four hours, and we've got enough. Even though he's 90 and almost blind Mr Vestermanis is still working almost every day, still active on Holocaust issues.

Daiga and I walk him several blocks to the tramlines at Krišjāņa Barona iela and help him onto a tram home to Jugla. Then we walk back to our hotel, stunned by the stories we have just heard.*

Note

1   Interview with author, Easter 2015.

---

*   I discovered in the final stages of writing this book that the interview Mr Vestermanis sent me in English was an extract from something he'd prepared for Susan Beilby Magee, the biographer of the American artist Kalman Aron, who was also a prisoner at Dundaga. A painting prodigy, Aron migrated to America after the war and established a reputation as one of America's 100 most outstanding painters. One of his constant themes was the Holocaust – the Germans killed his parents in 1941 and Aron survived the Riga Ghetto and several concentration camps. Susan's biography of Aron is called 'Into the Light – the healing art of Kalman Aron' with a website at: www.kalmanaron.com.

25

Only the Memory of Victory
Remains

Having won the war, the Soviet commander Bagramyan reflected on the way he waged his battle against the Germans and Latvians. The German supply lines were cut by land but they were able to keep a supply channel open through Liepāja. Courland offered the most favourable of conditions for the creation of a stable defence, he wrote afterwards. Attacks in autumn and winter in bad weather hindered the use of tanks and artillery and often troops had to advance through swamps and woodland. Resistance was fierce and concentrated and his men had to fight for every metre. Defences were strong due to the defenders only having to cover a front 200 kms across. They had been prepared in depth, with first fallback positions then second, which allowed powerful counter-attacks to be launched. Most importantly, he noted, control of the Baltic ensured enemy troops received everything they needed to remain operational until the end of the war.[1]

I couldn't persuade any Latvian Red Army veterans to speak to me despite lots of word of mouth contact and appeals in the newspapers in Courland. I was disappointed: I felt this would have added a valuable perspective. One journalist contact said he knew of several men who fought in Courland but they declined to talk, preferring to keep their heads down. Since the second independence opinion has rather swung against them and they are reluctant to break cover, preferring a quiet life in their old age instead.

In a bar in the centre of Riga's Old Town I have coffee with a Digger, Yngve Sjødin, known to most as Inka. He has spent the weekend with *Legenda* volunteers digging for fallen soldiers in Courland and has recovered the remains of one man, a German soldier. Inka is Norwegian and lives on the west coast just north of the Arctic Circle. It takes him several days, a long drive and at least one plane journey to get here. He came to Latvia for the first time in 2013.

> I started doing it to find helmets and belt buckles, to find 'gold' – a Schmeisser machine pistol, a gun, something cool; a relic. The soldiers weren't important on my first trip. But that changed the moment we found our first soldier. Because at that moment I thought: 'Oh my God, a human being'. My hands started to shake.
>
> You can see bullets stuck in the bones, holes in the bones from shrapnel passing through them, bodies that are complete but everything is smashed because of a detonation close to them. We find perfect bones but only a few

centimetres of thigh: limbs missing, legs blown off. You see the reality of war. I am new to this. Every time we dig a soldier I am shaking. I find it fascinating to look at the bones and to try and understand what happened to him. It's very emotional.

Inka describes his experiences as a Digger with great reverence for the fallen. I ask if his experiences so close to the reality of war have changed him as a person.

It brings home to me the finality and loneliness of death in war. The soldier who is badly wounded who leans against a tree and then dies… and it's 70 years before he is found. At first it was important for me to put the relic on the shelf but now I don't care. It doesn't matter now. It's a bonus but it's not why I'm here any more. I feel like I'm paying something back to history.

We dug a field cemetery where there were 21 Germans buried. At the start of the line the bodies were very deep – 2.5 metres. But at the end of the line there was only a few centimetres of soil, like they had been in a rush to get the job finished and get out of there quickly. At the shallow end we found three or four beer bottle caps on the body, as though they'd had a final toast to the dead men and then thrown the bottle tops in there'.[2]

Inka tells me about a site in Courland *Legenda* has identified where they believe 150 Red Army soldiers are buried. All traces of the grave were obliterated when the war ended. Six months after our conversation, once winter had passed, teams of diggers moved onto the site and found exactly what the legends had spoken of: 150 Red Army men in a mass grave. The dead were exhumed and returned to Russian military officials.

Through Inka I have met Klaus-Georg Schmidt, whose grandfather Michael Zank died near Priekule and is buried in the vast German cemetery at Saldus. By a strange twist of fate I had photographed Michael Zank's grave during a visit there because it showed signs of recent tribute, indicating that the family was still alive.

With maps, photos and documents to hand we talk about his search for details about his grandfather's life and death.

Michael Zank, my *grossvater*, fought in the 11th *SS Freiwilligen Panzer Grenadier Division Nordland*, which stood in the centre of the defensive fighting in Priekule. This was a division with a reputation for being a powerful fighting force and was made up of men from all over Europe. There were Norwegians, Swedes, Danes, Dutch, men from Transylvania in Romania – men from everywhere. Michael Zank was a farmer from Romania who was mobilised into the SS. His unit retreated from Leningrad to Narva in Estonia, then Riga, followed by a withdrawal to Courland. They were one of the last divisions out of the capital. As well as a fighting man Michael Zank was a medical orderly and stretcher-bearer. He was a battlefield medic – he had to carry a bag with equipment to treat wounds. Probably he was shot trying to help some wounded soldier.

Michael Zank was 34 when he was killed at the start of the second battle of Courland in late October 1944. He was hit in the stomach – a wound which in those days was very often fatal. Mr Schmidt has pieced together his grandfather's final hours and last resting place through a remarkable and dedicated piece of research. We look at photographs of an old manor house that is in the final stages of decay.

> My grandfather was taken to a manor house in a place called Izriedes on the road between Bunka and Tadaiki. It was used as a soldiers' hospital. The wounded soldiers would probably have been safe here from the Russian artillery.
>
> He had a comrade, another soldier in the same division. This man survived the war and told my grandmother that he saw Michael being brought wounded to this hospital.
>
> They carried him in on a stretcher through the front door you can see there on the photograph. The second day he saw them take him from the hospital bed and carry him out and he was covered in a blanket.
>
> About 300 or 400 metres from this manor house there is a field where the original cemetery was. In this cemetery they buried 400 soldiers. That's where my grandfather was buried the first time.

We look next at a family picture of Michael Zank dating from 1943 when he joined the SS.

> Before he left for war he had this picture taken, probably knowing that's all the family would have of him. In the photograph he is 32 years old. Born in 1911, went to the war in 1943. He had no choice but to go. All the men under 35 years old received this order to be mobilised.
>
> I am born in Romania and we were called *Volksdeutsche*. The Germans in the homeland were called *Reichsdeutsche*. We were from the German diaspora.
>
> Until 1943 the German Reich wasn't interested in soldiers from Romania but then Goebbels declared total war and people from Romania going to the war were called 'volunteers'. But they were not volunteers. My father explained to me how it worked. Every man got a letter to go on a certain day to a certain place to be enrolled in the German Army. They were still called 'volunteers'.
>
> My grandfathers were farmers and had a lot of land. It was terrible for them to leave the family and go to war. They had a lot of work to do at home. I was trying to imagine what my grandfather might have been feeling in that wood in Latvia 2,000 kms from home fighting against the Russians and the crop in his field was waiting for him. But they probably thought they were doing the right thing – doing their duty. The feeling that we have to do our duty is very deep in my family.
>
> My grandmother didn't speak much about what happened after the war but it was a very difficult time for the family to survive on a farm without the father. He was the only member of the family who had to go.
>
> My grandmother never received an official notice saying her husband died on that day in Izriedes because the Russians occupied Romania in August

1944 and my grandfather died in October, and it wasn't possible to send official German letters on Russian territory. So that was a tragedy. This comrade explained to my grandmother a little about what happened but she didn't remember where it was, and it wasn't possible to travel to Latvia at that time to look for a grave.

In 2009 Mr Schmidt's family received notification of Michael Zank's reburial at the Saldus Friedhof. Along with other members of his family he travelled to Latvia for the dedication.

There was a very nice ceremony. Everybody was speaking about the terrible losses suffered – the Germans, the Russians and the Latvians. The German ambassador from Riga was there.

One man said a wise thing: 'Don't try and judge the people lying here starting from your knowledge base. Try to judge them from the situation they had in the 1940s'.

That's something we should think about when we say: 'All the Germans were criminals and all the guys from the *Waffen-SS* were the biggest criminals. And the Russians and the Americans and the English were the good ones'. They had no option. They had to go.

I met an old Latvian gentleman at the reception afterwards. He was 80-something and had been in the 19th Latvian *Waffen-SS* Division. He enrolled because he had a choice: to join the partisans to support the Russians, or to go on the German side. He decided to take the less wrong decision.

Another German soldier was 18, serving in a *Panzer* division in Latvia. His commander sent him to Germany to have specialist weapons training. Initially he refused because he wanted to stay and fight the Russians but the commander insisted he went. He knew the war was coming to an end so he saved his life.

When the commander left a family from a nearby farm brought him a big piece of ham as a gift for his parents in Germany. He asked why. The Latvians said: 'As long as you are here we will probably stay alive – but when the Russians come they will probably kill us'.

So that was the level of support that was coming from the normal Latvian people. They had to make a choice between the Germans and the Russians and the Russians had no mercy.

Mr Schmidt's search for links to his grandfather has led to him gathering a collection of materials from the manor house in Izriedes, which was demolished soon after 2009. He contacted the farmers who owned the land and asked if they would save him some mementoes. They put aside some stones, roof tiles, nails and even a metal bedstead – all of which he has cleaned up and put on display at his home in Germany. He shows me pictures.

Then we turn to a diagram marked 'Map of the cemetery'. There is a plan drawn in pencil of a row of graves, numbered.

The first map is made by the men who buried the soldiers. This graveyard is known as Izriedes 1 – there were also graveyards II and III. You'll see areas marked Block 1 to 9. My grandfather was Block 1, Row 1, Grave 1. He was the first to be buried – the first grave in the new field cemetery.

In the middle of the plan there is Row 2 which is an entrance and exit and an *ehrenmal*, a monument made of stone. This monument does not exist any more. There is only one big stone left. I want to bring that to Germany, to treat it with respect.

Looking at the plan of the graveyard gives me a strange feeling. To Mr Schmidt this is priceless evidence. His grandfather was on this exact spot in Latvia – in a grave, of course, but he had found him. I wonder what emotions he felt when he saw this map?

Something happened to me when I first visited the cemetery in Saldus in 2009. I felt like my grandfather was calling me – even though I never met him. I was born 19 years after he died. But there is a very strong bond between us. During my whole lifetime I will stay close to him and I will go again and again to Courland to be near to him. All the time I am looking for details.

Somebody said his soul probably didn't find rest and he selected me to communicate a few things. I can't explain what's happening with me. I am an electronics engineer so I am used to working in a very logical and established way, and this experience with Latvia, with my grandfather, is something else completely.

We have our senses and we think we can cover everything with them but there is much more. I call myself a tough guy. I have climbed Kilimanjaro, I've climbed mountains in the Alps. I ask a lot of myself. But always when I'm going to the grave of my grandfather my feelings overcome me. Something happens to me on a higher level of my awareness – it's a very strong feeling I can't explain.

There are still many families looking for information about relatives who died in Courland fighting for Germany, sometimes in the Wehrmacht, sometimes in the SS. A man who can often provide that information is Michael Molter, who runs a website detailing where German units served, *Kurland-Kessel.de*.[*] It has become a vast archive of reports about the German experience in Courland, gathering stories from families who have successfully located their ancestors. Mr Molter also runs trips to the battle-fields for the relatives of veterans.

But ironically – tragically – Mr Molter has been unable to find the grave of his own grandfather, *Obergefreiter* Hermann Faul. He was killed on 27 December 1944 aged 35 defending a fortified farmhouse near *Paugibelas* during some of the most fierce combat of the Christmas Battles.

Mr Molter believes he may be buried in a graveyard 25 kms to the north at Suntuli, where other soldiers killed in that engagement were buried. But since the war more

*   www.kurland-kessel.de.

people have been buried on top of those graves, and so Mr Molter may now never know the final resting place of his grandfather. His name is in the Book of Remembrance at the German cemetery at Saldus, but that's not the same as being able to go to the spot where he is actually laid to rest.[3]

Becoming part of the *Kurland Kessel* [Courland Pocket] network has brought Mr Schmidt into contact with other relatives in similar positions, including the nephew of a Dutch SS volunteer in the *Nordland* Division who also died. They work together to help remember family members who died in Courland.

> This Dutch gentleman's uncle died in Priekule too, in this hospital, and my grandfather and this gentleman's uncle are lying together in Saldus. The *Waffen-SS* tried to find people in every European country and he volunteered. When I go to Saldus I always put an orange flower on his grave – the national colour of Holland. Then I take photos and send them to him. He does the same for me. We also visit some Russian cemeteries because although we have our own memories the Russian cemeteries are also important.
>
> In Germany since the Second World War it's not been possible to discuss national pride in a public way because someone will immediately say: 'You are a Nazi'. That's wrong. All of the people I'm connected to know that Hitler was a crazy guy. We recognise that the people who fought in the Second World War had a very hard job. Perhaps they didn't want to do it, but they did it. At least they deserve to be commemorated.
>
> My grandfather had no intention to fight the Russians. He was called to do that: he had no choice. He probably thought he was doing a good job for Germany. Today we have some perspective on that history. I would like to have a level playing field where people can talk about what happened – German, Russian, Latvian, anyone.
>
> The tragedy of it is that it's very easy to say every German was a Nazi. Yes, there were a lot of Nazis, but in Hermannstadt, where I was born, the Nazis didn't go to the front. They stayed at home having safe jobs in administration. It was people like Michael Zank who went to the front and died.[4]

I return to Riga in New Year 2016 to find something has changed since my last visit. It is noticeably more vibrant, with more boutique hotels, upmarket restaurants and many more people speaking English. I can also hear more Russian spoken as well. An awful lot of money has come into Riga in the past decade. The number of special edition Land Rovers, BMWs and Mercedes has always caught my eye but that seems to be accompanied by a more general sense of consumerism – and even glamour.

A lot of buildings have been renovated. Even the former KGB building the Stūra Māja has been painted and now, resplendent in a smart light grey, looks quite a desirable place to live. The grim lower floor will remain as a reminder for future generations though.

Many new restaurants have opened in the city offering gourmet food in stylish surroundings. Over lunch with some friends I wonder whether this process is Riga returning to the way it was 100 years ago when it was stylish and buzzing, and known as 'the Paris of the East'.

My friend agrees. Latvians still fear the Russians coming back and what they did here is not forgotten. Even though some time has passed since Russia seized control over Crimea in 2014 and sent military support to pro-Russian separatist rebels in Ukraine those examples still raise dread of Russian ambition in Latvia.

Walking back through Riga in the snow I passed a memorial to independence fighter Oscars Kalpaks that had been meticulously swept and cleared. Considering that he died in 1919 and was killed by friendly fire from his own side, that is a measure of the enduring respect Latvians have for their freedom fighters.

Riga is developing from its initial post-independence period into a seriously stylish European capital. As my friend added: 'It's always been an exciting place'.

Somehow there is a different atmosphere in the air. The city feels more youthful, more bustling. It is vibrant and sophisticated now with an air of magic to it, especially in the winter, with snow on the ground and colourful Christmas lights twinkling in the parks.

Perhaps after a century of being crushed by first one side then another as the Nazi and Bolshevik empires squared up for their titanic struggle, this country has finally found its feet. Membership of NATO and the European Union has helped bolster a growing sense of national confidence. Perhaps the historians on the Commission looking at the war years can reach a dispassionate conclusion on the truth about what actually did happen in Latvia. Certainly the Latvian people have regularly been the collateral damage in the fights between tyrants, and without question certain Latvians have done their bidding and been the perpetrators of terrible crimes.

I sit pondering Latvia's fortunes through the past century in Kuze's, a small café tucked away in a quiet part of the Old Town. A sign outside says it opened in 1910, but that cafe wasn't on this spot.

Kuze's café is at the far end of Jekaba iela, by Arsenals and near to the Powder Tower; the older end of the Old Town, a little off the tourist track. The clientele tend to be older people. Nostalgic French songs from the 1960s are playing; among the selection 'Ne Me Quitte Pas'.

It may well be that many young men going to answer their call-up for military service in Courland stopped for one last coffee in a cafe in this area before crossing the park to the mobilisation office in Raina Bulvāris.

I finish my coffee and decide to walk that route now, to see what they would have seen. Little has changed. The Old Town has survived since the 13th Century and the Freedom Monument was opened in 1935.

On their way to Raina Bulvāris the soldiers-to-be would have walked through the small city park and over the canal. Their eyes would have lifted naturally to the top of the recently-finished Freedom Monument and its statue holding three stars, representing Latgale, Vidzeme and Kurzeme, the regions that make up Latvia.

Their fathers may have fought for Latvian independence and now perhaps they think it is their turn. They would certainly know the inscription on the monument's column, a quote from the famous Latvian writer Kārlis Skalbe: 'For Fatherland and freedom'. Another minute's walk would take them through the doors of the mobilisation office and onward to their fate.

I turn and walk back to the Old Town and catch a tram to my hotel on the other side of the river. As we cross on the stone bridge, I look left to the railway bridge blown up by the last German troops out, decorated now with pretty blue lights. I think a city like Riga, which has survived since 1200 and lived through revolutions, wars, massacres, occupations and mass deportations, will emerge from an episode like this. And Latvia too – having had its Jewish population murdered, its young men killed in battle, thousands more killed as partisans, tens of thousands more deported.

Latvia paid a high price in the 20th Century and the Courland Pocket was the final chapter of a power struggle between two rival tyrants played out on its land – with Latvians doing the fighting on both sides. No wonder they are fearful that it might happen again. Living at the crossroads of history is a precarious place for a nation to occupy.

Only the memory of victory remains.
Too much blood was shed for it.

In the countryside and the forests of Courland, the trees grow and the wind whispers through the woods, and the ghosts of the fallen linger on forgotten battlefields … and each year there are fewer people who remember.

Notes

1   Buttar, p.306.
2   Yngve Sjødin, interview with author.
3   Michael Molter, interview with author.
4   Klaus-Georg Schmidt, interview with author.

Appendix I

Otto Fischer and the 'Barcelona of the Baltics'

He was the Pep Guardiola or Jurgen Klopp of his day – a visionary coach with revolutionary new methods who brought beautiful football to the Baltics and unprecedented, unexpected sporting success to his club – but he died in a hail of bullets as a victim of the Holocaust a few miles from the scene of his glory.

The story of the Austrian coach Otto 'Shloime' Fischer at Olimpija Liepāja on Latvia's western Baltic coast has perhaps slipped from history because the city where this sporting transformation took place was locked behind the Iron Curtain for 50 years after the Second World War as a top secret Soviet Cold War naval base.

Fischer was a product of the golden age of Austrian football in the 1920s and early 1930s who learned his craft as a teenager and was a highly-regarded left-sided player until a knee injury cut short his career. Born in Vienna in 1901, the youngest of three brothers and two sisters from a family with roots in Moravia, he signed terms as an 18 year old at ASV Hertha Vienna before moving to Karlsbad in Germany in 1921 for two seasons. He made the first of seven international appearances in friendlies for Austria in a 2-0 defeat to Hungary in 1923.[1]

Between 1923 and 1926 he played for First Vienna 1894, the oldest club in Austria and nicknamed the Döblinger ('blue-yellows'). In his first season they were runners-up in the league to rivals Vienna Amateurs. The following year they reached the Cup Final where the Amateurs beat them 3-1. The 1926 final was a repeat, except this time the 'blue-yellows' narrowly lost 4-3.

In 1926 Fischer's growing reputation took him to the all-Jewish club Hakoah [Strength] Vienna.[2] They were one of the biggest sporting clubs in Vienna and drew their players from the 180,000-strong Jewish population in the city. There were also Hakoah teams for ice-hockey, wrestling, swimming, water polo and fencing.

They made a feature of touring, especially in America, to market themselves to Jews around the world, with security provided by the wrestling team. But many could see the stormclouds of war gathering over Europe and a US tour in 1926 ended with so many players deciding not to go home that the team's competitive edge was effectively lost.[3]

Fischer was among the new recruits who toured North America with Hakoah in 1927, staying until the following year when he made his last international appearance

250

and was sold in January to Wacker Vienna.[4] When the knee injury ended his playing days, he moved into coaching, taking a job in the Italian top flight in 1928-29 as manager of Napoli, but he was sacked before the end of the season.[5] He continued as a coach through the early 1930s in Yugoslavia and Switzerland without any notable success until he was alerted to a vacancy with FC Olimpija Liepāja, one of the strongest teams in the newly-created Latvian First Division, or *Virsliga*. Under the leadership of their previous Austrian coaches, Olimpija had taken the League title three years on the trot and also won the Riga Football Cup three times in a row between 1928 and 1930, on one occasion beating their opponents 9-0.[6]

The success of Olimpija was due in part to a succession of talented Austrian coaches working at the club from the mid-1920s onwards, and the links between Austria and Latvia would serve Olimpija Liepāja well. Fischer was the fourth Austrian trainer to move to Latvia.

The first was former Hertha Vienna player Villy Maloschek, who coached the 1924 Latvian champions RFK [from the capital Riga – *Rigas Futbola Klubs*, or *RFK* for short] and took the national squad to the Paris Olympics. In 1927 he switched to Olimpija Liepāja and won the *Virsliga* in its first year. He stayed only six months but re-structured the club with different age group squads all feeding into the first team.

He was succeeded by Bruno Zinger who stayed for two years and brought silverware and progress to the club. He did the League and Cup double, re-laid the playing surface, had seats fitted for fans, increased the capacity of the stadium and had a scoreboard installed. He also invited the leading Austrian teams to play Liepāja – Hertha visited four times in two years – and started a tradition of the city homecoming, its triumphant team welcomed back at the railway station with a brass band and flowers.[7]

When Zinger moved on he was replaced by fellow Austrian Fritz Hiringer, but he was not able to maintain the same standards of success and, apart from a further League title in 1933, Olimpija were edged out by the dominant Riga side RFK and the Army side ASK until Fischer's appointment.

In return for a good salary, half paid by the club and half by the Latvian Football Union, Fischer brought tactics, training and professionalism, overseeing development at all levels of the club from boys to the first team.[8]

Importantly, he introduced a new style of football – the short passing game known as 'Viennese Lace'. His opponents, schooled in the 'English' tradition of kick and rush, had no answer to this possession on the pitch, and the result was a period of footballing dominance in which Fischer's side won the League in 1936, 1938 and 1939.[9] In that third season they scored 45 goals in 14 games, an average of three a game.[10]

Certainly those who witnessed Fischer's side in action never forgot what they saw, or the pride he brought to this port city.

"They chaired him through the streets," remembers 94 year old Zanis Musins, as he looks though the pictures I have gathered of the club he supported as a boy. He was just 13 when he first sneaked in to watch Olimpija playing in the 1936-37 season in the Latvian First Division, or *Virsliga,* but what he saw has stayed with him all his life.

"Olimpija were completely different from what we used to call 'the long ball game', which was before. Usually the full backs would wallop it up the field and the strikers would be on their own, chasing and dribbling if they could get it. But when Fischer came, all of a sudden the players were trained to pass the ball to a team-mate, and that of course made a difference."[11]

Austrian football was the gold standard of the age, and three fellow Austrians had already made their way to coach in Latvia before Fischer. The game had been introduced in 1890 by Scottish gardeners working for the Rothschild banking family in Vienna, the centre of British influence in Central Europe, and four years later the first clubs were formed: First Vienna Football Club and The Cricketers.[12]

The professionalisation of the leagues in 1924 ushered in a golden age between 1930 and 1934 of the legendary Austrian *Wunderteam* under manager Hugo Meisl. He introduced a quick passing game based on the coaching of Jimmy Hogan, a forward who played for Burnley, Fulham, Swindon and Bolton in a playing career between 1902 and 1913 then coached in Hungary, Switzerland and Austria.[13]

Between April 1931 and June 1934, *Das Wunderteam* lost just three of 31 games, scoring 101 goals in that time. Their slick interplay and swift movement off the ball made them favourites to win the 1934 World Cup, but in the semi-finals they were smothered by an Italian defence making the most of a muddy pitch at the San Siro, and the winning goal came in the 19th minute when the Italians bundled both the ball and the Austrian keeper over the line.[14]

The final of the 1936 Berlin Olympics was a repeat of this fixture, with the Austrians taking the game to extra time. Unfortunately for the *Wunderteam*, the Italians then scored a second to win the game 2-1 and take the gold medal.[15] That was the last high point for the *Wunderteam*, which qualified for but then withdrew from the 1938 World Cup in France after the Anschluss unified both Austria and Nazi Germany. The unification of the two teams, with the emphasis on retaining German players, effectively ended the *Wunderteam*.

These events would certainly have been on Fischer's radar not only as a former Austrian international but also because Latvia was the runner-up in Austria's qualifying group and his Olimpija team was full of international players. However, Latvia was not invited to replace Austria and Sweden progressed to the quarter-finals by default.[16] Italy won the competition, and retained the World Cup until 1950.[17]

Until World War One the ice-free port of Liepāja was a cornerstone of the Tsarist economy. Connected to the vast internal market of the Soviet Union by rail, endless lines of wagons delivered timber, butter, eggs, grain and hides to the Liepāja docks for shipping abroad and returned laden with coal, machinery, cotton, rubber, tea and especially herrings. Liepāja alone accounted for 33 million roubles of imports and 48 million roubles of exports in 1913: trade that year through Riga, Ventspils and Liepāja combined accounted for 28 per cent of total Tsarist exports and 20.6 per cent of imports.[18] Alongside the merchant vessels in the port huge warships emptied cadets into a vast barrack city built on the other side of the Trade Canal as Liepāja developed into an important naval base for the Russian Empire.

In the early part of the 20th century the city was best known to Eastern Europeans by its German name of Libau, a port with a direct boat to New York and a gateway away from the violent anti-semitism of the time. From 1906 when the liners began running hundreds of thousands of Jewish families passed through its doors. In the first year alone 40,000 passengers made the trip. Demand was so great that the boats sailed non-stop for 18 years between Liepāja and New York, and then on to Halifax in Canada, until the service ended in 1924.[19] They were days of revolution, dislocation, relocation and eventually independence for Latvia from the Tsarist Empire and the Bolshevik regime which replaced it.

Fischer was encouraged to take the job in Liepāja because friends recommended the team, blessed with stability as most of the players were local. Not only that, seven in the side he inherited had played for Liepāja since Maloschek's League-winning team of 1927.

There was the fearless goalkeeper Harijs Lazdins, a Latvian international who stayed in the team until 1944. Defender Karlis Tils won the League six times with Olimpija and made ten international appearances for Latvia. His defensive partner Fricis Laumanis played from 1927 to 1940, including several seasons where he didn't miss a game. Striker Voldemars Žins became the first Latvian footballer to score an international hat-trick following the country's independence in 1918.[20]

Lazdins, Tils, Laumanis, Žins and Stankuss, Dudanecs and Kronlaks would be the backbone of Fischer's new Olimpija. What he brought to the club was a professional attitude and football philosophy which was difficult to instil at first.[21]

Until Fischer took over, Liepāja played physical 'kick and rush' football, and crowds became used to powerful clearances by defenders followed by charges by strikers en masse. The precise passing combinations of Fischer's 'Viennese Lace' were at odds with this style, with possession and intelligence being more important than power. It took some time for the grumbling to die down from spectators and players alike: they complained it was boring to play that way, hour after hour. But Fischer stuck to his principles. The first phrase he learned in Latvian was 'The team that plays on the ground never loses'. Those among the playing staff who wouldn't adapt were sometimes slapped physically until they did, or were shown the door.[22]

Results improved – Liepāja didn't lose a game in the 1936 season and scored 37 goals - and before long those watching this transformation began to back the team.[23] Crowds of 5,000 became regular. President Karlis Ulmanis sent the team a telegram complimenting them on their 'beautiful and masculine game'.

'Fischer made Liepāja the pride of Kurzeme [the western Baltic region of Latvia], and the only way Liepāja could compete with [the capital] Riga and win,' wrote veteran sports journalist Andžils Remess in his book *Liepāja Sporting Legends*.

Taking charge for the 1936 season Fischer successfully guided Olimpija to the league title without losing a game. The following season football was suspended, but he won the league a second time in 1938 and then again in 1939.

"He was doing something new, something exciting," says Zanis Musins, as we look at pictures of Fischer in his trademark dark suit being hoisted onto the shoulders of his players at the Daugava Stadium.

"All the other Latvian teams were still playing the long ball and of course it knocked six bells out of them. With short passes it's very difficult to stop, if you play it well.

"He was like a god around town. He really was. The local people chaired him through the streets. If he ever turned up anywhere people would be cheering him and carrying him on their shoulders. There wasn't that much going on in Liepāja but here was the football team beating everyone. International teams were coming to Liepāja and getting beaten: that was unheard of - and so his popularity soared. That seemed to be about the only good thing that was happening in the town."

He laughs at the memory. Mr Musins has supported Manchester United since 1949 after coming to the UK post-war to work. He fought in the Second World War in the Latvian Legion but was among the thousands of soldiers able to surrender to the Allies rather than the Red Army. He is casting his mind back 75 years here: I show him some pictures of the players.

"Do you remember this man, Fricis Laumanis?" I ask.

He laughs even louder.

"Oh yes! Everyone remembered him – he was a big man, a massive bloke, and if you got too close to him he had such a mighty swipe he'd take you and the ball as well. Boom! You didn't joke with him. If you were fleet-footed you got away with it, but if you weren't you'd had it."

"And the goalkeeper Harijs Lazdins?"

"He actually worked as a cashier in a bank. I was working as a peatcutter on a marsh during summer holidays after school time. Guess who came in to pay our wages? Harry Lazdins! He was a massive bloke: 6 ft 4, 6 ft 5 (1.82 metres) ... and he was bloody agile for a man of that size.

I mention that at least seven men from this side played from 1927 to 1936 and they were all local.

"Yes, they were all locals. In Liepāja we had districts and we'd play each other. If you were a good side you'd often smash your opponents and they'd return the favour by chasing you out of their district, throwing stones and beating you up. Your life was in your feet!

"I grew up on a farm and my grandfather always tried to keep me reading and doing maths, so I got into college at 13 rather than 15, and at college I met the Zingis brothers. I already knew the younger brother Voldemars but at college I met Ernests, who was in the year in front. He was the left-footed one and he was already in the first team. I wasn't very well off and I couldn't afford to pay the entrance fees, so we'd sneak through the fence, but there might be guards there who chase you, and of course, where do you run – into the crowd! And the crowd is cheering and pulls you in and people hide you so the guards will never get you after that. Sometimes of course you got caught halfway under the fence and you'd get a wallop on the backside – but there wasn't much spare money and football was a luxury. If you could sneak in, you could watch it.

"They were very good at that time. There were four big teams in Riga and they dreaded coming to Liepāja. We were very partisan and gave them a tough reception. There was one time when a Riga team were playing and beating the Liepāja team and the crowd was nearly rioting, so they closed the stadium and the Riga team got back on the bus. What happened was that by Grobina (a town about 20 kms back to Riga) the coach was stopped on the road and all the windows were smashed! So they didn't get away with it![24]

When the Soviets occupied Latvia in 1940-41, Olimpija Liepāja was disbanded. In June 1941, the Nazis replaced them as occupiers. Now the Holocaust would begin.

"Otto Fischer," Ilana Ivanova says almost absent-mindedly, leafing through the pictures as we talk in her office at the Jewish Heritage Foundation in Liepāja, on the southwestern tip of Latvia's Baltic coast.

"My mum knew him. He was a small man, well-dressed in elegant suits. My mum was training as a track and field athlete at the Olimpija stadium. He held regular training sessions for his Olimpija Liepāja football teams at the same time. When the Nazis occupied Liepāja in June 1941, the extermination of the Jews started a few days later."

The local stories are that Jewish refugees from Europe were the first to be killed. They were rounded-up, held in overcrowded conditions in jails and then systematically murdered: in town parks, on the beach, sometimes in small groups, sometimes in larger numbers.

Ilana points at the picture of a small man in a suit, surrounded by footballers.

Everyone looks happy, and no wonder. This is the team Fischer coached to the Latvian League championship three times in four years.

Perhaps fearing for their future, on 10 June 1941 Otto married his Latvian bride Anna Lemkina who came from Pāvilosta, a short distance up the coast from Liepāja. Two weeks later the Nazis invaded Latvia. Two weeks after that, Fischer was dead.

"The football team leaders went to the Nazis to ask them not to shoot him," says Ilana. "He was not a refugee but an invited guest coach from Austria."

Despite his status as an invited guest and regardless of the protests by his club, Fischer was arrested and shot in the first mass executions of the Holocaust in Latvia.[25] Anna was murdered five months later in the massacre of thousands of Jews in the sand dunes at Šķēde as Nazi death squads and their Latvian auxiliaries systematically wiped out almost all of Latvia's 70,000-strong Jewish population.[26] Fischer's older brother Hugo would die the following year, having been deported from Vienna to Auschwitz.[27]

Ilana Ivanova's father, David Zivcon, was the man who discovered photographs of the slaughter at Šķēde beach in a German officer's flat he was working in. He hid them and then went into hiding, recovering the pictures when the war ended. They were subsequently used as evidence at the Nuremberg trials of Nazi war criminals.

Olimpija Liepāja continued during the war years until 1944, when the city was the focus of repeated military onslaughts by the Red Army in efforts to break the Nazi supply lifeline through the port to the Baltic and so to Germany. Battered by endless bombing and shelling for six months, Liepāja was a ruin at the war's end. It became a secret city under the Soviets, sealed to outsiders for nearly half a century with even locals needing passes to move around.

But Fischer's legacy and methods lived on. Many coaches applied his philosophy of possession and passing and players referred to 'Fischer's time'.

After the end of the war nine of Olimpija's players joined Daugava Liepāja, coached by former Fischer defender Karlis Tils. With Voldemārs Sudmalis and another Fischer player in the team, striker Ernests Zingis, they won the Latvian Soviet League in 1946. Sudmalis, who began his playing career with Olimpija in 1942, is considered one of Latvia's greatest footballers of all time.[28]

Merging with another Liepāja team and taking the name *Sarkanais Metalurgs* [the Red Metalworkers, after the famous Liepāja metalworks] they won the League seven times in 10 years between 1948 and 1958, a dominance greater than their time under Fischer.

For a while during the Soviet occupation they reverted to the name Olimpija Liepāja and even made the qualifying rounds of the Europa Cup in 2011-12 with an almost entirely Latvian playing squad, but went bankrupt in 2014. City council sponsorship revived the team, and they play today as FK Liepāja.

The Liepāja Jewish Heritage Foundation marked the 75th anniversary of Fischer's death in 2016 with an exhibition about him produced in collaboration with the Austrian Embassy in Latvia.

There is no statue of Fischer around the town he brought such pride to, nor at the stadium by the beach where those glorious seasons were played out. There are, however, some faded images of him and his players on a public display board.

But Otto Fischer has not entirely been forgotten by football. The First Vienna FC 1894 'Dream Team' of pre-1945 players includes him as their left winger.

Notes

1   <https://www.worldfootball.net/player_summary/otto-fischer/>.
2   Austrian playing career: National Football Teams website [Austria] <http://www.national-football-teams.com/player/43292/Otto_Fischer.html>. International career. <http://www.worldfootball.net/player_summary/otto-fischer/>.
3   Bowman, W. D. *Hakoah Vienna and the International Nature of Interwar Austrian Sports*, p.654, paper for the Conference Group for Central European History of the American Historical Association, 2011 doi:10.1017/S0008938911000677
4   <https://www.worldfootball.net/player_summary/otto-fischer/>.
5   Napoli historical website: <http://www.sscnapoli.it/static/content/Rose-degli-anni--20-25.aspx>.
6   Latvian historic football league tables at foot.dk website at <http://www.foot.dk/Letstilling.asp?SeasonID=24?> (accessed 25.12.2019).
7   *Liepāja Sporting Legends* by Andzils Remess. (Translated)
8   *Liepāja Sporting Legends* by Andzils Remess. (Translated)
9   List of Latvian champions from <http://www.rsssf.com/tablesl/letchamp.html> by Almantas Lauzadis, Hans Schöggl and RSSSF.
10 Figures from Latvian football league standings <http://www.foot.dk/Letstilling.asp?SeasonID=24> (accessed 25.12.2019).
11 Interview with author, November 2017.
12 Goldblatt, D. *The Ball is Round*, p.139.
13 BBC Sport article By Chris Bevan 24 April 2013: *Jimmy Hogan: The Englishman who inspired the Magical Magyars* (accessed 24.12.2019).
14 Goldblatt, *The Ball is Round*, pp.258-259 and Fifa.com <https://www.fifa.com/worldcup/matches/round-3492/match=1107/index.html#overview#nosticky> (accessed 24.12.2019).
15 Wallechinsky, D and Loucky, J. *The Complete Book of the Olympics* [2008 edition] p.656.

16 Fifa.com: FIFA World Cup draw details at <https://www.fifa.com/mm/document/fifafacts/mcwc/ip-201_10e_fwcdraw-history_8842.pdf> (accessed 25.12.2019).

17 FIFA.com: 1938 World Cup in France: *Double joy for Pozzo's men* at <https://www.fifa.com/worldcup/matches/round=3487/match=1174/classic-match/index.html> (accessed 25.12.2019).

18 Karnups, V.P. 'Latvia as an Entrepôt Prior to WWI: Effects of Trade and Industrialisation' (*Humanities and Social Sciences Latvia*) Volume 21, Issue 1 (Spring–Summer 2013), pp 18-30.

19 Special Economic Zone website: <http://www.Liepāja-sez.lv/en/Liepāja-port/history/>.

20 Player biographies from Miķelis Rubenis, *History of football in Latvia*, 2002.

21 *Liepāja Sporting Legends* by Andzils Remess. (Translated)

22 *Liepāja Sporting Legends* by Andzils Remess. (Translated)

23 Final Tables of Latvia Championships (Arvids Stashans) at <http://web.archive.org/web/20020816042350/>, <http://www.geocities.com/Colosseum/Loge/8133/lat-meistars.html> (accessed 25.12.2019).

24 Interview with author, Coventry, November 2017.

25 From <http://www.Liepājajews.org/ps12/ps12_151.htm>.

26 Nollendorfs, V. (ed) (2012) *1940-1991*. p.61.

27 From Liepāja Jewish Heritage website <http://Liepājajewishheritage.lv/en/otto-schloime-fischer/> (accessed 27.12.2019).

28 Miķelis Rubenis, *History of Football in Latvia*, 2002.

Bibliography

Goldblatt, D. (2006) *The Ball is Round: A Global History of Football* Penguin Books, London.

Nollendorfs, V. (ed.) (2012) *1940-1991*, published by the Museum of the Occupation of Latvia, Riga.

Remess, A. *Liepāja Sporting Legends* Kurzemes Vārds, 1996 (Translated)

Wallechinsky, D and Loucky, J. (2008) *The Complete Book of the Olympics* [2008 edition] Aurum Press.

Other sources:

Drawn from A. Remess *Liepājas sporta leģendas*, Kurzemes Vārds, 1996, and from I.G. Körner *Lexikon jüdischer Sportler in Wien 1900–1938,* courtesy of Ronald Gelbard at SC Hakoah, Vienna.

Author correspondence with Latvian Football Federation.

EU football website.

Player biographies from Miķelis Rubenis, *History of Football in Latvia*, 2002.

Thanks to Kristine Zuntnere at the Latvian Football Federation.

Bibliography

E. Anders *Amidst Latvians During the Holocaust* The Occupation Museum Association of Riga, 2011.

E. Andersons, L. Silins *Latvija un Rietumi [Latvia and the West – The Latvian Central Council: Kurland after the Capitulation]* Latvijas Universitates zurnala, 2002.

A. Angrick, P.Klein, R.Brandon *The Final Solution in Riga: Exploitation and Annihilation, 1941-1944,* Berghahn Books, 2009.

G.H. Bidermann *In Deadly Combat: A German Soldier's Memoir of the Eastern Front* translated and edited by Derek S. Zumbro. University Press of Kansas, 2000.

Daniel Blatman *The Death Marches: The Final Phase of Nazi Genocide*, Belknap Press, 2010.

M. Blosfelds *Stormtrooper on the Eastern Front,* edited by Lisa Blosfelds. Pen and Sword Books, 2008.

C.R. Browning *The Origins of the Final Solution: The Evolution of Nazi Jewish Policy, September 1939-March 1942,* Random House, 2014.

P. Buttar *Between Giants: The Battle for the Baltics in World War II,* Osprey Publishing, 2013.

S. Dorril *MI6: Inside the Covert World of Her Majesty's Secret Service,* Touchstone 2002.

A. Ezergailis *The Holocaust in Latvia,* Historical Institute of Latvia, 1996.

G. Fleming *Hitler and the Final Solution,* University of California Press, 1987.

J. Gilmour *Sweden, the Swastika and Stalin: The Swedish experience in the Second World War*, Edinburgh University Press, 2011.

D.M. Glantz and J.House *When Titans Clashed: How the Red Army Stopped Hitler,* University Press of Kansas, 1998.

A. Gribuska *Ways of the Soldier in the Latvian Legions (Kareivja Gaitas Latviešu Leģionā)* Latgale Kulturas Centrs, 2012.

D. Grier *Hitler, Dönitz, and the Baltic Sea: The Third Reich's Last Hope, 1944-1945* Naval Institute Press, 2007.

J.P. Himka and J.B. Michlic *Bringing the Dark Past to Light: The Reception of the Holocaust in Post-Communist Europe*, University of Nebraska Press, 2013.

J.P. Kauffmann *A Journey to Nowhere: Among the Lands and History of Courland,* Hachette UK, 2012.

C.W. Koburger *Steel Ships, Iron Crosses and Refugees*, Praeger, 1989.

N. D. Kondrat'ev *The Great Soviet Encyclopedia, 3rd Edition (1970-1979).* The Gale Group, Inc, 2010.

F. Kurowski *Bridgehead Kurland: The Six Epic Battles of Heeresgruppe Kurland* JJ Federowicz Publishing, 2002.

V. Lācis *Kurzeme (1944-1945): Latviesu Gara un Patveruma Cietoksnis [Courland Stronghold 1944-1945]* Jumava, 2010.

R. Landwehr *Siegrunen 81* Merriam Press, 2012.

J.D. Lepage, *An Illustrated Dictionary of the Third Reich*, McFarland, 2013.

W. Ludde-Neurath *Unconditional Surrender: the Memoir of the Last Days of the Third Reich and the Dönitz Administration*, Frontline Books, 2010.

V. Lumans *Latvia in World War II*, New York, Fordham University Press, 2006.

S.M. McAteer *500 Days: The War in Eastern Europe, 1944–1945* Red Lead Press, 2009.

J. Matthäus, J.Böhler, K.M. Mallmann *War, Pacification, and Mass Murder, 1939: The Einsatzgruppen in Poland* Rowman & Littlefield, 2014.

F. Michelson, *I Survived Rumbula* (edited by Wolf Goodman) Holocaust Publications, 1979.

R. Moorhouse *Ship of Fate: The Story of the MV Wilhelm Gustloff* Endeavour Press E-book, 2008.

M.H. Murfett *Naval Warfare 1919-45: An Operational History of the Volatile War at Sea,* Routledge, 2008.

G.J. Neimanis *The Collapse of the Soviet Empire: A View from Riga*, Greenwood Publishing Group, 1997.

V. Nollendorfs, U.Neiburgs et al: *The Three Occupations of Latvia 1940–1991: Soviet and Nazi Takeovers and their Consequences*, Occupation Museum Foundation, Riga 2005.

V. O'Hara *The German Fleet at War, 1939–1945,* Naval Institute Press, 2013.

A. Ozola *Savējo stāsti, ne svešo*, Tukuma muzejs, 2014.

M. Paldiel *The Path of the Righteous: Gentile Rescuers of Jews During the Holocaust,* KTAV Publishing House,1993.

S. Payne, *A History of Fascism*, University of Wisconsin Press, 1996.

A. Plakans, *The Latvians: A Short History*, Hoover Press, 1995.

A. Plakans (ed) *Experiencing Totalitarianism: The Invasion and Occupation of Latvia by the USSR and Nazi Germany 1939–1991*, Author House (2007).

D. Pormale, *Lūcija Garūta. Andrejs Eglītis. Dievs, Tava zeme deg!* [God, Thy Earth is Aflame!] Foreword. (7-12). Rīga, *Musica Baltica, 2012.*

B. Press, *The Murder of the Jews in Latvia: 1941-1945* Northwestern University Press, 2000.

C.J. Prince, *Death in the Baltic: The World War II Sinking of the Wilhelm Gustloff,* Palgrave Macmillan, 2013.

G. Roberts: *Stalin's Wars: From World War to Cold War, 1939-1953*, Yale University Press, 2008.

A. Rubiks (ed); O.Mačs, A.Zusāne. *Patiesiba ir Dziva: Dokumenti Liecina*, Latvijas Socialistiska partija, 2010.

G. Schneider *The Unfinished Road: Jewish Survivors of Latvia Look Back* ABC-CLIO, 1991.

A.Silgailis *Latvian Legion*, R.J. Bender Publishing, 1986.

J.D. Smele *Historical Dictionary of the Russian Civil Wars 1916 – 1926* Rowman and Littlefield, 2015.

J. Thorwald *Defeat in the East*, Bantam, 1980.

Z. Turcinskis *The Unknown War: The Latvian National Partisans' Fight Against the Soviet Occupiers 1944 – 1956* HTP Publishing, 2011.

D. Williams *In the Shadow of the Titanic: Merchant Ships Lost With Greater Fatalities*, The History Press, 2012.

D.T. Zabecki, *Germany at War: 400 Years of Military History*, ABC-CLIO, 2014.

Articles

Aces of the Luftwaffe website (http://www.luftwaffe.cz/rudorffer.html)

S. Alexievich War's Unwomanly Face at World Literature Forum: http://www.world literatureforum.com/forum/showthread.php/59637-Svetlana-Alexievich-War-s-Unwomanly-Face?s=23a8d33263cc9eb891f091b1f8b1096f

Swain, G. (2009) 'Latvia's democratic resistance: a forgotten episode from the Second World War'. *European History Quarterly*, 39 (2). pp. 241-263. ISSN 0265-6914.

Kvon Lingen Soldiers into Citizens: Wehrmacht Officers in the Federal Republic of Germany (1945–1960) page 45, German Historical Institute London Bulletin Volume XXVII, No. 2 November 2005. Web archive: https://web.archive.org/web/20060626010113/http://www.ghil.ac.uk:80/bul/bu2005_no2.pdf

Report from 16.05.15 on Latvian Public Broadcasting website quoting foreign ministry article 'Fallen Legionnaires remembered at Lestene cemetery' http://www.lsm.lv/en/article/societ/society/fallen-legionnaires-remembered-at-lestene-cemetery.a121777/

Latvian History website, http://latvianhistory.com/2013/10/27/the-soviet-victory-monument-in-riga/ and Barricades: https://latvianhistory.com/2013/01/20/omon-against-latvian-independence-1990-1991/

Janis Blivis memoirs from the Jelgava Museum, kindly translated for this book by Astrid Zandersons.

M. Vestermanis: The SS Seelager Dondagen – a model for the planned Nazi new order in Europe, Military History 2/1986, pp 145-146, in LEXIKON DER WEHRMACHT. DE www.lexikon-der-wehrmacht.de/Karte/TruppenubungsplatzeSS/TruppenubungsplatzeSSSeelager.htm) (translated)

JewishGen.org: 'Report on an inspection trip by BJ Hoekstra' to Popervale at http://www.jewishgen.org/yizkor/Popervale/pop002.html

Article, ShotgunNews.com (Sept 28, 2011) at http://www.shotgunnews.com/uncategorized/musical-chairs-of-modern-sniping-part-2/

Article marking the 100th anniversary of the birth of Veronika Strelerte in Australian Latvian newspaper *Laikrasts*. Issue 223, 10 October 2012. At http://www.laikraksts.com/raksti/raksts.php?KursRaksts=2836

The Baltic Course 02.06.13 Harmony Center/Honor To Serve Riga win 39 seats on City Council at website http://www.baltic-course.com/eng/analytics/?doc=75667

The Guardian 05.10.2014: http://www.theguardian.com/world/2014/oct/05/latvia-ruling-coalition-russia-leaning-party-election

The Guardian 15.06.2015 http://www.theguardian.com/world/2015/jun/15/riga-mayor-im-a-russian-speaking-latvian-patriot-nils-usakovs

The Guardian 14.03.2014: Latvia minister faces sack in Nazi memorial row http://www.theguardian.com/world/2014/mar/14/latvia-minister-einars-cilinskis-nazi-memorial-row

The Guardian, 21 January 1991: https://www.theguardian.com/world/1991/jan/21/eu.politics

The Baltic Times: article 11.05.15: May 9 commemoration in Riga attended by 220,000: organisers at http://www.baltictimes.com/may_9_commemoration_in_riga_attended_by_220_000__organisers/

Russia Today Online: Latvian party calls for demolition of Soviet Liberator Memorials 3 May, 2013: http://www.rt.com/news/latvia-liberators-monument-demolition-776/)

The Latvian Centre for Human Rights article 07.02.2012 Radical nationalist Igors Siskins invited representatives of the ultra-right movements from Ukraine, Russia, Germany and Poland to Riga on 16 March: http://cilvektiesibas.org.lv/en/monitoring/date/2012-02-07/

Press statement by Simon Wiesenthal Center 16 March 2014, titled: Wiesenthal Center Israel Director Among Leaders Of Protest Against March Of Latvian SS Veterans And Hundreds Of Supporters
http://www.operationlastchance.org/PR.htm

Wiesenthal Center statement 16 March 2015: Wiesenthal Center Protests March of Latvia SS Veterans at http://www.wiesenthal.com/site/apps/nlnet/content.aspx?c=lsKWLbPJLnF&b=8776547&ct=14546335

Other Sources

Author interviews with Arta Dumpe, Andris Lelis, Toms Altbergs, Ilgmar Brucis, Herbert Knēts, Vaira Vīķe-Freiberga, Antons Leščanovs, Fricis Borisovs, Žanis Grīnbergs, Gunita Freiberga, Austra Sunina, Oscars Lejnieks, Aigars Pūce, Dmitrijs Mežeckis, Rita Krūmiņa, Andžils Remess, Juris Raķis, Ilana Ivanova, Artūrs Tukišs, Mārtiņš Cerins, Zigmārs Turčinskis, Aija Abens, Margers Vestermanis, Inka Sjodin, Klaus-Georg Schmidt, Michael Molter, Roberts Sipenieks, Roberts Miķelsons, Biruta Sipeniece, Jānis Blums, Lidija Treide.

Interviews with Lydia Doronina, Valentina Lasmane, Boris Mangolds and Pēteris Jansons with permission from the National Oral History archive at the University of Latvia, Riga, with grateful thanks to Māra Zirnīte.

Personal archive of Herberts Knēts, Kuldiga, November 2014.

Latvian Legion film from film studio Devini (2000) produced by The Soros Fund, script by Uldis Neiburgs.

http://www.jwmww2.org/vf/ib_items/1400/LatvianJewsAtTheFrontsOfStruggleAgainstNazism.pdf

Dundaga tourist information website: http://visit.dundaga.lv/en/various/pieminekli/

UNESCO World Heritage list. http://whc.unesco.org/en/list/852

Latvia University of Agriculture website: http://eng.llu.lv/?mi=579

Latvian Art History website www.makslasvesture.lv

http://www.jelgava.lv/for-visitors/sightseeing/historical-sites/

Occupation Museum website:http://www.occupation.lv/#!/en/eksponats/05VI.3

German information site for relatives of those killed in Kurland: http://www.kurland-kessel.de

Liepāja city history http://www.Liepāja .lv/page/936

Liepāja Special Economic Zone history website http://www.Liepāja -sez.lv/en/Liepāja -port/history/

Latvians.com website, quoting *Latvia—Our Dream is Coming True* published by Soviet Booklets, London, England, in December, 1959. http://www.latvians.com/index.php?en/CFBH/LatviaLācis/LācisA-05-author.ssi

www.laikraksts.com, Australian Latvian online newspaper. Issue 223, 10 October 2012.

Latvian Football federation and SC Hakoah, Vienna.

Riga Barricades: Waymarking memorial website: http://www.waymarking.com/waymarks/WMPNCQ_Barikades_Memorial_Riga_Latvia

Index

Index of People

Abens, Aija 227-229
Altbergs, Toms 31-33
Ancāns, Roberts 102-103
Anders, Edward 143
Andžāns/Andžāne family 131
Ansons, Žanis 103
Arājs, Viktors 18-19, 82

Bagramyan, Ivan Khristoforovich 42, 48,
  54, 64, 242
Balodis, Jānis 137-138
Bangerskis, General Rūdolfs 20, 50, 70,
  72-73
Barkāne/Barkāns family 131
Barševskis, Aldis xii, xv, 41, 43-45
Baumgards/ Baumgarte family 130
Benjamin family 64
Bidermann, Gottlob Herbert 50, 52, 95-96,
  100, 179, 194, 210-211
Blīvis, Jānis 41-42
Blosfelds, Mintauts 49
Blūmentāls, Arvīds 44, 174-175
Blums, Jānis 196, 198-199
Bogdanova family 127
Bonitz, Woldemar 138-139
Braunbergs, Emīls 65-69
Brucis, Ilgvars 57, 59

Čakste, Jānis 43, 151
Čakste, Konstantīns 151-152, 163
Cebergs, Arvids 218-219
Cerins, Mārtiņš 189-192
Čevers, Pēteris 224
Churchill, Winston 81, 197

Dankers, General Oskars 48, 70-71
Dönitz, Admiral Karl 22, 92-93, 195-196
Doronina, Lydia 152, 165
Dumpe, Arta 25-26, 105, 176, 185

Eglītis, Andrejs 37-38, 45

Fabriciuss, Jānis 162-163
Fischer, Otto 'Shloime' 142, 150, 250-257
Fonzelis, Jānis 156-157
Freimane, Jautrite 171, 174-175
Frost, Matis 169, 174

Garūta, Lūcija 37-38
Gataulin, Pilot Captain Anvar 216-217
Grigoriev, Ivan Yakovlievich 189
Grīnbergs, Žanis 79, 82
Gustovskis, Artis 76, 82-83, 85, 117, 119,
  126, 128-130, 196, 198-199

Hilpert, *Generaloberst* Carl 195, 215
Hitler, Adolf 20-22, 25, 31, 46-48, 62, 65,
  70, 87, 92, 136-137, 149, 184, 195, 213,
  226, 247

Ivanova, Ilana 148-150, 255

Jeckeln, *SS Obergruppenführer* Friedrich 19,
  50, 70-71, 116-118, 125-126, 132-133,
  135, 161, 230, 235
Jēkabsons/Jēkabsone family 124, 127-128
Juris, Andrejs 63-64

Kalniņš, Alfrēds 37
Kalpaks, Oscars 203, 248
Ķeizars family 127, 129
Klinke, Egon/Egons 170, 238-240
Knēts, Herberts 117, 119, 123-126,
  128-132, 161
Konovalov, Vladimir 135-136
Krauze brothers 63-64
Krišanovskis/ Krišanovska family 125, 127
Kröschel, Max 167, 169
Krüger, *Obergruppenführer* Walter 213

263

Index of Places

Index of Military Formations & Units, Paramilitary Organisations, Partisans

Index of General & Miscellaneous Terms